16, 95

(100)

The Population
Explosion

▲

The Population Explosion

▼

PAUL R. EHRLICH
& ANNE H. EHRLICH

HUTCHINSON

LONDON SYDNEY AUCKLAND JOHANNESBURG

This edition first published in 1990 by
Hutchinson

Random Century 20 Vauxhall Bridge Road,
London SW1V 2SA

Century Hutchinson Australia (Pty) Ltd
20 Alfred Street Milsons Point, Sydney, NSW 2061, Australia

Century Hutchinson New Zealand Limited
PO Box 40–086, Glenfield, Auckland 10, New Zealand

Century Hutchinson South Africa (Pty) Ltd
PO Box 337, Bergvlei, 2012 South Africa

British Library Cataloguing in Publication Data

Ehrlich, Paul R. (Paul Ralph), *1932*–
    The population explosion.
    1. Population. Growth
    I. Title   II. Ehrlich, Anne H.
    304.62

ISBN 0–09–174551–9

Printed and bound in Great Britain by
Mackays of Chatham PLC, Chatham, Kent

The Population Bomb

was for Lisa;

this is for

Lisa's daughter,

Jessica,

and Jessica's sister,

Mara

▲

Contents

▼

Preface

1 Why Isn't Everyone as Scared as We Are? 13

2 The One-Time Bonanza 24

3 Critical Masses 46

4 Food: The Ultimate Resource 66

5 The Ecology of Agriculture 88

6 Global Ecosystem Health 110

7 Population and Public Health 136

8 Population, Growthism, and National Security 158

9 The Bang, the Whimper, and the Alternative 174

10 Connections and Solutions: I 185

11 Connections and Solutions: II 203

12 What You Can Do 226

Take-Home Messages 237

Samples of Letters Sent to Influential People 239

Organizations Working to Solve Population Problems 246

Books for Further Reading 249

Appendix: Aspects of How Earth Works 252

Notes 263

Acknowledgments 305

Index 307

▲

Preface

▼

In 1968, *The Population Bomb*[1] warned of impending disaster if the population explosion was not brought under control. Then the fuse was burning; now the population bomb has detonated. Since 1968, at least 200 million people—mostly children—have perished needlessly of hunger and hunger-related diseases, despite "crash programs to 'stretch' the carrying capacity of Earth by increasing food production."[2] The population problem is no longer primarily a threat for the future as it was when the *Bomb* was written and there were only 3.5 billion human beings.

The size of the human population is now 5.3 billion, and still climbing. In the six seconds it takes you to read this sentence, eighteen more people will be added.[3] Each hour there are 11,000 more mouths to feed; each year, more than 95 million. Yet the world has hundreds of billions *fewer* tons of topsoil and hundreds of trillions *fewer* gallons of groundwater with which to grow food crops than it had in 1968.

In 1988, for the first time at least since World War II, the

9

United States consumed more grain than it grew. About a third of the country's grain crop was lost to a severe drought—roughly the fraction that is normally exported. Over a hundred nations depend on food imported from North America, and only the presence of large carryover stocks prevented a serious food crisis.

It is not clear how easy it will be to restore those stocks. World grain production peaked in 1986 and then—for the first time in forty years—dropped for two consecutive years. In just those two years, the world population rose by the equivalent of the combined citizenry of the United Kingdom, France, and West Germany. Global food production per person peaked earlier, in 1984, and has slid downward since then. In Africa south of the Sahara, production per capita has been declining for more than twenty years and in Latin America since 1981.[4] And the prospects for unfavorable weather for agriculture may be rising as burgeoning populations add more and more "greenhouse" gases to the atmosphere.

The Population Bomb tried to alert people to the connection of population growth to such events. The book also warned about the greenhouse warming and other possible consequences of "using the atmosphere as a garbage dump." It concluded: "In short, when we pollute, we tamper with the energy balance of the Earth. The results in terms of global climate and in terms of local weather could be catastrophic. Do we want to keep it up and find out what will happen? What do we gain by playing 'environmental roulette'?"[5]

What indeed? We've played, and now we're starting to pay. The alarm has been sounded repeatedly, but society has turned a deaf ear.[6] *Meanwhile, a largely prospective disaster has turned into the real thing.* A 1990s primer on population by necessity looks very different from our original work. *The Population Explosion* is being written as ominous changes in the life-support systems of civilization become more evident daily. It is being written in a world where hunger is rife and the prospects of famine and plague ever more imminent; a world where U.S. consumption is so profligate that the birth of an average American baby is hundreds of times more of a disaster for Earth's life-support systems than the birth of a baby in a desperately poor nation; and a world in which most people are unaware of the role that overpopulation plays in many of the problems oppressing them.

Even people far removed from the pangs of hunger must suspect that something is amiss, must feel a sense of foreboding for their own future well-being and that of their children. Television shots of tropical forests afire, sewage-smeared beaches, and drought-stricken farm fields cause unease. Pictures of starving Africans in desolate relief camps rend the heart.

In the United States, drivers in virtually every large metropolitan area now can encounter gridlock at practically any hour of the day or night. Visitors to our nation's capital find homeless people sleeping in the park opposite the White House, and drug abuse and crime sprees fill the evening news. News about the AIDS epidemic seems to be everywhere, as is talk of global warming, holes in the atmosphere's ozone layer, and acid rain.

These may seem to be isolated problems, but they are all tied together by common threads—threads that also link them to food-production statistics, to the prospect of a billion or more deaths from starvation and disease, and to the possible dissolution of society as we know it. Chief among the underlying causes of our planet's unease is the overgrowth of the human population and its impacts on both ecosystems and human communities. Those impacts are the threads linking all the seemingly unrelated problems mentioned above, and others besides. The explosive growth of the human population, its meaning for you and your children and grandchildren, and what you and your friends can do to make a better future are what this book is all about.

PAUL R. EHRLICH
ANNE H. EHRLICH

Rocky Mountain Biological Laboratory
Gothic, Colorado
July 26, 1989

1

▲

Why Isn't Everyone as Scared as We Are?

▼

In the early 1930s, when we were born, the world population was just 2 billion; now it is more than two and a half times as large and still growing rapidly.[1] The population of the United States is increasing much more slowly than the world average, but it has more than doubled in only six decades—from 120 million in 1928 to 250 million in 1990.[2] Such a huge population expansion within two or three generations can by itself account for a great many changes in the social and economic institutions of a society. It also is very frightening to those of us who spend our lives trying to keep track of the implications of the population explosion.

► **A SLOW START** ◄

One of the toughest things for a population biologist to reconcile is the contrast between his or her recognition that civilization is in imminent serious jeopardy and the modest level of concern that population issues generate among the public and even among elected officials.

Much of the reason for this discrepancy lies in the slow development of the problem. People aren't scared because they evolved biologically and culturally to respond to short-term "fires" and to tune out long-term "trends" over which they had no control.[3] Only if we do what doesn't come naturally —if we determinedly focus on what seem to be gradual or nearly imperceptible changes—can the outlines of our predicament be perceived clearly enough to be frightening.

Consider the *very* slow-motion origins of our predicament. It seems reasonable to define humanity as having first appeared some four million years ago in the form of australopithecines, small-brained upright creatures like "Lucy."[4] Of course, we don't know the size of this first human population, but it's likely that there were never more than 125,000 australopithecines at any given time.

Our own species, *Homo sapiens*,[5] evolved a few hundred thousand years ago. Some ten thousand years ago, when agriculture was invented, probably no more than five million people inhabited Earth—fewer than now live in the San Francisco Bay Area. Even at the time of Christ, two thousand years ago, the entire human population was roughly the size of the population of the United States today; by 1650 there were only 500 million people, and in 1850 only a little over a billion. Since there are now well past 5 billion people, the vast majority of the population explosion has taken place in less than a tenth of one percent of the history of *Homo sapiens*.

This is a remarkable change in the abundance of a single species. After an unhurried pace of growth over most of our history, expansion of the population accelerated during the Industrial Revolution and really shot up after 1950. Since mid-century, the human population has been growing at annual rates ranging from about 1.7 to 2.1 percent per year, doubling in forty years or less. Some groups have grown significantly faster; the population of the African nation of Kenya was estimated to be increasing by over 4 percent annually during the 1980s—a rate that if continued would double the nation's population in only seventeen years.[6] That rate did continue for over a decade, and only recently has shown slight signs of slowing. Meanwhile, other nations, such as those of northern Europe, have grown much more slowly in recent decades.

But even the highest growth rates are still *slow-motion changes compared to events we easily notice and react to.* A car swerving at us on the highway is avoided by actions taking a few seconds. The Alaskan oil spill caused great public indignation, but faded from the media and the consciousness of most people in a few months. America's participation in World War II spanned less than four years. During the last four years, even Kenya's population grew by only about 16 percent—a change hardly perceptible locally, let alone from a distance. In four years, the world population expands only a little more than 7 percent. Who could notice that? Precipitous as the population explosion has been in historical terms, it is occurring at a snail's pace in an individual's perception. It is not an event, it is a trend that must be analyzed in order for its significance to be appreciated.

▶   **EXPONENTIAL GROWTH**   ◀

The time it takes a population to double in size is a dramatic way to picture rates of population growth, one that most of us can understand more readily than percentage growth rates. Human populations have often grown in a pattern described as "exponential."[7] Exponential growth occurs in bank accounts when interest is left to accumulate and itself earns interest. Exponential growth occurs in populations because children, the analogue of interest, remain in the population and themselves have children.[8]

A key feature of exponential growth is that it often seems to start slowly and finish fast. A classic example used to illustrate this is the pond weed that doubles each day the amount of pond surface covered and is projected to cover the entire pond in thirty days. The question is, how much of the pond will be covered in twenty-nine days? The answer, of course, is that just half of the pond will be covered in twenty-nine days. The weed will then double once more and cover the entire pond the next day. As this example indicates, exponential growth contains the potential for big surprises.[9]

The limits to human population growth are more difficult to perceive than those restricting the pond weed's growth. Nonetheless, like the pond weed, human populations grow in a pattern that is essentially exponential, so we must be alert to the treacherous properties of that sort of growth. The key point to remember is that *a long history of exponential growth in no way implies a long future of exponential growth.* What begins in slow motion may eventually overwhelm us in a flash.

The last decade or two has seen a slight slackening in the human population growth rate—a slackening that has been prematurely heralded as an "end to the population explosion." The slowdown has been only from a peak annual growth rate of perhaps 2.1 percent in the early 1960s to about 1.8 percent in 1990. To put this change in perspective, the population's doubling time has been extended from thirty-three years to thirty-nine. Indeed, the world population *did* double in the thirty-seven years from 1950 to 1987. But even if birthrates continue to fall, the world population will continue to expand (assuming that death rates don't rise), although at a slowly slackening rate, for about another century. Demographers think that growth will not end before the population has reached 10 billion or more.[10]

So, even though birthrates have declined somewhat, *Homo sapiens* is a long way from ending its population explosion or avoiding its consequences. In fact, the biggest jump, from 5 to 10 billion in well under a century, is still ahead. But this does not mean that growth couldn't be ended sooner, with a much smaller population size, if we—all of the world's nations— made up our minds to do it. The trouble is, many of the world's leaders and perhaps most of the world's people still don't believe that there are compelling reasons to do so. They are even less aware that if humanity fails to act, *nature may end the population explosion for us*—in very unpleasant ways—well before 10 billion is reached.

Those unpleasant ways are beginning to be perceptible. Humanity in the 1990s will be confronted by more and more intransigent environmental problems, global problems dwarfing those that worried us in the late 1960s. Perhaps the most serious is that of global warming, a problem caused in large part by population growth and overpopulation. It is not clear whether the severe drought in North America, the Soviet Union, and China in 1988 was the result of the slowly rising surface temperature of Earth, but it is precisely the kind of event that climatological models predict as more and more likely with continued global warming.[11] In addition to more frequent and more severe crop failures, projected consequences of the warming include coastal flooding, desertification, the creation of as many as 300 million environmental refugees,[12] alteration of patterns of disease, water shortages, general stress on natural ecosystems, and synergistic interactions among all these factors.[13]

Continued population growth and the drive for development in already badly overpopulated poor nations will make it *exceedingly* difficult to slow the greenhouse warming—and impossible to stop or reverse it—in this generation at least. And, even if the warming should miraculously not occur, contrary to accepted projections,[14] human numbers are on a collision course with massive famines anyway.

► **MAKING THE POPULATION CONNECTION** ◄

Global warming, acid rain, depletion of the ozone layer, vulnerability to epidemics, and exhaustion of soils and groundwater are all, as we shall see, related to population size. They are also clear and present dangers to the persistence of civilization. Crop failures due to global warming alone might result in the premature deaths of a billion or more people in the next few decades, and the AIDS epidemic could slaughter hundreds of millions. Together these would constitute a harsh "population control" program provided by nature in the face of humanity's refusal to put into place a gentler program of its own.

We shouldn't delude ourselves: the population explosion will come to an end before very long. The only remaining question is whether it will be halted through the humane method of birth contol, or by nature wiping out the surplus. We realize that religious and cultural opposition to birth control exists throughout the world; but we believe that people simply don't understand the choice that such opposition implies. Today, anyone opposing birth control is unknowingly voting to have the human population size controlled by a massive increase in early deaths.

Of course, the environmental crisis isn't caused just by expanding human numbers. Burgeoning consumption among the rich and increasing dependence on ecologically unsound technologies to supply that consumption also play major parts. This allows some environmentalists to dodge the population issue by emphasizing the problem of malign technologies. And social commentators can avoid commenting on the problem of too many people by focusing on the serious maldistribution of affluence.

But scientists studying humanity's deepening predicament recognize that a major factor contributing to it is rapidly worsening overpopulation. The Club of Earth, a group whose members all belong to both the U.S. National Academy of Sciences and the American Academy of Arts and Sciences, released a statement in September 1988 that said in part:

Arresting global population growth should be second in importance only to avoiding nuclear war on humanity's agenda. Overpopulation and rapid population growth are intimately connected with most aspects of the current human predicament, including rapid depletion of nonrenewable resources, deterioration of the environment (including rapid climate change), and increasing international tensions.[15]

When three prestigious scientific organizations cosponsored an international scientific forum, "Global Change," in Washington in 1989, there was general agreement among the speakers that population growth was a substantial contributor toward prospective catastrophe. Newspaper coverage was limited, and while the population component was mentioned in *The New York Times*'s article,[16] the point that population limitation will be essential to resolving the predicament was lost. The coverage of environmental issues in the media has been generally excellent in the last few years, but there is still a long way to go to get adequate coverage of the intimately connected population problem.

Even though the media occasionally give coverage to population issues, some people never get the word. In November 1988, Pope John Paul II reaffirmed the Catholic Church's ban on contraception. The occasion was the twentieth anniversary of Pope Paul's anti-birth-control encyclical, *Humanae Vitae*.

Fortunately, the majority of Catholics in the industrial world pay little attention to the encyclical or the Church's official ban on all practical means of birth control. One need only note that Catholic Italy at present has the smallest average completed family size (1.3 children per couple) of any nation. Until contraception and then abortion were legalized there in the 1970s, the Italian birth rate was kept low by an appalling rate of illegal abortion.

The bishops who assembled to celebrate the anniversary defended the encyclical by announcing that "the world's food resources theoretically could feed 40 billion people."[17] In one sense they were right. It's "theoretically possible" to feed 40 billion people—in the same sense that it's theoretically possible for your favorite major-league baseball team to win every single game for fifty straight seasons, or for you to play Russian roulette ten thousand times in a row with five out of six chambers loaded without blowing your brains out.

One might also ask whether feeding 40 billion people is a worthwhile goal for humanity, even if it could be reached. Is any purpose served in turning Earth, in essence, into a gigantic human feedlot? Putting aside the near-certainty that such a miracle couldn't be sustained, what would happen to the *quality* of life?

We wish to emphasize that the population problem is in no sense a "Catholic problem," as some would claim. Around the world, Catholic reproductive performance is much the same as that of non-Catholics in similar cultures and with similar economic status. Nevertheless, the *political* position of the Vatican, traceable in no small part to the extreme conservatism of Pope John Paul II, is an important barrier to solving the population problem.[18] Non-Catholics should be very careful not to confuse Catholics or Catholicism with the Vatican—most American Catholics don't. Furthermore, the Church's position on contraception is distressing to many millions of Catholics, who feel it morally imperative to follow their own consciences in their personal lives and disregard the Vatican's teachings on this subject.

Nor is unwillingness to face the severity of the population problem limited to the Vatican. It's built into our genes and our culture. That's one reason many otherwise bright and humane people behave like fools when confronted with demographic issues. Thus, an economist specializing in mail-order marketing can sell the thesis that the human population could increase essentially forever because people are the "ultimate resource,"[19] and a journalist can urge more population growth in the United States so that we can have a bigger army![20] Even some environmentalists are taken in by the frequent assertion that "there is no population problem, only a problem of distribution." The statement is usually made in a context of a plan for conquering hunger, as if food shortage were the only consequence of overpopulation.

But even in that narrow context, the assertion is wrong. Suppose food *were* distributed equally. If everyone in the world ate as Americans do, less than half the *present* world population could be fed on the record harvests of 1985 and 1986.[21] Of course, everyone doesn't have to eat like Americans. About a third of the world grain harvest—the staples of the human feeding base—is fed to animals to produce eggs, milk, and meat for American-style diets. Wouldn't feeding that grain directly to people solve the problem? If everyone were willing to eat an essentially vegetarian diet, that additional grain would allow perhaps a billion more people to be fed with 1986 production.

Would such radical changes solve the world food problem? Only in the *very* short term. The additional billion people are slated to be with us by the end of the century. Moreover, by the late 1980s, humanity already seemed to be encountering trouble maintaining the production levels of the mid-1980s, let alone keeping up with population growth. The world grain harvest in 1988 was some 10 percent *below* that of 1986. And there is little sign that the rich are about to give up eating animal products.

So there is no reasonable way that the hunger problem can be called "only" one of distribution, even though redistribution of food resources would greatly alleviate hunger today. Unfortunately, an important truth, that maldistribution is a cause of hunger now, has been used as a way to avoid a more important truth—that overpopulation is critical today and may well make the distribution question moot tomorrow.

The food problem, however, attracts little immediate concern among well-fed Americans, who have no reason to be aware of its severity or extent. But other evidence that could make everyone face up to the seriousness of the population dilemma is now all around us, since problems to which overpopulation and population growth make major contributions are worsening at a rapid rate. They often appear on the evening news, although the population connection is almost never made.

Consider the television pictures of barges loaded with garbage wandering like The Flying Dutchman across the seas, and news stories about "no room at the dump."[22] They are showing the results of the interaction between too many affluent people and the environmentally destructive technologies that support that affluence. Growing opportunities to swim in a mixture of sewage and medical debris off American beaches can be traced to the same source. Starving people in sub-Saharan Africa are victims of drought, defective agricultural policies, and an overpopulation of both people and domestic animals— with warfare often dealing the final blow. All of the above are symptoms of humanity's massive and growing negative impact on Earth's life-support systems.

▶   **RECOGNIZING THE POPULATION PROBLEM**   ◀

The average person, even the average scientist, seldom makes the connection between such seemingly disparate events and the population problem, and thus remains unworried. To a degree, this failure to put the pieces together is due to a taboo against frank discussion of the population crisis in many quarters, a taboo generated partly by pressures from the Catholic hierarchy and partly by other groups who are afraid that dealing with population issues will produce socially damaging results.

Many people on the political left are concerned that focusing on overpopulation will divert attention from crucial problems of social justice (which certainly need to be addressed *in addition* to the population problem). Often those on the political right fear that dealing with overpopulation will encourage abortion (it need not) or that halting growth will severely damage the economy (it could, if not handled properly). And people of varied political persuasions who are unfamiliar with the magnitude of the population problem believe in a variety of far-fetched technological fixes—such as colonizing outer space—that they think will allow the need for regulating the size of the human population to be avoided forever.[23]

Even the National Academy of Sciences avoided mentioning controlling human numbers in its advice to President Bush on how to deal with global environmental change. Although Academy members who are familiar with the issue are well aware of the critical population component of that change, it was feared that all of the Academy's advice would be ignored if recommendations were included about a subject taboo in the Bush administration. That strategy might have been correct, considering Bush's expressed views on abortion and considering the administration's weak appointments in many environmentally sensitive positions. After all, the Office of Management and Budget even tried to suppress an expert evaluation of the potential seriousness of global warming by altering the congressional testimony of a top NASA scientist, James Hansen, to conform with the administration's less urgent view of the problem.[24]

All of us naturally lean toward the taboo against dealing with population growth. The roots of our aversion to limiting the size of the human population are as deep and pervasive as the roots of human sexual behavior. Through billions of years of evolution, outreproducing other members of your population was the name of the game. It is the very basis of natural selection, the driving force of the evolutionary process.[25] Nonetheless, the taboo must be uprooted and discarded.

▶   **OVERCOMING THE TABOO**   ◀

There is no more time to waste; in fact, there wasn't in 1968 when *The Population Bomb* was published. Human inaction has already condemned hundreds of millions more people to premature deaths from hunger and disease. The population connection must be made in the public mind. Action to end the population explosion *humanely* and start a gradual population *decline* must become a top item on the human agenda: the human birthrate must be lowered to slightly below the human death rate as soon as possible. There still may be time to limit the scope of the impending catastrophe, but not *much* time. Ending the population explosion by controlling births is necessarily a slow process. Only nature's cruel way of solving the problem is likely to be swift.

Of course, if we do wake up and succeed in controlling our population size, that will still leave us with all the other thorny problems to solve. Limiting human numbers will not alone end warfare, environmental deterioration, poverty, racism, religious prejudice, or sexism; it will just buy us the opportunity to do so. As the old saying goes, whatever your cause, it's a lost cause without population control.[26]

America and other rich nations have a clear choice today. They can continue to ignore the population problem and their own massive contributions to it. Then they will be trapped in a downward spiral that may well lead to the end of civilization in a few decades. More frequent droughts, more damaged crops and famines, more dying forests, more smog, more international conflicts, more epidemics, more gridlock, more drugs, more crime, more sewage swimming, and other extreme unpleasantness will mark our course. It is a route already traveled by too many of our less fortunate fellow human beings.

Or we can change our collective minds and take the measures necessary to lower global birthrates dramatically. People can learn to treat growth as the cancerlike disease it is and move toward a sustainable society. The rich can make helping the poor an urgent goal, instead of seeking more wealth and useless military advantage over one another. Then humanity might have a chance to manage all those other seemingly intractable problems. It is a challenging prospect, but at least it will give our species a shot at creating a decent future for itself. More immediately and concretely, taking action now will give our children and their children the possibility of decent lives.

2

▲

The One-Time Bonanza

▼

More people would be demanding action now if they realized that global civilization is behaving in a manner they would not tolerate in themselves, their families, or a corporation they work for or invest in.

Think of it this way. Suppose there were two brothers who as young men each inherited a great fortune from their father. Suppose the elder brother invested his fortune in sound enterprises that yielded regular dividends and in an interest-bearing savings account in a bank. The dividends and interest from his invested capital would provide this young man with an income on which he could live comfortably, if not munificently, for the rest of his life. Mindful of the many decades of effort and work by his father and earlier forebears to build up the fortune, he was always careful to husband his capital and invest in ways that would further enlarge it if possible, in order to pass on the inheritance to his children and their descendants.

Suppose the younger brother, by contrast, was more interested in enjoying the present than in planning for the future.

He invested his money, too, but with a less careful eye to protecting and enhancing his inheritance. He lived beyond the income from his investments, becoming increasingly dependent on inroads on his capital to support himself and his large family in luxury. In addition, some of his inheritance was lost through unwise investments. As the capital diminished, so did the income; so he was forced to depend more and more on capital to maintain his affluent lifestyle. The younger brother had run through his entire fortune well before his death and had nothing left to support himself in his old age or to hand on to his children, who instead were left with the burden of supporting their profligate parent.

► **SQUANDERING OUR INHERITANCE** ◄

Homo sapiens, like the two sons in our story, "inherited" a priceless fortune: the planet Earth and the riches it contained. Part of that one-time bonanza is, of course, the great deposits of fossil fuels that have powered industrial civilization. Even politicians and economists have gradually become aware of the finite nature of the fossil-fuel supply. But there are other riches, less obvious, perhaps, but even more valuable.

Arguably the greatest treasure consists of the millions of other kinds of organisms—plants, animals, and microbes— with which people share the planet. These other living beings have provided us with all our foods; with wood, fibers, and skins for clothing and shelter; and with medicines, oils, soaps, resins, rubber, and uncountable other useful items. Many organisms, of course, we domesticated and often improved by selective breeding to make them even more useful to us. Here we "invested" wisely; but we weren't investing income, we were investing part of our inheritance to increase income.

More important, that treasure of other species plays critical roles in providing us a hospitable environment. That environment includes such essentials as a favorable climate, breathable air, and deep, fertile soils. All these came into existence over eons, in part as outcomes of the evolution of the Earth's diversity of life forms. Similarly, the fossil fuels—coal, oil, peat, and natural gas—are the geologically processed and preserved remains of ancient plants and microorganisms. The human inheritance also includes inorganic treasures, such as vast underground supplies of pure fresh water as well as concentrated deposits of dozens of useful metals, from copper, iron, and mercury to zinc, all of which our clever species eventually learned to exploit.

For the first several million years of their existence, human beings, like other animals, were dependent for their resources (apart from air to breathe and water to drink) almost entirely on other living organisms—the plants and animals they ate or used for fuel or to fashion simple tools, shelter, and clothing. All these are renewable resources, naturally reproducing themselves, or, in the case of water, continually being replenished by natural processes that involve plants, animals, and microorganisms. In a real sense, early people, like the prudent elder son of our analogy, were living on the *income* from their inheritance.

With the invention of agriculture, things began to change. Human beings not only learned to manipulate their biological environment to enhance their food supplies, they soon discovered the value of metals—the first significant use of nonrenewable resources. Agricultural people later overexploited some renewable resources such as soil (by depleting it of nutrients, failing to control erosion, or allowing irrigated fields to accumulate salts) and forests (by cutting them faster than they could regenerate). These resources, once naturally replenished, were thus effectively made nonrenewable. By using metals and converting renewable resources to nonrenewable ones, human beings unwittingly began making inroads on their capital endowment. And those inroads, slightly at first and then more and more, provided the support for humanity's expanding populations.

►   **CAPITAL DEPLETION**   ◄

Human beings greatly accelerated their shift from living on income (renewable resources) to depleting capital (nonrenewable resources) with the advent of the industrial age and the harnessing first of coal and then of petroleum and natural gas as fuels. These seemingly abundant and cheap sources of energy permitted large-scale replacement of human labor in both manufacturing and agricultural production. They also allowed more rapid exploitation of other nonrenewable resources, making extraction easier and remote deposits more accessible.

The availability of "cheap" energy also made possible the development of powerful farm machinery, and abundant oil and gas allowed development of synthetic fertilizers, pesticides, and other products to boost crop yields (production per acre) considerably above those achieved with traditional methods. Similarly, we can thank fossil energy for facilitating the production of many useful goods[1] and for stimulating unprecedentedly rapid expansion of economies and of food production. In effect, fossil energy facilitated the population explosion of the twentieth century.

Finally, cheap energy has accelerated humanity's conversion of resources from renewable to nonrenewable, both through overuse and through pollution. Overuse converts renewable resources to nonrenewable ones by using them faster than they can be "renewed." Pollution, on the other hand, can simply render them unusable.

Overexploitation of two essential "renewable" resources, topsoil and groundwater, has resulted from efforts to maximize agricultural production in the short term to support ever-increasing numbers of people. Because the necessary actions to conserve soil have been neglected, enormous amounts of priceless topsoil have been washed or blown away.[2] Soil is irreplaceable on any time scale of interest to society today; centuries or millennia (depending on the situation) are normally required to produce a few inches. Losses of soil to erosion in natural ecosystems,[3] such as grasslands and forests, are negligible and are usually compensated by natural processes of soil generation. In agricultural systems, by contrast, losses can be measured in inches per decade or tons per acre per year.

Contrary to popular impressions, manufactured fertilizers are not substitutes for natural fertility in soils, and certainly not for soils themselves. The use of fertilizers can temporarily mask losses due to erosion, but they ordinarily provide only two or three of the twenty or so nutrients required by crops. Nor do they supply needed soil structure or the complex living community of soil organisms that often are involved in the uptake of nutrients by the crops.[4]

While certain tilling and planting methods can dramatically reduce rates of erosion, short-term economics commonly works against soil protection. Global soil losses in excess of new soil formation have been estimated at 24 to 26 billion tons per year.[5] As agricultural economist Lester Brown, president of Worldwatch Institute, has observed, civilization might survive the exhaustion of petroleum reserves, but not exhaustion of the world's agricultural topsoil.[6]

Similarly, water is being withdrawn from underground stores (aquifers) many times faster than it is being replaced by nature—all to support the expanding human enterprise. Most people realize there are limits to how much oil can be pumped, but few realize that humanity is also mining a finite reservoir of groundwater. A good example is the rapid depletion of accessible portions of the Ogallala aquifer underlying the Great Plains of the United States. That water accumulated during the last ice age; in some places (especially in the southern high plains) where the Ogallala takes in about a half inch of water a year, the water level drops four to six *feet* annually as pumps empty the aquifer to irrigate cropland. Mining southern parts of the aquifer to economic exhaustion in less than half a century amounts to the greatest overdraft of groundwater in human history. The rate of *net* withdrawal today is roughly equal to the flow of the Colorado River.[7]

That overdraft is deliberate, a policy established on the assumption that an infinite number of tappable water resources exists. As the state engineer of New Mexico put it, "We can always decide to build some more water projects."[8] But we can't if the water isn't there. The draining of accessible portions of the Ogallala aquifer in the next few decades will result in bankruptcy for many farmers in the Great Plains and a loss of production of much of the grain that the United States now exports. Overdrafts can destroy aquifers permanently. The water-filled cavities in rock formations sometimes collapse after the water is pumped out, or, in coastal areas, aquifers may be infiltrated by salt water.

The Ogallala overdraft is just one case of turning a renewable water resource into one that is, in essence, nonrenewable. In California's San Joaquin Valley, aquifers are being pumped at a rate that exceeds recharge by more than 500 billion gallons annually—and the rate is rising. That enormous overdraft to support irrigation in one California valley is difficult to visualize. It can perhaps best be pictured as roughly double the flow of oil into the American economy each year. Think of it. Double the number of arriving supertankers, double the flow of all those oil wells offshore and onshore, just to represent the drainage of the supply of groundwater under the southern half of California's Central Valley!

How long it can continue is not clear, although as the aquifer is depleted, the cost of pumping will rise substantially. As water analyst Marc Reisner put it, "It depends on a lot of things, such as the price of food and the cost of energy and the question of whether, as carbon dioxide changes the world's climate, California becomes drier."[9] All those factors, of course, partly depend on the size of the human population.

Overdrafts on aquifers are a worldwide problem; in India, for example, tube wells are lowering water tables under much of the nation. One Indian scientist recently noted about India's "water crisis":

Natural resources of the drought-affected and drought-prone lands become too limited to sustain and nourish the vastly multiplying human populations and the livestock . . . we shall have to put in a herculean endeavour to maintain any viable balance between the hungry people and the remnants of fertile land. . . . Our scientific know-how has no potential to increase the natural water supply. At the same time we are exerting too much pressure on the ground water for irrigating semi-arid lands without replenishing it.[10]

In China, per-capita water consumption is only one-fifth that of the United States, and demand is increasing rapidly. Industrial water use is expected almost to double from 1980 to 2000, and that by urban residents to quadruple. Water shortages are expected in 450 of China's 644 cities by the turn of the century; by 1989, the aquifers supplying Beijing and Tianjin had already been drained.[11]

Overdrafts on aquifers are one reason some of our geologist colleagues are convinced that water shortages will bring the human population explosion to a halt. There are substitutes for oil; there is no substitute for fresh water.[12] Unfortunately, the mindless attitudes of some engineers (and economists and politicians) are found worldwide: "We can always decide to build some more water projects."

Overdrafts are not the only problem facing aquifers. They can also be poisoned by human activities and their contents thus rendered unusable. The expanding U.S. economy produces more and more products whose manufacture creates toxic wastes. Poisons seeping into the ground from accidental spills and unsealed dumps can more or less permanently pollute aquifers. Sunlight and microorganisms are essential to natural purifying processes, but the former is absent underground and the latter in short supply. Some aquifers have even been poisoned by long-lived radioactive materials seeping into them from sites of nuclear-weapons manufacturing and processing facilities scattered over a dozen states.[13]

Our growing population also "demands" more highways, streets, sidewalks, and parking lots. Paving over large areas often results in rainfall streaming into rivers or the sea directly or through sewers, rather than percolating into the ground to recharge aquifers. So at the same time that we are draining aquifers for agriculture, industry, and drinking water, we are interfering with the processes that replenish them.

▶   **THE ASSAULT ON BIOTIC DIVERSITY**   ◀

Perhaps the most crucial part of humanity's inheritance being squandered to support rising overpopulation is Earth's biotic diversity ("biodiversity"). The planet's plants, animals, and microorganisms are now threatened with a colossal extinction epidemic.[14] It may prove to be a crisis even more severe than the natural episode that ended the reign of dinosaurs some 65 million years ago. There are aesthetic and ethical reasons for deep concern about the decimation of humanity's only known

living companions in the universe, but most people will probably feel the impacts of lost biodiversity through repercussions
on the economic system.

Humanity has already borrowed the very basis of its civilization from nature's "genetic library"—including all crops and
domestic animals, important industrial materials, and the active ingredients of numerous prescription medicines. A handful of species of scruffy grasses from that library, through
thousands of years of selective breeding, have been turned into
wheat, rice, maize (corn), and other grains. The 1.7 billion or
so tons of those grains produced annually are the feeding base
of humanity.

Even so, the potential of the library to provide such useful
items has barely been tapped. In exterminating genetically
distinct populations and species, *Homo sapiens* is foreclosing
myriad opportunities to improve the health and welfare of its
exploding population through as-yet-undiscovered new foods,
medicines, and industrial materials.[15] Indeed, we are even re-
moving the raw material on which genetic engineering depends, threatening to close down a technology that many are
counting on to improve the human condition. Genetic engineers do not create brand-new genes, they transfer genes of
known function from one organism to another. They are dependent on nature's library to provide the genes they transfer.

Even more worrisome, the reduction of genetic diversity
threatens humanity's capacity to maintain high-yielding strains
of its most important crops, which often can be improved only
by transferring genes from wild relatives. In many parts of the
world, close relatives of crop plants are being wiped out. As a
result, the crops may become increasingly vulnerable to pest
attacks and adverse weather.

But the most serious impacts of extinctions on society are
not these direct economic losses, but the consequences of dis-
rupting ecological systems, which support humanity by supplying us with indispensable "ecosystem services."[16] All of these
services depend on the participation of plants, animals, and
microorganisms. Two vital services are control of the proportions of gases in the atmosphere (which influences the climate)
and regulation of the hydrologic cycle—the circulation of

water through oceans, atmosphere, and land (including flood control and aquifer recharge). Additional services are generation and maintenance of soils, disposal of wastes, and recycling of nutrients; the pollination of crops and control of the vast majority of pests that potentially could attack them; and the provision of forest products and food from the sea.

One of the main reasons that many people are able to avoid facing the population problem is that they remain ignorant of the functioning of those most critical parts of the human inheritance—the ecological systems that support civilization. (A brief review of some basics of "how earth works" can be found in the Appendix.)[17]

Without the necessary biological background, laypeople are not in a position to understand either the constraints within which humanity must operate or the origins of those constraints. They can't understand why the human population has exploded or why the exploding human population threatens the very existence of civilization. They have little awareness of interactions between themselves and populations of other living beings and their nonliving environment.

This lack of understanding represents a colossal failure of education, a failure that goes unrecognized by most "educated" people. Years ago, the great naturalist Aldo Leopold observed that ecologists live in a "world of wounds" that thinks itself whole.[18] Today that world is bleeding to death, yet the average person goes about his or her business quite oblivious to it.

▶   **EXTINCTIONS AND NATURE'S GENETIC LIBRARY**   ◀

Let's look more closely at a major part of that hemorrhage, the loss of biotic diversity. Evolution and coevolution (the reciprocal evolutionary interactions of ecologically intimate organisms)[19] have produced the vast variety of life forms that make up Earth's biotic resources and that comprise the extraordinary richness of tropical forest communities.[20] Evolution and coevolution are also responsible for the enormous variety of chemical compounds that organisms, especially microorganisms and plants, produce to serve their own ends—especially defense against their enemies. That diversity of life forms constitutes the genetic library that we have already found so valuable; the biochemicals produced by organisms are among its chief benefits.

The library also contains those wild relatives of crops that serve as sources of genes to help the crops keep winning their coevolutionary races with the pests that attack them. Genetic variability is an essential tool of the plant evolutionists who are responsible for maintaining agricultural productivity. For instance, new wheat strains resistant to rust fungi have a life expectancy of only about five years in the northwestern United States. Then a new variety of fungus evolves that can attack the strain, and a new crop strain that is resistant to the rust must be ready for planting. But creation of that new strain is possible only if the requisite genes are available.

Genetic variability is also necessary to permit crops (and domestic animals) to adjust to variations in climate. The importance of being able to do that is highlighted by the prospect of extremely rapid climate change in coming decades as a result of global warming.

As humanity destroys biodiversity in tropical forests and elsewhere, it reduces the pool of genetic variability needed to stay in the game of high-yield agriculture. The loss of biodiversity also deprives us of tools that might help in the struggle to feed ever-increasing numbers of people. For example, only a few of the more than a quarter-million kinds of plants that exist have been investigated for their potential as crops. Some, such as some Central American grain amaranths (cereals in the pigweed family), appear capable of greatly increasing food production in some tropical areas.[21] Many other opportunities for creating new foods are doubtless "out there" in the library, awaiting discovery and development. But the destruction over the next few decades of the tropical forests promises to remove permanently virtually all possibilities of benefiting from that part of the genetic library.

Growing human populations are not only eroding the basis of agriculture, they are destroying the source of many of the most effective medicines (compounds such as aspirin and quinine were evolved as plant defenses). About a third of all prescription medicines are either plant defensive chemicals or chemicals modeled on them. Moreover, the chemicals present vary both from one plant species to another and among populations of the same species, so preserving different populations is as important as preserving representatives of each species. Conceivably, every time a square mile of tropical rain forest is burned, a drug with potential to help treat cancer or AIDS or some other deadly or crippling disease is lost forever.

Human overpopulation contributes in many ways to the destruction of rain forests and the species they contain, ironically compromising the chances for those increasing numbers of people to live long and productive lives. But the extinction of populations of plants and animals often disrupts ecosystem services well before entire species are seen to be threatened. The extermination of plant populations, for instance, can change the climate locally and also have severe regional effects through disturbance of the hydrologic cycle.

Human population growth in the Himalayas of central Asia after World War II has led to the disappearance of many populations of trees on the mountain slopes. The ecosystem's control of the hydrologic cycle was impaired, as exposed soil, no longer held in place by roots and sheltered from the force of downpours, eroded away. Much of that soil was washed downstream and has ended up in the joint delta of the Ganges and Brahmaputra rivers—the nation of Bangladesh.

Bangladesh is vastly overpopulated by any standard, its 115 million people jammed into a country the size of Wisconsin. Many Bangladeshis have been forced onto low-lying siltbars ("chars"), built partly of Himalayan soil.[22] There the people are especially vulnerable to the larger and more frequent floods originating in the now denuded parts of the Himalayas, and to storm surges caused by cyclones in the Bay of Bengal. In 1970, at least 150,000 people in Bangladesh perished when a storm surge swept over the coastal lowlands.[23] In 1984, tens of thousands were killed in a similar disaster, and the toll from the 1988 flooding (caused first by rising rivers and then by another cyclone) probably was at least that high. That disaster, which inundated three quarters of the country, left at least 50 million people homeless and destitute.

► COMPETING WITH NATURE ◄

Such events are among the consequences of the ever-increasing scale of human activities. Most people are unaware of the degree to which humanity has taken over Earth's land surface. Eleven percent of the world's land is used to grow crops; perhaps 2 percent is paved over or covered by cities and towns; a quarter serves as pasture for livestock; and most of the 30 percent that is still forested is exploited at some level by humanity or has been converted to tree farms.[24] Nearly all the remaining third of Earth's land is in arctic or antarctic regions or desert, or it's too mountainous or otherwise too inhospitable to be of much use to civilization.

Expanding human populations everywhere are replacing natural plant communities with ones that serve human needs, competing with populations of other animals for Earth's bounty, and destroying natural communities outright. As a consequence, the natural ecosystems upon which the human economy is utterly dependent are being degraded as myriads of their living components are exterminated.

The extent of this replacement, competition, and destruction is vast. Humanity directly or indirectly is appropriating a large and growing fraction of the sun's energy that is harnessed through the process of photosynthesis, which is carried out by green plants, algae, and many kinds of bacteria. Virtually all animals and other nonphotosynthesizing organisms ultimately depend on that energy, which they acquire in their food.[25] All the solar energy annually captured worldwide by photosynthesizers and not used by them to run their own lives is known as net primary production (NPP).

Human beings and domestic animals directly consume (as food, fodder, and timber) about 4 percent of the NPP produced on land and about 2 percent of that in the oceans.[26] This is certainly a disproportionate share for only one of 30 million or so species of animals. Yet an even greater proportion of NPP on land is diverted into human-directed systems, such as vast stretches of land planted in genetically similar crops, with their attendant pests. This widespread replacement of natural communities with human-created ones thus multiplies the human impact on terrestrial NPP to over 30 percent. Included in this calculation are the NPP produced in recently converted pastures, the NPP consumed when grazing lands are burned to improve forage, and the NPP in plant materials that are killed though not used in timber harvesting or when land is cleared for agriculture. Thus almost eight times as much of the NPP on land as is directly consumed is changed or diverted by human activities into human-controlled systems, featuring different kinds of organisms than live in natural ecosystems.

But that's not all. The conversion from natural to human-dominated ecosystems more often than not results in diminished productivity. Cropland (except when irrigated) usually yields less NPP than the grassland or forest it replaced; pasture is less productive than forest. In addition, people have reduced or eliminated productivity in many areas by paving them over or by creating deserts (a process called desertification), usually through overgrazing, overcultivation, or poorly managed irrigation. Just in the last forty years, global terrestrial NPP has been cut back in these various ways by roughly 13 percent,[27] and the reduction is proceeding at an accelerating pace.

Humanity's direct consumption, indirect cooption, and suppression of photosynthetic production thus add up to *nearly 40 percent* of the planet's potential NPP on land. Including the lesser effects on oceanic systems, the total global impact is about 25 percent. This enormous diversion of the energy resource of all life on Earth goes a long way toward explaining why the vital services supplied by natural ecosystems are deteriorating, why the expansion of food production is becoming increasingly difficult, and why, as a consequence, all nations are less and less secure.

Laypeople might get the mistaken impression that there's no problem if 60 percent of Earth's basic food resources are not directly affected by humanity; but to ecologists these are frightening figures. Perhaps more frightening than the level of takeover, indeed, is the rising fraction of potential productivity that is being lost—literally a reduction in total carrying capacity for *all* animal life, including ourselves.

Humanity is not only rearranging the biotic systems of Earth, its impact on the planet's physical makeup is far from negligible. For some time, civilization has been mobilizing many minerals at rates much faster than geologic processes such as erosion and weathering. Even in the mid-1960s, humanity was mining iron at a rate roughly twelve times faster than it was being eroded from Earth's crusts by rain and rivers; four times as much manganese was being mined, fifteen times as much lead, and thirty times as much phosphorus.[28] Those rates have continued to rise in the last two decades.

This evidence from physical systems, as well as changes in cycles of nutrients such as carbon, nitrogen, and phosphorus and in concentrations of atmospheric gases, reinforces conclusions based on the scale of the diversions and losses of biotic production. Altogether, they show unequivocally that humanity has truly become a global force threatening the very habitability of Earth—its ability to support civilization.

The fraction of terrestrial NPP already lost or diverted into human systems becomes all the more impressive when one realizes that our species seems to be "planning" to double its population again well before the end of the next century. Many people talk of a *quintupling* of economic activity, in order to allow for taking care of the additional people *and* raising standards of living.[29] Such an expansion implies an assault on global NPP far beyond that already observed. Given current technologies and those that can be foreseen, the planet could not support a quintupled level of human activity for even a brief time.

As any banker or businessman knows, one cannot continue to spend capital at a rapid and increasing rate for very long without going bankrupt—no matter how rich one is at the start. But society seems unaware that it is swiftly squandering its inheritance. *Worse yet, in the process of expending its capital, humanity is steadily degrading the systems that supply it with income.* We're eating the goose that lays our golden eggs. Not a very clever course for a species with the hubris to call itself *Homo sapiens*.[30]

▶   **OVERPOPULATION**   ◀

Having considered some of the ways that humanity is destroying its inheritance, we can look more closely at the concept of "overpopulation." All too often, overpopulation is thought of simply as crowding: too many people in a given area, too high a population density. For instance, the deputy editor in chief of *Forbes* magazine pointed out recently, in connection with a plea for *more* population growth in the United States: "If all the people from China and India lived in the continental U.S. (excluding Alaska), this country would still have a smaller population density than England, Holland, or Belgium."[31]

The appropriate response is "So what?" Density is generally irrelevant to questions of overpopulation. For instance, if brute density were the criterion, one would have to conclude that Africa is "underpopulated," because it has only 55 people per square mile, while Europe (excluding the USSR) has 261 and Japan 857.[32] A more sophisticated measure would take into consideration the amount of Africa not covered by desert or "impenetrable" forest.[33] This more habitable portion is just a little over half the continent's area, giving an effective population density of 117 per square mile. That's still only about a fifth of that in the United Kingdom. Even by 2020, Africa's effective density is projected to grow to only about that of France today (266), and few people would consider France excessively crowded or overpopulated.

When people think of crowded countries, they usually contemplate places like the Netherlands (1,031 per square mile), Taiwan (1,604), or Hong Kong (14,218). Even those don't necessarily signal overpopulation—after all, the Dutch seem to be thriving, and doesn't Hong Kong have a booming economy and fancy hotels? In short, if density were the standard of overpopulation, few nations (and certainly not Earth itself) would be likely to be considered overpopulated in the near future. The error, we repeat, lies in trying to define overpopulation in terms of density; it has long been recognized that density *per se* means very little.[34]

The key to understanding overpopulation is not population density but the numbers of people in an area relative to its resources and the capacity of the environment to sustain human activities; that is, to the area's *carrying capacity*. When is an area overpopulated? When its population can't be maintained without rapidly depleting nonrenewable resources (or converting renewable resources into nonrenewable ones) and without degrading the capacity of the environment to support the population. In short, if the long-term carrying capacity of an area is clearly being degraded by its current human occupants, that area is overpopulated.[35]

By this standard, the entire planet and virtually every nation is already vastly overpopulated. Africa is overpopulated now because, among other indications, its soils and forests are rapidly being depleted—and that implies that its carrying capacity for human beings will be lower in the future than it is now. The United States is overpopulated because it is depleting its soil and water resources and contributing mightily to the destruction of global environmental systems. Europe, Japan, the Soviet Union, and other rich nations are overpopulated because of their massive contributions to the carbon-dioxide buildup in the atmosphere, among many other reasons.

Almost all the rich nations are overpopulated because they are rapidly drawing down stocks of resources around the world. They don't live solely on the land in their own nations. Like the profligate son of our earlier analogy, they are spending their capital with no thought for the future.

It is especially ironic that *Forbes* considered the Netherlands not to be overpopulated. This is such a common error that it has been known for two decades as the "Netherlands Fallacy."[36] The Netherlands can support 1,031 people per square mile only because the rest of the world does not. In 1984–86, the Netherlands imported almost 4 million tons of cereals, 130,000 tons of oils, and 480,000 tons of pulses (peas, beans, lentils). It took some of these relatively inexpensive imports and used them to boost their production of expensive exports—330,000 tons of milk and 1.2 million tons of meat. The Netherlands also extracted about a half-million tons of fishes from the sea during this period, and imported more in the form of fish meal.[37]

The Netherlands is also a major importer of minerals, bringing in virtually all the iron, antimony, bauxite, copper, tin, etc., that it requires. Most of its fresh water is "imported" from upstream nations via the Rhine River. The Dutch built their wealth using imported energy. Then, in the 1970s, the discovery of a large gas field in the northern part of the nation allowed the Netherlands temporarily to export as gas roughly the equivalent in energy of the petroleum it continued to import. But when the gas fields (which represent about twenty years' worth of Dutch energy consumption at current rates) are exhausted, Holland will once again depend heavily on the rest of the world for fossil fuels or uranium.[38]

In short, the people of the Netherlands didn't build their prosperity on the bounty of the Netherlands, and are not living on it now. Before World War II, they drew raw materials from their colonies; today they still depend on the resources of much of the world. Saying that the Netherlands is thriving with a density of 1,031 people per square mile simply ignores that those 1,031 Dutch people far exceed the carrying capacity of that square mile.

This "carrying-capacity" definition of overpopulation is the one used in this book.[39] It is important to understand that under this definition a condition of overpopulation might be corrected with no change in the number of people. For instance, the impact of today's 665 million Africans on their resources and environment theoretically *might* be reduced to the point where the continent would no longer be overpopulated. To see whether this would be possible, population growth would have to be stopped, appropriate assistance given to peasant farmers, and certain other important reforms instituted. Similarly, dramatic changes in American lifestyle *might* suffice to end overpopulation in the United States without a large population reduction.

But, for now and the foreseeable future, Africa and the United States will remain overpopulated—and will probably become even more so. To say they are not because, if people changed their ways, overpopulation might be eliminated is simply wrong—overpopulation is defined by the animals that occupy the turf, behaving as they naturally behave, *not by a hypothetical group that might be substituted for them.*

▶   **UNEQUAL ACCESS TO THE**   ◀
                  HUMAN INHERITANCE

Thus far, for simplicity's sake, we've mostly treated humanity as a single family squandering its inheritance. In many ways, that unitary view is accurate, but it leaves out one of the major features of global society: the division of the human species into haves and have-nots, rich nations and poor nations. Even that, of course, is still a simplification; countries like Argentina and Portugal do not fit readily into either category, and almost all countries have both rich and poor segments in their populations.

The economic division of the world has changed somewhat in the four decades or so that we have been intellectually involved with population issues. In 1960, the rich–poor division of nations was sharper. In the 1990s, more countries are "semideveloped," and fewer of them still have the kind of total poverty typical of developing nations in the 1950s and 1960s. Still, the absolute numbers of people living in such poverty are much greater today, and the poorest of the poor have lost ground. Dividing humanity into rich and poor nonetheless remains a convenient simplification for considering how our one-time bonanza is being squandered. And recognizing the basic elements of the gross economic inequities that afflict the world is absolutely critical both to understanding the bind we are in and to finding ways out of it.

The numbers can be summarized briefly. Slightly over one billion people, less than a quarter of the world's population, live in nations whose standard of living—health, education, diet, housing, and quantity of material possessions—has improved dramatically over what the vast majority of the world's population enjoyed a century ago. But some four billion people don't. They live in nations where average per-capita wealth is only about a fifteenth of that of the rich nations and where their babies are some five to twenty times as likely to die by the age of one. Of those, nearly a billion live in "absolute poverty"—defined as being too poor to buy enough food to maintain health or perform a job.[40]

Rich and poor nations also differ drastically in their rates of population increase. The poor nations, except China, are growing at an average rate of 2.4 percent a year, which, if continued, would double their populations in about twenty-nine years.[41] The poorest populations are among the fastest-growing ones. In contrast, the populations of rich nations are growing at only approximately 0.6 percent annually, which gives a doubling time of some 120 years. These numbers are, remember, averages—they conceal considerable differences between nations within these groups, just as national statistics do not show the very different states of individuals within countries.

We must always also keep in mind that buried in dry statistics about differences between rich and poor is an enormous amount of human misery, an endless series of almost incomprehensible tragedies. But, even if you don't care about starving children and overburdened parents who live without hope for a future, selfishness alone demands attention to the problems of the poverty-stricken. That is because the plight of the underprivileged of Earth is probably the single most important barrier to keeping our planet habitable.

Without the cooperation of the poor, the most important global environmental problems cannot be solved; and at the moment the poor have precious little reason to listen to appeals for cooperation. Many of them are well aware that the affluent are mindlessly using up humanity's common inheritance—even as they yearn to help us do it. And all poor people are aware that the rich have the ability to bear the suffering of the poverty-stricken with a stiff upper lip. To remove such attitudes and start helping the less fortunate (and themselves), the rich must understand the plight of the poor not just intellectually but emotionally.

Our own *emotional* involvement with the sorrows of poor nations began with a visit to India in 1966. The desperate situation of that nation, exacerbated that year by the Bihar famine, left a lasting impression. There was no sign of profligate use of Earth's capital in the form of superabundant consumer goods, but there was abundant evidence of the loss of soils and biodiversity.

In 1989, Paul returned briefly to India and found some

things improved, some much worse, and the situation of the world's largest democracy even more precarious. The population of 500 million in 1966 had expanded by 325 million, and the results in urban sprawl and poverty were horrifying. But other aspects of the nation remained impressive: the admirable qualities of the Indians, both peasants and sophisticates, with whom he had contact, the rise of a substantial middle class (widely evident in Delhi), and success in increasing agricultural production (people looked comparatively well fed).

But an Indian government report estimated that 2.5 million Indians live their entire lives in the streets and that, of the urban poor, 65 percent have no tap water, 37 percent have no electricity, and 50 percent must defecate in fields and vacant lots.[42] India has managed to "keep it together" better than many (including us) expected. Whether it will continue to do so even more overpopulated, with much less topsoil, groundwater, and biodiversity, and in the face of the greenhouse warming and other global ecological problems, is questionable. We cannot be optimistic about the future of that nation—or ours—if current trends are allowed to continue.

For one thing, some superficial differences between the two nations have faded. Among the shocking things we saw in our original trip to India were huge numbers of people living in the streets and an army of beggars. Now, in any large American city, one can see many homeless people sleeping in bus stops and on park benches and street gratings. Beggars in New York's Pennsylvania Station are as persistent as those in Old Delhi. In the wake of the Reagan years, several hundred thousand Americans are homeless, and the income gap between the rich and the poor in the United States has grown.[43]

Many of the consequences of overpopulation in the United States, especially the plight of America's own poor and the nation's huge contributions to global environmental deterioration and resource depletion, are too easily overlooked. But, as we've noted, signs of too many overconsuming people, such as gridlock on freeways and city streets, severe air pollution, growing mountains of garbage, ubiquitous toxic wastes, and escalating crime rates,[44] are increasingly apparent.

The United States and India, the rich and the poor, face

the same basic choice: either to shift in an orderly, planned way to a sustainable human life-support system or to be brutally forced into that shift by nature—through the untimely deaths of large numbers of human beings. Population control in both rich and poor nations is absolutely essential. If that were achieved, and the rich chose to restrain themselves and to help the poor, the remaining nonrenewable resources could be used to build a bridge to that sustainable future. At the same time, the damage currently being done to nominally replenishable resources would have to be curbed and their replenishment encouraged. Otherwise, those resources will be capable of supporting even fewer people in the future. Sustainable development is needed not just in poor nations, but in rich nations as well (that certainly is *not* what they have now).[45]

In short, human numbers and human behavior must be brought into line with the constraints placed upon *Homo sapiens* by the limits of Earth and the laws of nature. People who think those can be ignored or evaded are living in a dream world. They haven't reflected on the four *million* years it took for humanity to build a population of two billion people, in contrast to the forty-six years in which the second two billion appeared and the twenty-two years it will take for the arrival of the third two billion. They have overlooked the most important trend of their time.

▶   **THE END OF THE GAME**   ◀

Rich nations have developed an economic system that increasingly depends on consuming humanity's stored inheritance, but which provides very unequal access to it, a system that has encouraged humanity to reach an astonishing level of overpopulation. It is a temporary game.

It should be obvious that an economic system based on consuming our limited capital is inherently self-destructive, but our short-term vision blinds us to the results of our actions. Society has already received warnings that the party may soon be over. Among the most obvious signs in addition to increasing environmental deterioration are the rapidly rising costs of discovering and exploiting new reserves of petroleum and other resources, and growing difficulty in expanding supplies of groundwater. The petroleum situation was spotlighted by the *Exxon Valdez* disaster, which underlined the price to be paid for exploiting oil fields in ecologically sensitive areas. Still, humanity seems incapable of reading the signs properly or of reaching a consensus on appropriate actions to avoid a disastrous final reckoning.[46]

Instead, each nation seems bent on competing for and quarreling over the pieces of the shrinking resource pie—even diverting large portions of it into dangerous and wasteful arms races. One need only contrast the great efforts expended to find and defend access to petroleum reserves in the 1980s with the negligible efforts to increase energy efficiency and control population growth. The world might yet be plunged into nuclear war over the Persian Gulf, and the petroleum situation is often discussed in the media. But few people protested the Reagan administration's pro-natalist population policies, its relaxation of fuel-efficiency requirements for new automobiles, or its dismantling of research and development programs for energy efficiency and alternative energy sources—all of which were senseless policies when viewed in a long-term perspective.

Serious consequences arising from such irresponsible behavior will sooner or later overtake us. The depletion of the one-time bonanza of resources will eventually force humanity to return to dependence on renewable resources—to live on income rather than burn capital.

Could a population as large as today's—let alone one much larger—*ever* be supported only on income? At the moment, we don't know how to do it, and it may not be possible. Among the things that may make it impossible will be the social and political responses to increasing scarcity and environmental deterioration.

But before looking at these questions, let's get some background by tracing how we got into our current predicament. How did we ever get ourselves into a situation of squandering our capital and calling it "growth"?

3

▲

Critical Masses

▼

We now turn to how humanity rose to a position of dominance on the planet and to its chances for staying there. How, after billions of years of Earth's history, did we get to the place where we could consume our inheritance and destroy the global environment in the process? That story starts with our origins and reveals that the behavior of past civilizations has differed from ours not so much in kind as in scale. By necessity, it will also lead us to consider the demographic facts of life.

Human beings are a very recent form of life, with a history of only a few million years.[1] During most of those years, the human forms that arose were fairly obscure omnivores (animals that eat both plants and animals) in warm parts of Africa and Asia, sharing habitats with their close primate relatives, monkeys and apes. Early members of our species evolved during the "ice age" era known as the Pleistocene, surviving intermittent glaciations in the northern continents. These primitive hunter-gatherers wandered and foraged in small groups, probably much as do chimpanzees today.

▶ **TREADING LIGHTLY** ◀

The total populations of the early human forms were quite small, probably not exceeding a few tens of thousands. Females probably bore several young during their lifetimes, but most likely at intervals of several years. Because the available foods were not easily digested by very young children, breast-feeding may have continued for three years or more, thus delaying the return of fertility after childbirth. Moreover, the wandering lifestyle and the need to carry very small children probably reinforced the long intervals between births. The birthrate in early hunter-gatherer groups was therefore lower than would be expected if births simply occurred as closely together as was biologically possible.

The birthrate is defined as the average number of children being born per 1,000 people in a population per year.[2] In 1989, the human population of roughly 5.2 billion (5,200 million)[3] produced about 144 million children, or an average of 28 children per 1,000 people.[4]

The counterpart of the birthrate is the death rate. In 1989, about 51 million people died in a population of some 5.2 billion, giving a death rate of 10 deaths per 1,000.[5]

The growth rate of the human population (or that of any other animal) is simply the difference between the birthrate and the death rate.[6] So in 1989 the growth rate of the human population was 28 births minus the 10 deaths to equal 18 per 1,000. That is, for every 1,000 human beings alive in the middle of that year, 28 more were born and 10 died during the year. Just to make things more complicated, while birth and death rates are conventionally given as rates per thousand, population growth rates are normally given per *hundred*—that is, percent. Thus the growth rate of the human population in 1989 was about 1.8 percent.

"Natural increase" of populations of human beings (or other animals) ceases when the birthrate and the death rate are the same. Then, if there is no immigration or emigration, the population growth rate (births minus deaths) is equal to zero, and there is "zero population growth" (ZPG).[7]

The growth rate of early human beings must have been very, very close to zero over millions of years; otherwise, there would have been a prehistoric population explosion equivalent to today's. Even a growth rate as small as only 0.1 percent annually would have produced a population of over 6 billion from a starting population of, say, 100,000 individuals, in less that twelve thousand years. That is less than half of one percent of the stretch of time from Lucy to us.

This means that over most of our history death rates must have been much higher than they are today. And no doubt they were, due to accidents, exposure, and predators, as well as diseases. Then, as always, infants and small children must have been most vulnerable; yet even adults probably rarely survived to very old age. With a very small gap between average birth and death rates, growth of these early human populations was extremely slow in the best of times. And sometimes groups of people must have declined or even died out when food was scarce, diseases struck, or other human groups slaughtered them.

Over hundreds of thousands of years, the characteristics that distinguish human beings from other animals evolved: a larger brain, the ability to create and use tools, and, above all, the development of language and culture—the capacity to transmit information from one generation to the next, nongenetically. Cultural evolution, the process of change in that nongenetic information, indeed was the key to the phenomenal success of human beings. Adjustment to environmental changes or new environments no longer depended solely on the slow process of adaptation through natural selection of better-suited genetic types of individuals. People could simply change their behavior and tell others about the improvement in life brought by the change.

Cultural change in early human beings, while lightning-quick by the norm of biological evolution, was very slow by recent historical standards. Refinements in tool and weapon designs, hunting and gathering techniques, shelter-building, fire-preserving, etc., occurred rarely, but occur they did. Genetic evolution continued as well, and several human species appeared and thrived for a time. The brains of the earliest forms were roughly the same size as those of modern apes, and the use of tools was scarcely more advanced. Physical and cultural evolution seem to have advanced step by step and in tandem for a long time.

The resources used by the earliest human beings were primarily food, water, and resting places. Their food probably consisted mainly of fruits, nuts, and vegetables, with insects, eggs, and occasional small animals providing a protein supplement. Meat most likely was not a major element in human diets until hunting skills had developed sufficiently to produce regular kills of large game animals. Besides consuming food and water, early people may have used tree branches or leaves to construct crude shelters, skins for clothing and other uses, and bones, sticks, and stones for tools and weapons. The discovery of how to control fire, of course, must have led to an appreciable use of wood for fuel.

Except for the stones, the resources used by the early human groups therefore were consumed no faster than natural processes produced them. The raw material for stone artifacts, however, was abundant. Thus, few in number and relying all but entirely on naturally replenished resources, the first human creatures "trod lightly on this Earth." They were not capable of doing more.

►   **THE FIRST IMPACTS**   ◄

Perhaps 300,000 years ago, *Homo sapiens* appeared, eventually supplanting the other human forms. During the most recent ice age, these modern human beings spread to occupy most of the planet's continental areas, and their population expanded accordingly. With superior hunting skills and much more sophisticated tools and weapons than those of earlier groups, the expanding human population began to exert a noticeable impact on the rest of the planet's flora and fauna. It has been suggested that the extensive savannas of Africa are a result of repeated forest-burning by human groups to facilitate hunting; if so, it was a significant alteration in biotic communities over a wide area.

The impact of hunting seems to have been even greater on animal populations, however. Increasingly skillful human hunters are thought by many biologists to have caused, or at

least abetted, the extinction of many species of large herbivorous (plant-eating) mammals, including wooly rhinoceroses
and mammoths, giant sloths, and one kind of bison. The disappearance of these animals occurred gradually in Eurasia and
might have been caused by the changing climate as glaciers
retreated. But similar large mammals in the New World vanished relatively suddenly and suspiciously soon after human
beings with fully developed hunting abilities invaded North
America about twelve thousand years ago.[8] It is likely that the
substantial widespread climate changes taking place during
that period, as the glaciers retreated, played a role in the extinctions of these large herbivores—as well as of some of their
other predators such as saber-toothed cats—but the additional
hunting pressure from human groups seems to have dealt the
final blow.[9]

The demise of the giant herbivores is the first instance we
know about in which human populations exploited a resource
with such ferocity that it was extinguished, although at a lower
level of exploitation it would have survived. The loss of that
important resource may have led to a renewed dependence by
human groups on plant foods for sustenance and consequently
spurred the invention of agriculture as the ice age waned about
ten thousand years ago. At that time, the population had
reached perhaps 5 million people.[10] Agriculture, of course,
opened the door to exploitation of renewable resources on a
scale and in ways never seen before.

▶   **THE FOOT GROWS HEAVIER**   ◀

The deliberate cultivation of plants for food is thought to have
been first practiced in Asia Minor and the Near East. The
earliest farming communities grew wheat, barley, and rye—all
grasses native to the region—as well as pulses (various kinds
of beans and peas) and fruits. A second center of agricultural
development, based on rice, is believed to have originated at
about the same time in Southeast Asia. A third (and possibly
fourth) independent invention of agriculture, based on potatoes
and maize, occurred in the New World several thousand years
later.

Although the archaeological record shows farming villages in the Near East appearing rather suddenly, the development of agriculture was very likely a gradual process, arising from the increasingly intimate knowledge by the food gatherers of the ecology of their preferred food plants. Deliberate planting of seeds and casual "weeding" of competing plants in favorable places presumably led, through repeated beneficial results, to human groups carrying out these activities in a more and more systematic fashion. And over many centuries, by choosing and planting seeds primarily from individual crop plants with desired traits, early farmers slowly transformed plant species from their wild forms to much more productive ones—to the domesticated crops familiar today.

Exactly when people began to control herds of herbivorous animals in order to maintain access to steady supplies of meat, and perhaps to facilitate the animals' reproduction, isn't known. But nomadic herding cultures in some semiarid regions unsuitable for cultivation may date as far back as the earliest farming. Like the development of agriculture, that of herding may have been a gradual process, as groups of people following migrating herds step by step asserted control over the animals, while protecting them against other predators.

However the processes may have occurred, farming and herding represented a radical new departure in the ability of human beings to manipulate their environments and the renewable resources on which they depended. The planting of crops meant, first, a replacement of the natural flora. By extension, it also spelled the displacement of much of the animal life that had depended on the flora, although some other animal species—pests—were favored by the bountiful new plantings.

The advantages of the new way of life to the first farmers were quite clear. Food supplies were more dependable and much more abundant; many times more people could be supported by the agricultural production of a given area of land than through hunting and gathering. A settled way of life, as necessitated by farming, was a more secure existence than constant wandering in search of food.

Whether death rates declined because of the greater security is a matter of debate, because the denser populations may have been more susceptible to communicable diseases. But the settled life and the more easily digested foods produced by agriculture may have enabled mothers to wean their children earlier and thus to bear infants more often. In any case, some combination of these factors—an increased, more dependable food supply, greater security, and more frequent childbearing —led to a gradual expansion of the human population.

After a time, farming became so efficient that one farmer could produce enough food for several people, a circumstance that permitted some people to specialize in other occupations and eventually made possible the development of towns, cities, and governments. Mining and metalworking were among the new occupations; these marked the first important use of non-renewable resources—the first inroads on our capital inheritance. The use of metals undoubtedly contributed to more efficient farming, as well as providing weapons for protection against other, hostile human groups. Because metals are unevenly distributed in Earth's crust, their use also presumably stimulated trade over long distances and, quite likely, the spread of ideas and technologies among different groups.

Not long after cultivation of crops began, people learned to channel supplies of surface water in areas where rainfall was sparse or unreliable. Some very early farming cultures developed complex irrigation systems to divert water from streams and rivers to the fields—another instance of human manipulation of a renewable resource. The ancient Sumerian culture of the Tigris and Euphrates valleys (in what is now Iraq), some five thousand years ago, was based on irrigation. One cause of the demise of that early civilization is believed to have been the result of centuries of irrigation: an inexorable accumulation of salts in the soil and siltation of the extensive irrigation systems.[11]

The increasingly efficient use of both renewable and non-renewable resources to support people and the expansion of farming to ever larger areas fueled an increase of the human population from 5 million before the invention of agriculture around 8000 B.C. to 200–300 million some two thousand years ago. That population growth, while imperceptibly slow by today's standards, represented an unprecedented outbreak of a single animal species, namely us. Moreover, it was accompanied by substantial changes in the biotic communities over much of the planet's land surface, especially in southern Europe and parts of Asia. Agriculture increasingly replaced natural ecosystems in favorable areas, and forests were cut down for fuel, for construction materials, and to clear more land for farming.

The Mediterranean basin, once heavily forested and well watered, then converted to agriculture, supported the ancient Egyptian, Phoenician, Greek, and Roman civilizations, among others. But, over the centuries, deforestation, overcultivation, and overgrazing by domestic animals led to a gradual depletion of soils and possibly contributed to a gradually drier climate. The fading of those once-brilliant civilizations may have been due in part to such environmental damage and depletion of the renewable resource base, although sources are not adequate to make judgments on the degree of responsibility. The exception was surely Egypt, whose civilization outlasted many others because the fertility of its soil was continually restored by the annual floods of the Nile.

Historians trying to explain why past civilizations rose, flourished for a time, then usually declined or fell prey to some conquering outside force have customarily looked for causes in social, economic, or political factors. Rarely have they considered population pressures, and their contributions to environmental deterioration and depletion of resources, as underlying causes of a civilization's downfall. Yet numerous contemporary accounts documented problems with soil erosion, recurring floods and droughts associated with deforestation, and so forth. The Greek philosophers described such processes and warned of the consequences of continued deforestation and of overgrazing, especially by goats. The warnings went unheeded; Greece today is nearly a desert, its soils thin and poor, the vast majority of its original forests long vanished.[12]

Similar trends were described by Roman writers, who also mentioned serious air and water pollution in Rome that may have caused significant but subtle public-health problems such as lead poisoning. The fall of Rome may have had less to do with the growing power of the barbarians who overcame it than with the declining health and vigor of the Romans themselves. The quality and abundance of food supplies may have declined as well, and it seems possible that the region's population, after a considerable expansion during Rome's heyday, may have dwindled with the decline and collapse of the empire and the onset of the Dark Ages.

Such phenomena were not confined to the Mediterranean basin. Similar damage to natural resources, though even less well documented, seems to have destroyed a thriving early civilization in the Indian subcontinent, now the Thar Desert in Pakistan. Deforestation, followed by floods and droughts and other environmental changes in densely populated areas, was also recorded by the ancient Chinese; they are problems that plague China to this day. And some scientists think that intensive cultivation of erosion-prone tropical soils was a major factor that led to the collapse of the Mayan civilization in Central America.[13]

Processes of environmental deterioration and degradation of the natural-resource base, which in various forms are known today as "desertification," evidently have occurred locally numerous times in human history. A human tendency toward overexploitation of renewable resources seems to have been established almost as early as agriculture—if not before. The current human predicament, in which this pattern has become worldwide and is threatening to go out of control, can thereby be seen to be an outgrowth of our history.[14]

Despite some setbacks (such as the bubonic-plague epidemic, which reduced the population of medieval Europe by at least a quarter) and the rise and fall of various civilizations, the human population as a whole continued to grow throughout the historical period, reaching 500 million around 1650. From the advent of agriculture some ten thousand years earlier, the human population had increased about 100-fold, doubling its size approximately every 1,500 years.

After 1650, the growing human dominance of the planet became even more obvious. The New World had been "discovered" and was settled by more numerous and agriculturally more advanced Europeans, who displaced the indigenous societies. The occupation of all the habitable continents by increasingly efficient agricultural societies was only the beginning, however. As European forests shrank in the late Middle Ages, first peat and then coal were discovered and put to use as fuels, and water was harnessed as a source of power. The stage was set for the Industrial Revolution and a new surge in human population growth.

►   **TREADING HEAVILY**   ◄

By sometime around 1800, the world population had grown to a billion, having doubled again in well under two hundred years. The Industrial Revolution was under way in western Europe and North America by then; in a multitude of ways, it transformed the world over the next century. Generally improving living conditions, including better housing and food along with advances in sanitation, accompanied industrialization in the West. These changes led to declines in death rates, especially among infants and small children, many more of whom survived their early years than before.

Annual birthrates of around 40 to 45, and death rates of 38 or more, per 1,000 in the population are characteristic of agrarian societies without modern sanitation and medicine. Such rates were typical in eighteenth-century Western Europe and North America, as well as the rest of the world. During the nineteenth century in some Western nations, however, death rates crept downward to 30 per 1,000 and below. The widening gap between the persisting high birthrates and falling death rates led to an acceleration of population growth in those countries, and growth rates climbed to previously unknown levels of 1.5 percent (15 per 1,000) per year or more in the late nineteenth and early twentieth centuries. Led by this population growth spurt in the industrializing West, the population worldwide doubled in a little over one hundred years to 2 billion in 1930.[15]

But, a generation or two following the onset of declining death rates in the West, birthrates too began to fall slowly. This even more remarkable change was apparently the result of individual couples perceiving that more of their offspring were surviving and that large numbers of children were an economic burden in industrializing societies,[16] and therefore limiting their families. Other factors, such as later marriage— thus reducing the years of a married woman's reproductive activity—and moderately high rates of nonmarriage, also played a part. Later, the feminist movement and the rising participation of women in employment outside the home probably helped to reduce birthrates even further.

Although the precise causes of the decline in fertility are still being debated by demographers, it occurred in nation after nation in the industrializing West and came to be called the "demographic transition."[17] By the 1930s, both birth and death rates in most European countries, the United States, and Canada had reached unprecedentedly low levels. For a few years during the Great Depression, birthrates in some industrial nations fell well below 20 per 1,000, with death rates around 12– 15, producing growth rates well under one percent per year. Indeed, demographers of the time worried about an end to growth and the prospect of population shrinkage.

Despite the lowering of population growth rates in the West, however, the average worldwide rate of growth continued to rise after 1930 as the benefits of industrialization— especially modern medicine and the control of insect-borne diseases—reached societies far from the West. With the prosperity of the post–World War II years, birthrates in the industrialized West rose again, particularly in the English-speaking nations such as the United States, Canada, and Australia: the famous postwar baby boom.

By the early 1960s, there were spectacular declines in death rates in the less developed nations of Asia, Africa, and Latin America, caused largely by the use of antibiotics and of synthetic pesticides against malarial mosquitoes. Helped a little by the Western baby boom, the plummeting death rates (accompanied by no change in the high birthrates) produced a global population explosion.[18] Growth of the world population peaked in that decade at an average rate of about 2.1 percent per year.

Although falling birthrates in a majority of countries since then have led to a slackening of the average growth rate, the annual population increment in 1990 is at an all-time high—

some 95 million people. In contrast, twenty years earlier the
population was increasing by only some 75 million per annum,
in spite of the higher growth rate. The reason, of course, is
that 1990's lower rate is applied to a much larger population
base; then it was only 3.5 billion, now it's past 5.3 billion.

▶   **MULTIPLE IMPACTS**   ◀

The Industrial Revolution brought improved conditions of life
in many ways, leading to a longer life expectancy for the average person. Similarly, discovery of an entire new category of
resources, the fossil fuels, underwrote the huge twentieth-cen-
tury expansion of the human population. But that also marked
the change from human dependence primarily on renewable
resources, constantly replenished by nature (even with human
manipulations), to an enormously enhanced dependence on
nonrenewable resources. By 1900, coal and peat had been sup-
plemented by petroleum, an even more convenient fuel, and
natural gas. The availability of these cheap, apparently abundant energy sources led to an acceleration in the extraction
and use of metals as well. And the fossil fuels subsidized far
more intensive agricultural practices, because of their use in
the manufacture of fertilizers and pesticides and to fuel farm
machinery.

By the 1980s, the depletion of accessible reserves of many
nonrenewable resources—notably, but not exclusively, petroleum—was becoming more and more evident. Expansion and
intensification of agriculture were approaching their limits.
Both processes were increasing the damage to soils and depletion of groundwater reserves. Natural communities of plants,
animals, and microbes were vanishing or being impoverished
as humanity took over more and more of the planet's land
surface, converted natural ecosystems to human-dominated
ones, and coopted their net primary production. As a result,
the life-supporting services performed by natural ecosystems
have been impaired or lost. Human beings now occupy and
use, at one level or another, some two thirds of the planet's
land surface, and are striving to find ways to exploit the remaining inhospitable third.

As we have seen, in the decades since World War II humanity has undeniably become a global force. The assault that we are carrying out upon the environment and resources of the planet is not just a matter of brute numbers of people. Rather, it is what those people *do;* it is their *impact* on the things we care about—on each other, on nonrenewable resources, and above all on the environmental systems that sustain us.

The impact of any human group on the environment can be usefully viewed as the product of three different factors. The first is the number of people. The second is some measure of the average person's consumption of resources (which is also an index of affluence). Finally, the product of those two factors—the population and its per-capita consumption—is multiplied by an index of the environmental disruptiveness of the technologies that provide the goods consumed. The last factor can also be viewed as the environmental impact per quantity of consumption. In short, Impact = Population × Affluence × Technology, or $I = PAT$.[19]

The $I = PAT$ equation is the key to understanding the role of population growth in the environmental crisis. It tells us why, for example, rich nations have such serious population problems (because the A and T multipliers for each person are so large). That is why it is so important that those nations begin shrinking the size of their populations by lowering birthrates until they are below death rates. It also tells us why a little development in poor nations with big populations like China can have an enormous impact on the planet (because the P multiplier on the A and T factors is so large).

Note that the total impact of a society can be lowered by decreasing any of these three factors, as long as the others are not increased so as to offset the reduced factor. In the case of the attack on the ozone layer by chlorofluorocarbons (CFCs), the impact eventually could be made negligible by operating on the technology factor alone—that is, by banning the use of the offending CFCs, which might result in a slight decrease in affluence if substitutes were more expensive or less convenient.

But the injection of the major greenhouse gases carbon dioxide (CO_2) and methane into the atmosphere, which threatens to change the climate and, among many other things, wreck agricultural production, is not so easily corrected. The atmospheric concentrations of these gases are tightly tied to population size. Consequently, there is no practical way to achieve the necessary reduction in greenhouse emissions without population control.

To illustrate how this interaction works, suppose that, by dint of great effort, humanity managed to reduce the average per-capita consumption of resources on the planet (A in the $I = PAT$ equation) by 5 percent and improved its technologies (T) so they did 5 percent less damage, on the average. This would reduce the total impact (I) of humanity by roughly 10 percent. Unless population growth (P) were restrained, however, its growth would bring the total impact back to the previous level in less than six years.

▶   **POPULATION MOMENTUM**   ◀

Of course, the size of the human population is not under control. In 1989, the world population appeared committed to at least doubling its size—lacking any concerted effort to accelerate reductions in reproductive rates or a significant rise in death rates. That commitment is based on "demographic momentum"—the tendency of a previously growing population to keep expanding long after reproductive rates have been reduced. A supertanker requires several miles to come to a stop after reversing its propellers; only a nuclear torpedo (or an Alaskan reef!) could stop it in its tracks. Similarly, only the demographic equivalent of such a torpedo, a sudden and dramatic rise in the death rate, could produce instant ZPG in a fast-growing population.

The reason for demographic momentum is the youth of rapidly growing populations. In 1989, 40 percent of the population of the average less-developed nation was under fifteen years of age.[20] Well over a billion young people in those nations have yet to enter their prime reproductive years (fifteen through thirty) and make their contributions to the birthrate. They will then live alongside their children and watch the births of their grandchildren. It will be a half century before they reach old age (over sixty-five) and start making large contributions to the death rate.

When the average couple has slightly more than two children, the population has reached "replacement reproduction." That means each couple will be replaced by just two descendants in the next adult generation. The "slightly more" than two is to compensate for the children who die before they reach reproductive age. In countries with high infant and child mortality rates, slightly larger completed family sizes are needed for replacement than in nations with lower death rates. For instance, in the United States, replacement reproduction is an average completed family size of 2.1 (we're significantly below that now at 1.9). In India, where infant deaths are considerably higher, replacement would be about 2.4.[21] The average Indian family size in 1989 was 4.3.

Demographic momentum may seem complicated to understand at first, but it will become clear if you just remember that births take place primarily among young people and deaths primarily among the old. Thus if a population has a high proportion of young people, one must wait for the average age in the population to increase before death rates catch up with birthrates. The process normally takes about a life expectancy (some fifty to sixty years in most poor nations) from the time replacement reproduction is reached.

The bottom line on demographic momentum is simple: barring plunges in the birthrate that take family sizes well below replacement reproduction, or substantial rises in the death rate, it will take fifty to sixty years *after* a rapidly growing population reaches replacement reproduction to achieve ZPG. The exact length of time depends on the age composition of the population (that is, the proportions of people of various ages) at the time birthrates begin to fall, how long it takes to reach replacement reproduction, and what happens to family sizes afterward (do they stay just at replacement level or drop below?).[22]

In 1990, for instance, India had a population of some 850 million people. Suppose, over the next thirty to thirty-five years, India's average completed family size dropped from the 1990 level of about 4.3 to 2.4 (replacement level) and remained there, and death rates didn't rise. India's population would continue to grow for almost a century, and when it stopped there would be about 2 *billion* Indians—as many people living in that one nation as populated the entire planet in 1930!

That's what demographic momentum is all about; that's why knowledgeable people always think of population control first when they think of solving the human problems related to overpopulation. To stop human population growth humanely, by limiting births, will take a very long time—at least two generations, even if completed family sizes everywhere dropped substantially below two children in the next decade or so. By contrast, social behavior and economic systems can be modified in a few years.

Overall, the prospects for a birth-control solution to the human population dilemma do not appear good. In May 1989, demographers Carl Haub and Mary Kent stated:

Even to reach a stable world population size of 10 billion, double the current total, birth rates will have to begin a steady descent soon. Unless we see declines in high fertility rates in many African and Asian countries during the 1990s, the prospect for world population to level out at less than 10 billion seems very dim. As far as ultimate world population size is concerned, the 1990s will truly be a decade of decision.[23]

Their gloomy statement was partly based on an apparent reversal in the late 1980s of the long-established slowdown of population growth. In the mid-1980s, the worldwide population rate of increase had fallen to 1.7 percent annually; by 1989 it had risen again to 1.8 percent, driven largely by a resurgence of fertility in China (about which more later). The continued failure to gain control over population growth increases the prospect that humanity will suffer large rises in death rates over the next fifty years.

► **MIGRATION** ◄

So far, we have discussed the population situation as if people always stayed put. But they don't; they have wandered since their days as hunter-gatherers, and they still pick up and move to better hunting grounds. Unequal access to resources is, of course, one major reason people move from place to place.[24] When one is looking at global overpopulation, migration does not come into the picture, since we neither receive immigrants from space nor send emigrants to other planets.

In various regions of Earth, however, migration may be an important factor in population problems and may greatly influence how humanity uses its inheritance. Recently, more and more "ecological refugees" have been fleeing from areas where ecosystems are collapsing to seek better lives elsewhere. Much of this movement is toward cities, from rural environmental-disaster areas such as the Sahel. During the recent Sahel droughts, more than 250,000 people in Mauritania and nearly a million in Burkina Faso (about a sixth of the nation's population) migrated to cities.[25]

The Sahelian migrations probably will not have strong impacts on global systems—they amount mostly to relocation of poor people who will remain poor and do relatively little environmental damage. On the other hand, refugees from desertified northeastern Brazil are not just flooding into cities; they, along with migrants from southern Brazil, are moving into the Amazon basin, where they are helping to cut down the rain forest for farming. That deforestation, in turn, is an important factor contributing to global warming—which may well reduce the carrying capacity of the entire planet.

Migration from poor to rich nations represents a very different kind of threat, however. To the degree that immigrants adopt the lifestyles of their adopted countries, they will begin consuming more resources per person and to do disproportionate environmental damage. Net immigration to rich nations is the rough equivalent of natural population increase (more births than deaths) in those nations.

The United States faces very serious and complex problems with immigrants from developing countries. The nation has traditionally said that it welcomed the "poor and downtrodden" of the world, but unhappily the "poor and downtrodden" are increasing their numbers by some 80 million people a year. Many of these, of course, would like to come to the United States or other rich countries and acquire the standard of living of the average American (in the process greatly increasing their use of Earth's resources and abuse of its life-support systems). The United States, therefore, must reexamine how many such people should be admitted legally and how illegal immigration can be curbed.

In particular, Americans must find a way to integrate migration policy with a comprehensive population policy. This is especially important because net immigration now makes up something on the order of 25 percent of the growth of the American population.[26] If a national goal of ending and then reversing population growth is established, as it should be, then it will be important to decide how much of the input side of our population equation is to be made up by natural births, and how much by net immigration.

This is a particularly vexing problem because of our traditional welcoming attitude toward immigrants, because of many ethical and moral questions surrounding immigration policies, and because of the great difficulty of measuring the flow of illegal immigrants. If the United States is going to avoid even more serious problems of overpopulation, its people are inevitably trapped in a zero-sum game; every immigrant admitted must be compensated for by a birth forgone. This will require either a further lowering of American birthrates (which are already low enough to bring an end to natural increase eventually) or much more attention to the problems of restricting immigration in the future. Booming populations in desperately poor nations are bound to make the comparatively affluent United States a target for ever more migrants.

Much of the attention to immigration questions in the United States is focused around the flow of immigrants from Mexico. The United States is the only very rich nation that shares a long unfortified border with a poor nation.[27] Through much of this century, America has used Mexico as a "labor pool of last resort," opening its borders when there were shortages, especially in farm labor, and sliding them shut again when labor was plentiful. There have been disgraceful incidents in which children born to Mexican citizens in the United States, and therefore American citizens, have been illegally expelled from the country. Furthermore, a detailed study of the Mexican immigration situation indicated that the benefits for the United States of Mexican immigration have far outweighed its costs.[28] America has been able to profit greatly from the poverty of Mexico. In spite of that, the flow of immigrants into the United States should be damped, simply because the world can't afford more Americans. Because of the need for U.S. population shrinkage, immigration from Mexico and other nations must be held to a level that, added to a reduced number of natural births, keeps the number of births plus immigrants below the number of deaths plus emigrants.[29]

Achieving that goal will not be simple. And much of the complexity traces to the joint history of the United States and Mexico.[30] In our view, no policy of forcible exclusion is likely to prevent a steady flood of Mexicans seeking work from coming into the United States. The border is too long, the ties across it are too tight, and the difference in average wages is too great for a "Great Wall" policy to succeed. The *only* way that the tide is likely to be stemmed is through creative policies that simultaneously help Mexico to control its own population and substantially improve the standard of living of Mexicans within their homeland.

Indeed, it is high time to strengthen the bonds of cooperation among the three large nations of North America. Almost 150 years of peaceful coexistence[31] make the United States, Mexico, and Canada an ideal trio to show how cooperation could help solve transnational environmental and economic problems.[32] We should begin to think in terms of the carrying capacity of North America—not merely of three separate and disparate nations that just happen to occupy the continent. Family sizes, consumption patterns, and technological choices made over the entire continent should be coordinated. And an economic unification should include the goal of raising the standard of living in Mexico while reducing the total impact of North Americans on the environment and resources of Earth. Needless to say, that's a big order. But the alternatives, such as trying to turn the United States and Canada into fortress states against the influx from the south, are big orders, too.

The dilemma of the United States and Mexico, of course, is embedded in the global one and in many ways is a microcosm of that situation. Movement of people from poorer to richer areas—within or between nations—is a natural response to the rich–poor gap. And as that gap continues to widen, and as environmental deterioration makes staying home less feasible, the numbers of migrants can be expected to rise, perhaps dramatically. The United States is not the only developed nation facing the problem of immigrants, and especially of refugees, both political and ecological. As in North America, the problems will have to be addressed in terms of the root causes and through solutions jointly sought between the developing and developed worlds.

Now that we've explored the history of humanity's rise to planetary dominance and despoliation, let us consider what all this means for continuing to provide that most basic of resources for our massive and still expanding population: food. If the food supply is not what it ought to be now, what are the implications for a population twice as large fifty years from now?

4

▲

Food: The Ultimate Resource

▼

To ecologists who study animals, food and population often seem like two sides of the same coin. If too many animals are devouring it, the food supply declines; too little food, and the supply of animals declines. When thinking about population problems, ecologists quite properly focus much of their attention on food. The amount of food available restrains the size of any animal population, unless space, disease, predators, or some other factor sets lower limits. *Homo sapiens* is no exception to that rule, and at the moment it seems likely that food will be our limiting resource.

Compassionate people, especially those who are offended by the notion that there may be too many people, often subscribe to a pernicious fallacy about the human food supply. They are convinced that there is no "population problem," only a problem of maldistribution of food.[1] If only food production were better attuned to the nutritional needs of people and shared more equally, they say, no one would go hungry.

The fallacy is seductive, because in the short term and in

a limited sense this is correct. In Chapter 1 we mentioned a recent study showing that the 1985 food supply could provide an adequate basic diet, primarily vegetarian, to about 6 billion people.[2] The same food supply could provide a modestly improved diet, with about 15 percent of its calories from animal products (about what people in South America have available today), to 4 billion people. Some 1.3 billion people in the present population would get nothing at all to eat if that level of nutrition were given to the rest. A "full-but-healthy" diet, with approximately 35 percent of its calories from animal sources, could be fed to roughly 2.5 billion people, less than half the 1990 population.

With the present unequal distribution of food, a billion or so people are, if anything, too well fed. Most of them, of course, are in rich countries. About a third of the world's grain harvest is fed to livestock so that the diets of the well-to-do can be enriched with meat, eggs, and dairy products. Perhaps 3 billion other people get enough to eat, although meat may not often grace their dinner tables.

Nearly a billion of the world's poorest people, mostly in poor countries, are hungry.[3] An estimated 950 million people were getting deficient diets in 1988—roughly one out of three people living in developing nations outside China. About two out of five of those (almost 400 million people) were so undernourished that their health was threatened or their growth was stunted.

The great majority of the hungriest, of course, are infants and small children, whose parents are themselves living on the edge of survival. This daily food deprivation is a major factor behind the high infant mortalities in poor countries. One in ten babies born in these countries will not make it to its first birthday; two of the surviving nine can look forward to a lifetime of chronic hunger.

If the excess food of the rich were somehow made available to the poor, the poor would be better fed; but there wouldn't be much left to accommodate a population increase. Of course, food production worldwide has continued to increase somewhat faster than the population for the last four decades, and many agricultural experts expect that yearly rise to keep on materializing—despite setbacks increasingly encountered in the 1970s and 1980s.

What about the assertion of the Catholic bishops, cited earlier, that "theoretically" enough food could be produced to feed 40 billion people? The original estimate on which the bishops based their statement was made two decades ago and has long since been discredited. It was reached by assuming that all more or less flat land in the world could be farmed and would be as productive as the land on an experimental farm in Iowa. This condition can't even be met by the rest of Iowa!

In reality, all signs point in the opposite direction.[4] In Africa south of the Sahara, food production has fallen far behind population growth. Grain production per person has fallen by about 20 percent since 1970, and the average diet there was already woefully inadequate then. Rising imports of food have compensated in part for the shortfalls, but most of these very poor nations cannot afford to import all that is needed. The amount of food set aside for emergency donations is a pittance compared to the need in Africa alone.

Since 1981, per-capita food production has also been lagging in Latin America, where population growth rates are not too far below those in Africa. In short, population growth is already outstripping food production in two major regions of the world, in which live nearly a billion people. Could this alarming trend soon spread to encompass the entire globe?

Between 1950 and 1984, there was an unprecedented upward trend in *global* grain production, sufficient to stay ahead of population increase (in spite of the reverse trend in Africa south of the Sahara after 1970). There were only slight fluctuations, and until 1972 no actual declines in world production from one year to the next (local or regional declines were offset by bumper crops elsewhere). Before 1987, two consecutive years of substantial global declines were unheard of. Then, after a record grain harvest in 1986, *absolute* grain production worldwide dropped by 5 percent in 1987 and fell again in 1988 another 5 percent back to the level of the early 1980s. Meanwhile the population grew by 3.6 percent in those two years.

Part of the 1987 decline was "planned," as a result of conservation measures in the United States and as a strategy to reduce an accumulated grain glut, and part was due to a monsoon failure in India.[5] But the 1988 drop was the unexpected result of severe drought and crop failure in such supposedly secure granaries as the United States and Canada, as well as the Soviet Union and China. That took care of the grain glut.

Preliminary 1989 estimates indicate a return of production to the 1986 level, but a continuing drawdown of food reserves. It is especially ominous that population growth makes it difficult to replenish stocks even in "good" years. Unlike the gradual slippage of food production behind population growth in some less-developed regions over decades, the 1988 event signaled a different kind of vulnerability—one all but forgotten in the post–World War II era of "dependable" global food-production increases: *agricultural success still requires favorable weather and a stable climate.*

The tricks of modern agriculture (especially the adoption of high-yielding crop strains in Asia and parts of Latin America, known as the Green Revolution) that have more or less steadily resulted in ever bigger harvests for four or five decades may now be playing out for developed nations and are proving to be less readily transferred to poor countries than was hoped. They undeniably achieve substantial short-term gains, but possibly for too high a price—and the bill is coming due, in terms of depleted soils, salted fields, drained aquifers, and the like.

In the rest of this chapter, we summarize the current food situation in various regions of the world, focusing first on the developing nations, where the population–food ratio seems to be worsening.

▶   **ASIA'S FOOD PRODUCTION: SO FAR, SO GOOD**   ◀

Grain production in Asia continues to increase faster than the population, partly because population growth rates in many Asian countries are lower than in other developing regions and partly because of greater success with Green Revolution technologies. Even so, signs that food production may fall behind population growth have begun to appear in some of the world's most populous nations.

China's grain production peaked in 1984 at a level roughly

three times that of 1950; since then, production has fallen. After the drought-reduced 1988 harvest, China had to import about 15 million tons, some 5 percent of its domestic grain consumption that year.[6] In part, the decline in grain production reflects improvements in diets, as some land formerly planted in grain now produces a variety of other foods.

The development of nonagricultural sectors of China's economy, however, is also partly responsible for reduced grain harvests. Industry is diverting water from agriculture, and homes and factories are being built on scarce arable land. Each year some 4,000 square miles of farmland are taken out of production, three quarters of it for construction.[7] This is an alarming trend for a nation that has 7 percent of Earth's farmland but is trying to feed 21 percent of the human population.

Although China has been very successful in reducing its birthrate, housing and employment still must be provided for about 15 million more people each year. Unless the trend in land conversion can be reversed and steady growth in grain production restored, China will become a major food importer by the mid-1990s—if sufficient foreign exchange can be earned through industrial exports and *if* enough grain is available for sale on the world market. The latter, of course, will depend on production elsewhere.

India, the nation that in the next century may challenge China as the most populous on Earth, made dramatic increases in wheat production between 1965 and 1983, thanks to its Green Revolution. Since 1983, India's rising grain production has lost momentum, for reasons that aren't hard to find. About 40 percent of India's land is degraded from overuse.[8] Soil erosion is rampant, with an estimated annual loss of 6 billion tons of topsoil—the equivalent of 8,000 square miles of arable land (an area the size of Massachusetts) disappearing from India *each year*.[9]

In addition, 40,000 square miles of the nation's irrigated land is suffering from waterlogging and salinization, reducing its average productivity by about a fifth. And water levels in aquifers are dropping rapidly in some areas.[10] In the south in Tamil Nadu, water tables fell 80 to 100 feet between 1975 and 1985, and overdrafts of aquifers through tube wells may threaten India's breadbasket in Haryana and the Punjab.[11] The reduced water-holding capacity of eroded land leads to more runoff and less recharge of aquifers. On the positive side, considerable potential remains for expanding irrigated land on the plain of the Ganges River.

The recharge of aquifers now being drained is also hindered by deforestation, which also leads to accelerated soil loss and more rapid runoff in watersheds. Between 1960 and 1980, over 16,000 square miles of the Indian subcontinent's forests (twice the area of Massachusetts) were destroyed, leaving less than 15 percent of the land forest-covered—an area about the size of California. Rates of destruction have been accelerating, though, and if current ones continue, those forests will effectively be gone by early in the next century.[12] Once-dependable springs in the increasingly denuded mountains are becoming seasonal or drying up entirely. Dust blown from the Rajasthan desert is loading the atmosphere, possibly adding to regional climate change.

That the entire subcontinent is being deforested is of great concern to Indians. As environmentalist Mohan Dharia said in a report to the Indian government: "At the rate we are destroying our forests we will not have to wait for long to see India becoming the biggest desert in the world."[13] Roughly four fifths of India's land area is now subject to repeated droughts, often on a two- to five-year time scale.[14]

India suffered greatly from hunger in the early 1970s. Following the Soviet Union's decision to buy millions of tons of grain on the world market after a disastrous crop failure in 1972, India could not buy enough to make up for its own poor harvest caused by inadequate monsoon rains. In Uttar Pradesh, Bihar, and Orissa, the nation's poorest states, there were over 800,000 hunger-related deaths above the chronic level of child mortality.[15] Since then, observers who don't understand that India has increased grain production by "mining" its soils and underground water have been impressed by that nation's improved food security. But in fact, short-term security has been bought by risking medium-term disaster.

In 1987, environmental analyst R. N. Roy of the Catalyst Group in Madras described the outlook succinctly: "With two-thirds of India's land threatened by erosion, water shortages and salinity, and with the added threat of pollution and increasing urban industrial demand, the country appears to be facing a catastrophic problem in the 1990s, if not earlier."[16] And don't forget: with an annual population growth rate of 2.2 percent, India must somehow feed an additional 16 million people each year.

India is certainly not the only nation in trouble on the Indian subcontinent. The region is one of the two poorest in the world (Africa south of the Sahara being the other). Its population of more than a billion is also one of the most underfed, with about half of the people lacking sufficient food to carry on an active working life and one in five so deprived as to threaten health and (in children) growth. The majority of the world's hungry "absolute poor" live in South Asia.[17]

Bangladesh is much poorer than India, even more crowded, and more vulnerable, and has a population one-seventh as large but growing one-third faster. In the 1970s, Bangladesh suffered two sharp rises in death rates due to starvation, and more of the same can be expected in the decades to come. Every year, there are 3 million more hungry mouths in Bangladesh.

Pakistan, the third major nation in the Indian subcontinent, is not significantly better off than its neighbors. With a land area six times that of Bangladesh and about the same number of people, Pakistan's greatest agricultural problem is lack of water. More than three fourths of its arable land is irrigated, with all the difficulties that implies. Much formerly irrigated land has gone out of production as salts have accumulated in the soil. Lester Brown has noted "glistening white expanses of salt-covered cropland . . . now abandoned" seen from an airplane flying over Pakistan and other Middle Eastern countries.[18] Population growth in Pakistan is also on a par with that of Bangladesh, and per-capita grain production has dropped significantly in the 1980s.

Western Asia, more familiarly known as the Middle East, has seen remarkably large increases in grain production in recent years, largely as a result of agricultural inputs purchased by oil proceeds. Through extensive irrigation, fertilizers, and planting of high-yield grain varieties, production has leaped forward. But in a region of scant rainfall and restricted irrigation opportunities, there are clearly limits to this expansion—even with unlimited budgets. The current production glut of oil, with the low prices it commands, should have underlined the problem. Some Middle Eastern nations are modernizing rapidly, while others seem to be retreating full tilt to the seventh century; but all have very high population growth rates. The oil-producing nations now can afford to drill for water everywhere and import as much food as they wish, but problems will reappear if the quantities of food available for purchase diminish—or the oil runs out.

Southeast Asia, once a rich food-exporting region, has suffered destruction (including ecological destruction) as a result of the Vietnam War. Subsequent political turmoil in Kampuchea (Cambodia) has kept that nation from resuming its former role as an Asian breadbasket. Only Thailand has continued to export rice and maize; and that nation, despite a relatively successful family-planning effort, is beginning to have trouble, probably largely because of increasing deforestation in the northern part of the country.

The story in the Southeast Asian giant, Indonesia, is not much cheerier. The nation had become self-sufficient in rice and had large stored reserves in 1984.[19] Since then production has not kept up with population growth, partly because of diminishing returns to fertilizer application.[20] Indonesia already has 185 million people, and the population is projected to increase by over 100 million by 2020, despite a birthrate considerably lower than that of India or Bangladesh. If that projection, which assumes a further decline in the birthrate, is realized, in 2020 Indonesia will have a population density of almost 400 people per square mile. That is about the density of Switzerland or New York State—and more than five times that of the United States as a whole.

Some two thirds of those people are now crammed onto the island of Java, which has only about 7 percent of the nation's land area. Java therefore is one of the world's most densely populated areas (now about 2,400 per square mile, more crowded than Bangladesh). In response to that crowding, Indonesia launched an ambitious program of transplanting people from Java to the relatively sparsely occupied outer islands. Between 1985 and 2005, some 65 million people, somewhat more than the projected population growth during the period, were to be sent to agricultural settlements on Kalimantan, Sumatra, Sulawesi, and Irian Jaya.

But the program is failing; unlike the rich volcanic soils of Java, the rainforest soils on the outer islands are largely unsuitable for agriculture. Transported people often find themselves unable to make a living; many soon make their way back to Java. The program also has been enormously destructive ecologically, resulting in heavy deforestation, soil erosion, and stream siltation. And one of the most unfortunate side effects has been to divert the Indonesian government's attention away from the critical need for population control.[21]

The Philippines, with a population of 65 million, has enough land theoretically to feed twice that number of people under intensive irrigation for paddy rice. But the water to supply the irrigation for those paddies is disappearing, because the islands are being rapidly deforested—interfering with a crucial ecosystem service supplied by forest ecosystems: assurance of steady, dependable flows of water in streams. Only two thirds of the Philippines' original forest cover remains, and a third of that is severely degraded. Much of the denuded land is in critical watershed areas, and the watershed areas will suffer further as the rape of the forests continues. Lowland agriculture is being subjected to floods, siltation of irrigation canals, and dry-season water shortages, all related to deforestation, and the damage is bound to increase.[22]

Furthermore, the hybrid rice varieties that form the basis of the Philippines' Green Revolution have proven vulnerable to pests, which has led to an escalated use of pesticides. For instance, between 1966 and 1979 the amount spent on insecticides climbed from 2 to 90 pesos per hectare. Not only does such an increase in chemical control represent a heavy financial burden on a poor nation, it also creates nasty environmental problems. One of the most serious consequences in the Philippines, as elsewhere in Asia, is the poisoning of fishes that are raised in farm ponds and flooded rice paddies—denying some of the poorest people a key source of protein for their diets.[23]

At its current growth rate, the population will double in twenty-five years. Agricultural production in the Philippines is not likely to double in the foreseeable future; indeed, it may even decline. Conservative Catholic factions, whose views are shared by President Corazón Aquino, have effectively gutted the once-active family-planning program in the Philippines. This action has set the Philippines on a sure road to famine unless that nation somehow finds the means to buy food in the future and other nations have it to sell. In 1990, there were almost 2 million more Filipino mouths to feed than in 1989.

The industrial nations of the Far East—Japan, Korea, and Taiwan—have had declining grain harvests for over a decade. Industrialization itself is partly responsible. In these already crowded nations, industrialization pulls both land and labor out of agriculture. So far, the losses have been eased by reduced population growth and compensated by a rising ability to pay for imported food. All three countries can attribute much of their industrial success to having first developed and maintained sound agricultural sectors—a lesson unfortunately too seldom pointed out.

The previous pages have portrayed a troubled continent. Still, Asia is really the bright spot in the food picture among developing regions; in most countries, increases in food production have so far kept ahead of population growth. The portents for the future, however, are much less cheery.

▶ **LATIN AMERICA: FALLING BEHIND** ◀

The food situation in Latin America, especially in the tropical regions, is quite different from that in Asia. Recent trends have not been encouraging, yet the outlook could be much brighter if available resources were used more rationally. It should be remembered also that the average nutritional level of Latin Americans is considerably better than that of Asians, although great variation exists in both regions. Brazil, the largest nation in the region, illustrates the problems—and the variations—all too well.

At first glance, it is hard to imagine that a nation with three times the agricultural area of China and less than one seventh of its population could have difficulty feeding its people adequately.[24] But the combination of an inequitable social system (which also generates faulty government policies) and the intrinsic problems of tropical agriculture has produced exactly that situation.

Brazil's problems are rooted in history. The colonial economy was based on plantations growing crops for export.[25] Rich people ran the plantations; poor people and slaves worked on them. Producing food for the poor or slaves was never a high priority—just as food for the masses isn't today. Indeed, a lack of adequate diets for a major portion of the population has plagued Brazil since the seventeenth century. A disorganized economy and chronic shortages allowed the development of a class of *atravessadores*, dishonest middlemen, who managed to keep food prices low for farmers and high for consumers, and fattened themselves on the difference.

Despite wide recognition of the problem for a long time, and sporadic attempts at reform, curing it has proven extremely difficult. Labor unions are weak, which keeps both wages and thus effective demand for food low.[26] This situation has been exacerbated recently by industrialization of the agricultural system for growing crops for export at the expense of home consumption, especially in the subtropical and temperate south.

Between 1967 and 1979, the percentage of farmland dedicated to growing food for Brazilian consumption dropped from 63 to 55, as agriculture became a major source of foreign exchange to pay for imports and help to pay off the huge foreign debt. Industrial agriculture takes place on large holdings and is energy-intensive, not labor-intensive. Small farmers have been driven off their land, many into the cities. There they have swollen the urban labor pool and helped keep wages and food demand low. Success in producing export crops—soybeans, coffee, oranges, sugarcane, cacao (cocoa), and cotton —has resulted in production of less food for Brazilians. Indeed, as production of export crops has risen, so has importation of staples to feed the poor.

The running of Brazil's agricultural system for the financial benefit of a few rather than the feeding of the many is not the only agricultural problem the nation faces. Brazil has "modernized" its agriculture, using techniques developed for temperate climates. The result, especially when these methods are attempted in the tropics, often is an unsustainable system.

For example, plowing benefits the soil in temperate regions by raising its temperature in the spring and increasing the activity of beneficial soil organisms, but has the opposite effect in the tropics and subtropics. Rather, the soil is heated enough to kill bacteria, earthworms, insects, and mites that are essential for maintaining soil fertility. Furthermore, heavy mechanical working of the soil and planting in neat rows lead to serious erosion problems in the wake of tropical cloudbursts.

Soil loss in Brazilian soybean-growing regions has been estimated at about 100 tons per hectare per year, while soil conservationists believe that the "limits of tolerance" (*not* the replacement rate) are in the vicinity of 15 tons at most. The entire state of Paraná (which is in temperate southern Brazil) is eroding away at a rate of almost a half inch a year—soil that would take some four hundred years to regenerate.

Brazilian farmers have attempted to compensate for the horrendous erosion rate by escalating their fertilizer applications. These were increased *fivefold* between 1966 and 1977, while yields (production per hectare) increased only 5–15 percent. Fertilizers can partially compensate for and mask nutrient losses from erosion for a while, but sooner or later the piper must be paid, and yields will tumble. In short, "modernization" of agriculture in Brazil is a stark case of living on capital—using up a key renewable resource (topsoil) so fast as to make it nonrenewable.

Similarly, the adoption of temperate-zone chemical-control systems for pests has led to worsening pest problems in Brazil. Tropical and subtropical agricultural systems do not benefit from the natural "pest control" of a winter season; instead, tropical agricultural ecosystems must depend on the natural pest controls derived from the complexity of natural tropical ecosystems. Birds, predatory insects, fungi, and other enemies of crop pests normally help limit pest outbreaks, but these natural controls are seriously disrupted by routine pesticide applications.

Further problems in Brazil have been caused by the use of much potentially productive cropland as pasture for cattle—a result in part of Brazil's inequitable land-ownership patterns and outdated notions of appropriate land use. This pattern has been especially destructive when extended to the Amazon, where rainforest soils are often thin and unsuited to permanent agriculture or even pasture. Stripped of forest, the soil is eroded rapidly, and nutrients are leached by heavy tropical downpours.

In Brazil, moreover, the Amazonian "ranchers" include the Volkswagen and Ford companies, which have established gigantic ranches of low productivity that soon turn into wasteland. These enterprises have been subsidized by the Brazilian people as a whole through tax exemptions granted for the purpose of "opening" the Amazon frontier. Unfortunately, while using productive land for pasture in the subtropical and temperate parts of the country is wasteful (and morally dubious when millions of Brazilians are hungry and jobless), the application of such a policy to the rainforest region is a travesty, denying present and future generations any benefit from the forest's resources.[27]

In short, Brazil's agriculture is being pushed toward social and ecological failure, in part to satisfy the demand for export crops generated in the overpopulated developed world. In the absence of a drastic overhaul of its agricultural system, the country has scant prospect of being able to maintain its export potential in the long run, or to provide adequate diets for a population "scheduled" to double in thirty-five years or so. Each year, almost 3 million more Brazilians must be carried by the staggering food-supply system.

The reasons for a 10 percent decline in per-capita food production in Latin America since 1981 vary among the different nations, but some factors are common to many. Maldistribution of land ownership, irrational land-use patterns, ecological degradation, the debt crisis (which prevents capital from flowing into agricultural sectors), and rapid population growth (over 2 percent per year on average for Latin America) all contribute to the failure of agricultural production to keep up.

In the tropical Andes, particularly in present-day Peru and Ecuador, deforestation of the mountain ranges above the fertile valleys was well under way before the Spanish arrived in the sixteenth century. What the Incas had begun the Spanish colonial authorities continued, and today much of the land's productive capacity has eroded away with the soil. Stunted growth from malnutrition is obvious in the native Andeans, who live in what should be a healthy environment (compared with the disease-ridden lowland forests).

Argentina and Chile seem to have everything going for them: fertile lands, a temperate climate, and moderate population growth (currently about 1.5 percent per year). But corrupt or repressive politics and stratified societies with skewed landholding patterns have tripped them up. Nonetheless, Argentina remains the sole significant net grain exporter in Latin America.

Central America has suffered from extensive deforestation, much of it to create short-lived cattle ranches for exporting "cheap" beef for the North American fast-food market. As meat exports rose in the 1960s and 1970s, domestic meat consumption fell in several countries. For instance, in Costa Rica in those two decades, beef production quadrupled, but per-capita consumption declined by more than 40 percent (to a mere 35 pounds a year, barely one third of U.S. consumption). In recent years, political turmoil in El Salvador and Guatemala has prevented the needed land reform that might put domestic food production on a more secure footing, while Nicaragua's progress has been disrupted by U.S. intervention.

Mexico was the Green Revolution's first success story and a showcase. In the 1950s, Mexico went from being an increasing wheat importer to an exporter as yields multiplied. Grain production increased fourfold by the mid-1980s.[28] By the 1980s, Mexico's population growth, among the most rapid in the hemisphere, had overwhelmed those dazzling food-production increases, despite some progress in reducing the birthrate by a late-starting family-planning program.

Recently, Mexico's problems have been compounded by

its crippling foreign debt (largely a result of the oil-price bust in the 1980s), loss of 10 percent of its grain-producing farmland to other uses, an unfinished land-reform program, and chronic corruption. Mexico's agricultural system is probably sounder than many in Latin America, but its productive land is limited (the northern part of the country is largely desert), and the population is still growing fast; there are over 2 million more Mexicans to feed each year.[29]

It should be emphasized that, unlike most of Asia, Latin America is not yet pushing against physical or biological limits of agricultural production under available technology. The problems listed above are part of a generally inefficient use of resources, encouraged to a significant degree by demand from the overpopulated rich countries. Unfortunately, many trends (especially the destruction of rain forests and widespread unchecked soil erosion) are undermining the potential for future food production.[30] And population growth could quickly close the gap between food needs and the capacity to produce it.

▶   **AFRICA: FALLING BEHIND**   ◀

Africa is the world's nutritional "basket case." While deaths related to inadequate diets occur in poor nations everywhere, only in Africa have there been widespread famines in the last two decades. In the 1980s, more than 5 million infants—one of every five or six children born—have died each year in Africa from causes related to hunger.[31]

Periodically, the severity of African famines has been brought home to citizens of the rich nations through television programs showing starving children in hideous refugee camps. The coverage usually brings outpourings of empathy and donations, often generated with the help of celebrities and rock-music groups. Unfortunately, the acute situations publicized represent the iceberg tip of a continentwide tragedy: chronic hunger, spreading and intensifying year by year.

In the short term, donated food often does not reach the people it was meant for. In the Ethiopian famines of the mid-1980s, both sides in a ferocious civil war often used donated food as a weapon, preventing it from reaching starving people in territory controlled by "the other side." Similar tactics played a large role in the 1988 famine in Sudan, where some 100,000 perished.

Even in peacetime, food aid doesn't always reach its intended recipients. For food donations to reach the neediest famine victims, many things have to work right. Port facilities must be adequate, warehousing must be sufficient to store the food safely until it can be distributed, trucks and railroads capable of moving the food to the hinterland must be in working condition (along with their roads and railbeds). At the end of the line, there often must be four-wheel-drive vehicles available to take food to the more remote parts of the countryside where hunger may be most acute. The entire system must function smoothly in a time of stress, often in the face of massive corruption in the distribution system.

The magnitude of the problems that can plague a relief effort are exemplified by the Ethiopian situation in the mid-1980s. There were lots of television pictures of Hercules transports flying in much-needed food. Unfortunately, however, a Hercules can carry only 21 tons of grain, whereas Ethiopia needed 1.5 *million* tons.[32] Such mountains of grain can be carried only on ships, which may take months to reach Ethiopia from donor countries. Furthermore, at maximum capacity, Ethiopia's ports can handle only 3,500 tons per day; so even if the ships were perfectly lined up so that they never had to wait for space, and port facilities were never broken down or left idle, it would take fourteen months to unload that much grain. Meanwhile about 1.5 million Ethiopians are added each year to the ranks of those to be fed.

The barriers to distributing food aid to starving refugees only highlight problems of resource distribution and development that are endemic in Africa and other poor regions. While the starving victims of war and revolution have captured global attention, several hundred million victims of chronic rather than acute food shortages continue to be overlooked, and inefficient and impoverished agricultural systems fall ever farther behind in the race to stay ahead of population growth.

Since 1968, food production per person in Africa south of the Sahara has declined by some 20 percent. Tropical African nations are too poor and debt-burdened to make up all of the deficit with imports, and far too little food has been made available for donation. The result has been a continuous erosion of the nutritional status of Africans and in some areas a stagnation of progress in, among other things, reducing infant mortalities—a necessary prerequisite to reducing birthrates.

One example is Kenya, a country in some ways fortunate: it has a reasonably stable government, a well-established and remunerative tourist industry, and one of the better agricultural systems on the continent. Yet Kenya can't feed its people now, and population growth is so fast that, if it continues, there will be twice as many Kenyans in fewer than twenty years. Per-capita water supplies in that semiarid nation will be reduced by half soon after the turn of the century, and, despite a model soil-conservation program, erosion is unlikely to be brought under control before Kenya's population has doubled.[33] By then, it may be too late for a nation with limited arable land and so many people that a major preoccupation of men even today is squabbling over ever tinier, subdivided landholdings while the women do most of the farm and domestic work. Every year, Kenya must find food for a million more people.

Overall, the numbers for tropical Africa are grim. An estimated 44 percent of the region's people were inadequately fed in 1980, one in every four dangerously so.[34] Since 1980, the situation has become, if anything, worse, as per-capita food production has continued to slip and populations have continued to expand by an average of 3 percent per year.

Nigeria's population, 115 million in 1989, is projected to reach 160 million in 2000, some 270 million in 2020, and over 530 million before growth ceases sometime after 2050. This is as many people as lived in all of Africa in 1984. We don't take such projections very seriously, since they *ignore nearly certain rises in death rates* resulting from the manifold consequences of overpopulation.

Crop yields in Nigeria in the 1980s were lower than they had been thirty years earlier, in part because of soil erosion.[35] Corruption in government, mismanagement of resources (including revenues from oil), and failure to attend to agriculture have also contributed to Nigeria's problems. Imagine what they will be like if the Nigerian population doubles and redoubles in two generations, as projected!

The Sahel, a swath across Africa along the southern fringe of the Sahara cutting through a dozen countries, has been plagued with recurrent drought for nearly twenty years. The resultant, almost continuous famine has ceased to be "news" for the media, but is a prime example of the consequences of overpopulation. Overgrazing and overcultivation of the region's fragile lands have led to severe desertification. The effects of a naturally occurring drought were greatly intensified because so little vegetation remained to recycle the scant rainfall. Moreover, the denuded landscape's reflectivity had changed, leading to reduced cloud formation and thus still less rain.[36] Even with the return of more normal rains in the late 1980s, the rapidly growing Sahel populations remained dependent on imported food to meet their needs.[37]

North of the Sahara, the picture is not much better. The five nations of Africa's northern coast now import half their grain. Oil revenues in some cases have helped to finance the imports, and nutritional levels have improved during the 1980s. But the region's population is growing at an average annual rate of 2.8 percent, which does not bode well for future food self-sufficiency in those desert lands.[38]

Temperate South Africa is the continent's breadbasket—to the extent that there is one. South Africa sells grain to its neighbors, and sustained some of them when drought afflicted the southern part of the continent earlier in the decade. But South Africa's black and "colored" populations are increasing rapidly (a further source of tension between the races), and the country's agricultural resources are already under stress.[39] Given the disastrous governmental policies and uncertain future of the country, we can't hold out much hope for the long-term wise use of agricultural resources.

In sum, there are few nutritional bright spots in the Dark Continent.

▶   **THE OVERFED DEVELOPED WORLD**   ◀

We have until now concentrated on the food situation in the developing world, because that is where the biggest problems are—problems that are tightly tied to population growth. But in the modern world, food production is less and less matched to the distribution of people. Before World War II, international food trade was modest compared to the total amount produced. And the only region that imported substantial amounts of grain was Europe. Then, Asia, Latin America, and Africa were all net food-exporting regions, along with North America. Today the situation has almost completely reversed. As developing nations have lost ground in food production, they have become increasingly dependent on the world grain market to supply their needs.

Some industrialized nations are also food-deficit nations, heavily dependent on imports to feed their populations. Japan is an outstanding example, importing over two thirds of its grain. The Soviet Union and several Eastern European nations in recent years also have imported substantial portions of their grain supplies. But all these countries can comparatively easily afford the imports, and their populations are approaching ZPG. Hunger in these nations, when it occurs, is due to maldistribution, misallocation of resources (as in the USSR), and callousness about the plight of the poor. Many citizens of rich nations eat too much food for good health and waste too much of it.

Only a handful of nations today are reliable food exporters, nearly all of them developed nations: the United States, Canada, the European Common Market, Australia, New Zealand, Argentina, and Thailand. Americans, fond of viewing their country as a leading industrial power, are largely unaware that it also is by far the world's leading grain exporter and is economically dependent on those exports to keep its balance of trade from deteriorating even further. Three fourths of the world's grain shipments are from the North American granary; over a hundred nations around the world depend at some level on those resources.[40] This goes far to explain why the 1988 drought that hit the North American grain belt was a matter for global concern.

► **VACUUMING THE SEA** ◄

Now we turn to another important component of the world food system—fisheries. Two decades ago, it was fashionable among population optimists to say that the hungry millions could be fed by the boundless riches of the sea. But the boundless riches of the seas have been measured and the bounds found to be only too real.

In 1970 Peru harvested almost 13 million tons[41] of anchovetas, which provided a large amount of cheap protein for animal feed, mainly to rich nations. In 1972, the Peruvian anchoveta fishery collapsed. A combination of overfishing and an El Niño, the warming of the normally cool waters of the Humboldt Current, caused a drop of the fishery's harvest to just over 2 million tons in 1973.[42] This launched a decade in which increases in global commercial-fishery harvests lagged behind world population growth, with catches remaining below 70 million tons per year. Then, in the mid-1980s, there was a sharp upturn to about 84 million tons of fishes extracted from the oceans, plus another 7 million tons provided by fish-farming in 1986. The increase was due largely to the recovery, after almost two decades, of the Peruvian anchoveta fishery, combined with an expansion of the take of pollack, a codlike fish, in the northeastern Pacific.

Cheer at this news has to be tempered by the realization that many fish stocks are already overfished.[43] An ecologist in Alaska recently told us that the pollack fishery in the Bering Sea was being "strip-mined" and was expected to decline soon.[44]

Extraction of fishes from the oceans overall is approaching the maximum sustainable yield, thought to be in the vicinity of 100 million tons of conventional fishes (that is, not including such potential seafood sources as octopus and antarctic krill). Although 100 million tons of seafood seems small when contrasted with a global grain harvest some seventeen times bigger, fishes supply a critical protein supplement to many people who otherwise would have much less nutritious diets. Seafood is thus a vital element in the world food picture.[45]

If the approximately 24 million tons of fish caught each

year in sports and subsistence fishing, in addition to the commercial fisheries, are counted, the 100-million-ton estimate has been exceeded. Suppose, though, that estimate were low, and the maximum sustainable yield were actually 150 million tons. Suppose also that a miracle happened, and each stock was carefully harvested so as to maintain its maximum sustainable yield. Even under those circumstances, per-capita yields would fall again within a few decades as population growth overwhelmed those miracles.

Unfortunately, instead of miracles, fisheries are facing disasters. Demand for fish is climbing steadily, encouraging the destructive harvesting of stocks. Long before eastern-Pacific pollack became the fishermen's target, many stocks in the North Atlantic were seriously depleted; competition for the dwindling catches even led to a shooting war between the United Kingdom and Iceland during the 1970s.[46] The United Nations Food and Agriculture Organization recently estimated that, of 280 fisheries it monitors, only 25 could be considered underexploited or moderately exploited. The only underexploited fishing regions left are in the Southern Hemisphere.[47]

Meanwhile, ocean pollution is rising steadily, doubtless reducing the maximum sustainable yields for some stocks and contaminating many harvested fishes. Coastal waters are not only the sites of greatest marine pollution (being adjacent to the sources on land), they are also where most commercial fisheries are located—an unfortunate combination. Oil, sewage, and medical wastes washing up on American beaches tell us something about what's happening in the oceans.

Similar problems are occurring around the world. Off the coast of China, the total seawater fishing area has been reduced by a third as a result of the annual discharge of 400 billion gallons of domestic and 1200 billion gallons of industrial sewage.[48] According to Professor He Bochuan, whitebait, yellow croaker, prawns, and river crab are almost gone from the Bohai Sea (the northwestern corner of the Yellow Sea, the closest ocean to Beijing) and its estuaries.[49]

Fisheries productivity has also been indirectly threatened by pollution of estuaries and damage or destruction of coastal wetlands, which serve as important nursery areas and sources of food for numerous oceanic fish stocks. An even greater threat to estuaries and wetlands is posed by the prospect of global warming, which will cause the sea level to rise and flood them.

It seems the riches of the sea may not save us, after all. If humanity is lucky (or careful), it may be possible to maintain the present level of production in the face of the human assault on the oceans and associated wetlands. If not, seafood may increasingly become a luxury food as dwindling catches and rising prices put it beyond the reach of people of modest means.

In this chapter, we've assessed the current food-production picture and considered the precarious food situation of the developing world in particular. In the next chapter, we consider the ecological underpinnings of modern agriculture and the situation in developed nations—which may not be as secure as most Americans have been led to believe.

5

▲

***

The Ecology of
Agriculture

***

▼

We've now considered the precarious food situation in the developing world, as well as the rising pressures on the world's fisheries. Before looking in more detail at the issue of global food security, let's consider where food comes from. In order to understand the world food situation, it is necessary to have a grasp of the principal features of agricultural ecosystems and their resources.

First, agricultural systems necessarily are and will remain spread out—agriculture can't be concentrated in small areas. This characteristic traces to a fundamental circumstance: agriculture runs on photosynthesis, which in turn is driven by incoming solar energy. That energy arrives widely dispersed.[1]

Since humanity can do precious little about either the spread-out arrival of sunlight—the most fundamental agricultural resource—or the efficiency of photosynthesis, large areas must be farmed to feed a human population. Under extremely optimistic assumptions, a city of a million people would require almost 400 square miles of land in crops to "capture" enough sunlight to feed its citizens a basic, no-frills vegetarian diet. With realistic accounting for the fraction of the year that crops can be grown in most regions, the efficiency with which energy can be extracted from vegetable food, the pest losses and wastage between harvest and eating, the feeding of some crops to animals (and the pasture they require), and the need to produce some less calorie-rich crops to obtain variety and needed nutrients, that number could easily be multiplied five- or tenfold. The city therefore depends on thousands of square miles of farmland just to provide its food.

▶   **WEATHER AND CLIMATE**   ◀

A second key point for understanding the food problem is that agricultural productivity is extremely sensitive to the weather. A myth has arisen that modern agricultural techniques and irrigation have somehow freed agriculture from dependence on suitable temperatures and rainfall. If anything, the opposite is true. Modern high-yielding strains of crops often respond with larger variations in yield to changes in weather than do traditional strains.

The importance of a stable and suitable climate for agriculture today was clearly demonstrated in the United States in 1988. The drought slashed the nations's grain harvest from its usual 300 million tons or so to less than 200 million tons—even though the United States has as "modern" an agricultural system as there is.

The same source of energy that powers photosynthesis also creates the weather. The sun's energy drives the entire climatic system.[2] Hot air rises; and air near the equator is heated more than air near the poles. Cold air also can hold less moisture (water vapor) than hot air; so, as rising air cools by expansion in the thinner upper atmosphere, its moisture is squeezed out, resulting in clouds (made of tiny droplets of water) and rain (bigger droplets). Each puffy cumulus cloud that hangs over a summer landscape marks the cooling top of a rising column of hot air.

These characteristics of air, combined with Earth's rotation and the complex pattern of the planet's surface (water versus land; flat land versus mountains; differences in the re-flectivity of sunlight off various surfaces), create the behavior of the atmospheric system that we call "weather" and the long-term average weather called the "climate."

Climatologists can explain many major features of climate. A basic pattern is movement of warmed air poleward from the equator at high altitudes and of cooled air toward the equator from polar regions along the surface. This is not a simple loop, though. Hot air in equatorial regions spills out rain as it rises, cools, and then moves northward at high altitude, cooling fur-ther as it radiates away heat. The cooled dry air descends in subtropical latitudes, warming by compression as it falls and creating belts of desert north and south of the moist tropics. These desert regions include the Sahara, the American South-west, the Atacama of South America, the deserts of southern Asia, southern Africa, and the center of Australia. Their cli-mates are mostly too dry for productive agriculture, except where irrigation is practical.

Beyond the desert belts, strong prevailing westerly winds bring moisture from the oceans across the continents, provid-ing rain and snow for the world's most productive agricultural regions. It is no accident that the majority of the world's people live (and most of the grain is produced) in the temperate zones, mainly in the north, where the bulk of the land also is located. Nearer the poles, weather is too cold and often too dry to support most crops. An exception is Europe, warmed and watered by the Gulf Stream.

Of course, there is a lot more detailed action in the system than this brief description indicates, and therein lies the rub. For instance, climatologists now believe that weather in North America is heavily influenced by the temperature of the water surface in the tropical Pacific. But a combination of too few accurate temperature readings and inadequate computer models prevents them from predicting the exact nature of that relationship.[3]

Perhaps the most worrisome aspect of the weather–agri-culture relationship is that, as climatologists sometimes say, the climate runs on small differences between large numbers. Or, to put it another way, seemingly minor changes in such things as the relatively tiny amounts (less than one percent) of greenhouse gases in the atmosphere can have powerful influences on climate. In theory, small changes in weather patterns could sharply diminish the agricultural productivity of the U.S. Midwest. Similarly, alterations in atmospheric and oceanic circulation patterns could change the course of the Gulf Stream, producing an agricultural catastrophe in Europe as the climate there shifted toward that of subarctic Labrador, just across the Atlantic.

The threat to agriculture is severe even without a shift of climate into some dramatically new regime. Small changes in the *average* temperature, for example, might have little impact on agricultural production; but associated changes in *extremes* (such as blistering heat waves or out-of-season frosts) could wreak havoc. As the atmosphere warms from the greenhouse-gas buildup, variability in rainfall patterns might also increase, and extreme events (violent storms and severe droughts) might become more frequent.[4] Finally, rising sea levels from the greenhouse warming will certainly not benefit farmers in coastal or low-lying areas, which often are among the most productive farmlands.

▶   **INPUTS, OUTPUTS, AND DISTRIBUTION**   ◀

Because agriculture has to be a dispersed activity, while people are increasingly concentrated in cities (as is the manufacture of products needed by farmers), transport systems are vital components of agricultural systems. "Inputs" (fuel for farm machinery, seeds, fertilizers and pesticides) must be transported to farms, and farm products ("outputs") must be delivered to markets or to processing and storage centers and then sent onward to consumers. In the United States today, fewer than 2 percent of the population live on farms, and very few farmers grow all their own food. Indeed, food production more and more is regionally concentrated; nearly all of the lettuce and many other vegetables in the United States are grown in California and Florida (for East Coast markets) and shipped around the country, for instance. Virtually *everyone* in the nation depends on the smooth movement of trains and trucks to keep eating.

This dependency on the functioning of elaborate transport

systems applies between as well as within modern nations. Along with grain and other foodstuffs, the inputs for agriculture are important elements in world trade, although many developing nations have become increasingly self-sufficient in producing their own fertilizers and seeds.

The inputs used in modern farming have been vital to the nearly threefold increase in global food production that has been achieved since World War II (while the population has more than doubled). They are the essence of the Green Revolution: the use of specially bred high-yield varieties of major crops, which require large applications of fertilizer and abundant water in order to produce their high yields (more grain per acre). Because high-yield crops usually are planted in extensive, genetically uniform tracts, they also require extra protection against pests; hence, the emphasis on pesticides.

Increases of yields on already cultivated land, rather than the development of new land for farming, have been responsible for four fifths of the rise in crop production in the last few decades.[5] But humanity cannot rely on simply increasing inputs, especially fertilizers, to feed 95 million additional people every year indefinitely. First of all, fertilizers cost money. In much of the world, farmers now apply about all that is economically productive. In developing countries, this often means all they can afford or obtain, even though applying more might still be very helpful.

In much of the world, however, fertilizer applications have passed the point of diminishing returns. Fertilizers provide supplements of certain nutrients, mainly nitrogen, phosphorus, and potassium, to the soil. Yields of responsive crop varieties can be dramatically boosted by this enrichment, if sufficient water is supplied and other conditions are appropriate. But there are limits to how much of these nutrients crops can use. On the average worldwide in 1950, a ton of additional fertilizer used on grain crops produced 46 more tons of grain; in 1965, an additional ton of fertilizer produced only 23 more tons of grain; and by the early 1980s, the additional ton yielded only about 13 more tons of grain.[6] Fertilizer applications by the 1980s were so high and so widely adopted that most of the potential gains had already been made. Nowhere is this more true than in the United States, where the technology was pioneered. The increase in yield earned by applying one more ton of fertilizer to a field in the U.S. corn belt has fallen from 15–20 tons of grain in 1970 to 5–10 tons today.

In short, the "magic" of fertilizer is running out. In much of the world outside the poorest developing nations, increased fertilizer applications have become uneconomic because the rise in crop yield is too small to pay for the cost of the fertilizer. It would be folly to expect a surge in food production in the future to match that achieved with fertilizer-sensitive crops between 1950 and 1975, when the Green Revolution was established in industrialized nations and transferred, with mixed results, to the developing world.

One can, of course, imagine rich countries supplying more aid to increase fertilizer use in developing countries where ample room remains for yield improvements before the crop's responses to fertilizer start to plateau. The brightest remaining opportunities to raise yields are in some of the hungriest nations; but in the tropics, the potential for raising yields this way is probably quite limited. A repeat of the Green Revolution successes achieved in India, China, Mexico, and East Asia may not be feasible in Central Africa or the Amazon basin (leaving aside whether it's desirable).[7] Even if the Green Revolution should prove transferrable to the humid tropics, it's hard to see a way around the problem of diminishing returns from fertilizers. In drier areas, water may be a limiting factor, since to deliver their high yields heavily fertilized crops need plenty of it.

Along with the Green Revolution technologies, a major factor in the surge of food production since 1950 has been a massive increase in the acreage of land under irrigation. Much of this, of course, has been necessitated by the use of high-yield crop varieties. From 1950 to 1980, the amount of irrigated land expanded more than two and half times, but since then the expansion has definitely slowed, as the easy gains in production have been made and costs have risen. And, as aquifers have been drained and irrigated land has lost productivity from waterlogging and salt accumulations, land has been taken out of production. It is estimated that about a third of the world's irrigated cropland is losing productivity today because of these problems.[8]

It is seldom recognized that irrigation is usually a temporary game. Rainwater is essentially distilled water; it has been evaporated by the sun's heat and by the activity of green plants (in a process called "transpiration") and recondensed in the cool reaches of the atmosphere. It contains no significant amount of salts. Irrigation water, having run over or through Earth's surface after falling as rain, has had a chance to leach salts from the soil. When it is returned to the atmosphere from irrigated farm fields by evaporation and transpiration, the salts are left behind. Preventing their accumulation in most soils requires careful flushing. In the medium or long term, salvaging saline fields (when feasible at all) ordinarily costs more than farmers can pay—some $265 per acre, according to a United Nations estimate in the late 1970s.[9]

Even in rich nations where modern irrigated agriculture is practiced, land is often gradually ruined by the process. California's highly productive Imperial Valley is threatened by salinization, and may end up growing just a few salt-tolerant crops. Parts of the San Joaquin Valley are not too far behind. Over 600 square miles were affected by high, brackish water tables by 1980, and it was estimated then that 13 percent of the valley, some 1700 square miles, will ultimately become unproductive unless expensive subsurface drainage systems are installed.[10]

In the Soviet Union, the ill-advised diversion of water for irrigation from rivers that fed the inland Aral Sea has led to a regional ecological disaster. The sea, once a productive fishery, has shrunk in area by a third; two thirds of its former volume is gone. Shoreline towns have been stranded far inland, and the fishery has been destroyed. Worse, the irrigated cropland has been turned into a salt desert, described by a Soviet scientist traveling 200 miles across it as "what appeared to be a snow-covered plain stretching to the horizon without a sign of life."[11] Salt, dust, and dried pesticide residues have been carried and deposited thousands of miles away by winds and rain, causing health problems for the population and affecting agriculture over vast areas. The regional climate also has become less benign as the sea has dried up.

Of course, where water is obtained by overdrawing aquifers, as in parts of the southern high plains of the United States
that depend on the Ogallala, and in the desert Southwest,
irrigated agriculture will be greatly reduced or will come to a
halt as economically accessible groundwater is exhausted.
Similar stories can be told for every non-antarctic continent
(possibly excepting well-watered Europe). The problem of
aquifer overdraft threatens grain production in arid and semiarid regions around the world.

►   **RUNNING OUT OF OPTIONS**   ◄

Agriculture is adversely affected by many forms of human-
caused environmental damage. Climate change, deforestation,
and widespread pollution obviously will seriously interfere with
maintaining the crucial "genetic-library" service of natural
ecosystems—nature's inventory of species and genetic var-
iants that are used in so many ways by humanity. That function
is critical to the success of Green Revolution technology. Maintaining the genetic diversity of crop plants is essential so that
geneticists can modify them to be productive under a variety
of conditions. Genetic engineers can move genes from one
organism to another, but they need the genetic raw materials
found in existing plants and animals to do so.

As most of the productive land on Earth has been taken
over for human use and more or less drastically altered in its
biotic character, the remaining virgin forests, grasslands, and
other natural areas throughout the world increasingly are islands in a vast sea of human disturbance. Those islands are
the last reservoirs of genetic raw materials for use in agriculture and forestry to develop new crops or improve traditional
ones.[12]

If the possibilities for substantial further increases in
global yields on land already cultivated are limited, so are
those for increasing the amount of cultivated land. Virtually all
the reasonably arable land is being farmed. Indeed, much that
shouldn't be cultivated has been, and it contributes greatly to
statistics on land degradation from soil erosion and desertification.

As a consequence of humanity's massive takeover of

Earth's productive land (noted in Chapter 2), people are already using or coopting or have destroyed nearly 40 percent of
all the potential net primary production (NPP) on land.[13] And,
of course, most of that mammoth diversion of biotic energy is
accounted for by agriculture and livestock production. All this
must be viewed against the backdrop of a projected *doubling*
of the human population by the middle of the next century.

Clearly, there are limits to further expansion, both through
increasing yields on existing farmland and by opening up farmland in new areas. These limitations, indeed, are showing up
in land-use assessments. Even by the optimistic estimates of
"arable land" of the United Nations Food and Agriculture Organization (FAO), very little productive land exists in reserve
in the Near East, North Africa, and Asia.[14] FAO sees a lot of
land waiting for the plow in sub-Saharan Africa and Latin
America. But that assessment ignores the extremely poor,
fragile soils of much of that land. More important, it ignores
that much of it underlies tropical moist forests (especially in
Brazil and Zaire). Those forests are among the most important
elements of humanity's heritage, being critical both for the
preservation of biotic diversity and to help slow climatic
change, which threatens agriculture itself.

In the 1980s, more land went out of production (largely
because of exhaustion, desertification, or failed irrigation) than
was newly opened, and the world's cropland area shrank by
some 7 percent.[15] Perhaps a third of the cropland still in use is
estimated to have lost productivity, although much of the loss
has been masked by increased fertilizer applications. Sooner
or later, though, the mask will slip, and that land will no longer
produce a profitable crop.

Too much prime land is becoming marginal and then non-
arable. Erosion is a big problem even in the United States, the
"world's breadbasket." Around 1980, the United States was
estimated to be losing nearly 4 billion tons of soil a year,
enough to fill a freight train 600,000 miles long—twenty-four
times the circumference of Earth. About a third of America's
cropland is affected, and drops in yield attributable to erosion
have already been noted, including a 2 percent decline in grain
production per acre in Illinois—in the richest part of the grain
belt—between 1979 and 1984.[16]

▶   **SEESAWING U.S. POLICIES**   ◀

A major source of confusion about the world food situation has been the complexity and inconsistency of United States agricultural policies. Subsidies have been turned on and off in response to the politics of the moment rather than the overall needs for the food-production system.[17] In the early 1970s, the government was pumping huge amounts of money into maintenance and expansion of the irrigation system of California's Imperial Valley, while simultaneously paying other farmers to withhold their unirrigated land from production. Later, it paid the Imperial Valley farmers not to grow wheat, cotton, and other crops on the land it had paid to irrigate! Today western water is subsidized to the tune of about $1 billion to produce crops that, at least in some cases, other farmers are paid not to produce.[18]

American farm policy, unlike that of nations such as France and Switzerland, has encouraged the trend toward giant holdings and factory agriculture. This has sharply reduced the number of people who could make a living on the land. Every year between 1940 and 1960, a million Americans moved from farm to city, swelling the ranks of unskilled laborers and welfare recipients. In contrast, France and Switzerland avoided these social costs by adopting policies that kept small, relatively self-sufficient farms going, and accepting higher food prices. It has been argued that the savings in urban welfare and social costs more than compensated for the costs of subsidizing agriculture in this way.[19]

But there is an even bigger benefit to preserving family farms. Their owners are much more likely to conserve precious soil resources, to value the farm for its own sake, and try to pass it on to the next generation in superior condition. Large-scale farming, on the other hand, tends to focus on this year's "bottom line" and sacrifice the farm's long-term productivity for short-term gain. The family farmer is very much aware that his soil is precious capital; the accountant for a large corporation that bought a farm as an investment is not.

The achievement of an ecologically and socially sound agricultural policy for the United States, the leading food exporter, will be critical as the global population–food imbalance worsens. But such a policy won't be possible unless the nation's agricultural policies can be recaptured from their present dominance by agribusiness interests and made a concern of the public. Today, the system is so complex that almost no one in Congress understands it completely.

The Department of Agriculture is large, weak (compared to other executive-branch departments), and on occasion stunningly incompetent. The latter trait was displayed for all to see in the California Medfly disaster of the 1970s, in which the blame was largely and erroneously put on Governor Jerry Brown.[20] If the United States is to be able to continue supplying large quantities of food for export in response to rising global need, it must get its agricultural house in order.

Recently, though, the U.S. Department of Agriculture's new Conservation Reserve Program slashed the national erosion rate by a third in just a couple of years—one of the biggest conservation success stories of the century.[21] The establishment of this program under the Food Security Act of 1985 was a big step toward an ecologically sounder agricultural policy. Over five years, the program is subsidizing farmers who will permanently set aside highly erodible marginal cropland, some 11 percent of the cropland base. These fragile lands are to be restored as grassland or woodland. Farmers also will be penalized for permitting too much erosion. The Soil Conservation Service estimated that the program had already reduced the U.S. annual soil loss by almost a half-billion tons by the second year.[22]

The initiative for the soil-conservation program came from Congress, however, and was not much favored by the agricultural interests that usually determine policies. Rather, it was enacted largely at the behest of environmental organizations such as the Sierra Club.

For the most part, the American agricultural system is flying blind, too much of it controlled by large agribusiness corporations that by their nature cannot be concerned about the long-term viability of the system. Exhaustion of soils in a half century or so simply is not a factor in their financial planning.[23] Commodity prices are partly or largely in the hands of giant trading corporations that buy up grain from farmers and handle almost all grain exports. Their operations are so arcane that it seems impossible to determine who is buying the grain.[24]

In the context of today's changing world food picture, a major problem is that people can recall earlier American policies that seemed to convert surpluses to shortages and vice versa with ease. This created an impression that the productivity of American agriculture is now and forever boundless, and that proper policies will always be able to call forth all the food needed at home and abroad. But this may not always be so— as the 1988 drought brought home.

▶ **THE RISE OF EUROPE AS AN EXPORTER** ◀

In the 1980s, the United States was faced with competition on the world grain market from a new source: the European Common Market. Europe for generations had been a net grain importer; suddenly Western Europe was exporting and, using substantial subsidies for its farm sector, undercutting U.S. sales.

Most of the continent of Europe is blessed with a mild climate and evenly distributed, ample rainfall, all very beneficial for agriculture. Moreover, although the continent has been farmed for millennia, farming practices have mostly been sustainable. A long tradition of preserving soil and caring for the productivity of the land has resulted in little or no deterioration of farmlands and, in some cases, even improvement (proving that it is possible!). In addition, the continent's population is barely growing, on average; some countries have embarked on population shrinkage. So the increases in production achieved through modernization therefore were not consumed in the need to feed millions more people each year. Nevertheless, how carefully the modernization techniques have been applied in Europe is not entirely clear; if the centuries-old traditions of husbandry were abandoned as artificial fertilizers were embraced, the success might prove short-lived.

Of course, Western Europe's achievement has not extended to Eastern Europe, which, although potentially very productive, has suffered from the same inefficient, overcen-

tralized agricultural bureaucracies, as well as severe environmental problems, as have plagued the Soviet Union.

The result of the European Community's entry into the
export market, however, has been a wrangle, with the United
States trying to persuade the Europeans to reduce or eliminate
their subsidies. The wrangle was silenced by the grain-produc-
tion shortfall in 1988, but, if a new glut should build up, it may
recur. And the even more tightly integrated economic union
planned for 1992 may make the Europeans an even more formidable competitor.

If, as seems likely, food production continues to fall behind
population growth in developing regions (and possibly for a
time in the Soviet Union and its allies), the problems of competition may fade—and the world may be grateful that another
exporting region has turned up.

In an era in which global per-capita food supplies are likely
not to rise very much, and may even decline for a substantial
period, questions of distribution will become even more acute.
Some rationalization and international regulation of the grain
trade is clearly needed. When supplies are more than adequate, as they were during most of the 1980s, the unregulated,
market-driven system may function satisfactorily. But when
the crunch comes, as it inevitably will (all that's needed is a
second major drought before the grain stocks can be fully re-
built), some better mechanism for allocating the supply (especially enlarged emergency stocks for the poor) than higher
prices will be needed—unless we are prepared to accept a
multiplication of deaths from starvation in poor nations.[25]

▶   **FACING REALITY**   ◀

Just what is the outlook for feeding the expanding populations
of the developing nations? Even though agricultural conditions
and prospects (as well as rates of population growth) vary enormously among nations and regions, some conclusions can
nevertheless be drawn.

A few years ago, three international organizations collabo-
rated in a systematic study of "population supporting capacities of lands," to determine the prospects for developing

nations to increase their food production enough so they could feed their populations in the twenty-first century.[26]

The study concluded that the developing world (except East Asia, which was excluded from the study) could support twice its 1975 population, or 1.5 times the projected 2000 population, without significant modernization of agriculture. It also found that, with an intermediate level of modernization, four times the 1975 population could be supported. But these highly optimistic findings presumed an enormous unfettered trade in food between nations and regions—and a carload of other unlikely or unrealistic assumptions.

Among those assumptions were: people would be fed only a subsistence diet with a minimum of animal products; no land would be used for feed crops or nonfood crops (such as cotton, jute, rubber, palm oil, tea, or coffee); all potentially arable land would be planted to food crops (including all that is now in forest or woodland); maximum advantage would be taken of irrigation opportunities; and crops would be ideally matched to soils and climates in order to produce the maximum number of food calories per acre. Under low-input conditions, significant soil loss and land degradation were expected and accounted for. Presumably, no agricultural products were to be exported to or imported from the developed nations.

Some of the assumptions in this study, if followed, would precipitate environmental disaster. First and foremost, consider the assumption that all remaining tropical rain forests should be cleared and that they could be successfully converted to productive agriculture—an assumption that has been repeatedly proven wrong.[27] The removal of seasonal forests and woodlands would be disastrous for rural populations dependent on them for fuelwood—and would probably accelerate local cropland erosion and cause weather changes as well. The likely desertification that would result from such policies and the temporary nature of most irrigation projects appear to have been ignored. Finally, ruling out nonfood crops and assuming that "ideal" crops would be used everywhere (regardless of nutritional values other than calories, let alone differing traditions and tastes) are completely unrealistic.

Despite these incredibly optimistic assumptions, the study

concluded that some developing nations and regions couldn't feed themselves after 2000 without unrestricted access to surplus food from elsewhere, even if their agricultural systems were fully modernized. Nineteen of the 117 nations studied would fall short, with 47 million more people than they could feed in 2000. With agriculture only partially modernized (intermediate levels of inputs—fertilizers, pesticides, etc.), thirty-six countries would fall short, with an "excess population" of 136 million. With little modernization (low inputs), which, given the progress since 1975, is most likely for the majority of developing countries, sixty-five nations fail the test, being short of food for 441 million people.

If a carefully devised study of the agricultural-resource base of developing countries, using absurdly optimistic assumptions, shows an ominous food crunch facing the developing world as soon as 2000, what would a more realistic assessment reveal? What of the outlook beyond 2000, as populations continue growing and the modernization of agriculture has supposedly been accomplished? And what possible avenues remain for creating a brighter prospect?

Very few; most hungry countries are tropical, and growing more food in the tropics is not easy. The people doing this research appear to have fallen into an old trap—the assumption that, because tropical rain forests are luxuriant and extremely productive biologically, crops that replaced them would be similarly productive. Except in cases of rich volcanic soil (as in Java) or regularly flooded areas (as in parts of the Amazon Valley), the soils beneath rain forests are generally thin and poor. The forest's nutrients are stored largely in the vegetation, not in the soil; so when a forest is cleared, a substantial portion of the nutrients go with it, and those remaining in the soil are quickly leached away by heavy tropical rains.[28] Experience has shown that permanent agriculture in these areas is largely an illusion, but large numbers of people, including policymakers, still pin their hopes on it.

Even outside of tropical rainforest areas, agricultural development in the tropics has long been problematic, despite numerous attempts to transplant the all-too-successsful (in the medium term) technology of temperate regions. There are many reasons for this failure.[29]

The lack of a strongly defined winter (or dry season) to suppress pest populations is one important reason. Modern high-yield agriculture is based on planting in monocultures—a single crop, composed of thousands of genetically similar individual plants, covering large areas of land. Such a system is an open invitation to pests. With heavy rainfall typical of the tropics, soil erosion is often high, and fertilizers and pesticides are quickly washed away. Consequently, in order for them to be effective, large and frequent applications of both are needed, compounding the off-site pollution problems. Soil exposed to direct sunlight is often overheated and damaged, losing productivity. Small wonder attempts to farm this way have so often failed within a few years.

Another important reason for lagging food production in the tropics has been neglect until recently of indigenous crops by Green Revolution geneticists. Crop-improvement efforts have been concentrated on wheat, corn, and rice, which either do not grow well in many tropical areas, particularly in Africa, or are not part of local farming tradition and experience. Efforts are now under way to remedy this oversight by investigating and developing traditional tropical crops. But valuable time has been lost during which countless potential crops and wild relatives of existing crops have been unwittingly pushed to extinction in the rush to "develop."[30] Meanwhile, agricultural ecosystems in many poor regions are being overstressed in the desperate attempt to feed people this year, grinding down their capacity to produce more food in the future.

Successful traditional agricultural systems could be models for a new tropical farming approach. Many unfortunately have been all but forgotten or were corrupted beyond recognition under colonial regimes, but a few scientists are trying to recover some of the lore. Some have collapsed as population pressures made them unsustainable or because environmental degradation undermined their productivity. Belatedly, some tropical agricultural-research stations and nongovernmental organizations are now beginning to work toward a more ecological approach to agricultural development.[31]

Success has been met in some experimental research in the tropics, in which the structure of the original natural community is imitated in agriculture—for instance, tree crops with shade-loving shrubs or vegetables beneath them (so-called "forest farming").[32] Another often successful approach is to plant two, three, or even more crops together in a field. In one project in southern Mexico, for instance, corn, beans, and squash were planted together. Since the crops matured at different rates, the ground was never left bare. The result was a sharply reduced need for pesticides and fertilizers (the beans are nitrogen fixers) and very little soil erosion. Surprisingly, the yields of each of the three were only slightly less than they would have been if planted alone and supported by massive costly inputs.[33]

These efforts are still too few and scattered. Since they are necessarily small in scale, they must be multiplied thousands of times over if they are to make a real dent in the tropical food situation. Part of the problem is communicating the experiences of different groups to others that might benefit from them. And the preference of international assistance agencies is still for large-scale projects—despite the repeated failures and untoward environmental consequences—simply because they are easier to administer and monitor.

►   **BREAD AND CIRCUSES**   ◄

Whatever the technical problems of improving agricultural production and getting food to some 80 million more people in developing countries each year, they are not going to be solved without simultaneously dealing with the sociopolitical realities of Third World agriculture. These, of course, vary from region to region, but certain themes are nearly universal. One key difficulty is that national leaders live in cities, and national leaders have an aversion to being killed by mobs. That has generated an all-too-understandable tendency to give higher priority to placating urban masses than to taking care of the needs of rural people.

Nothing makes city folk more likely to get together and go politician-hunting en masse than food that is too scarce or too expensive. This is not just a rule in poor countries; Douglas MacArthur led U.S. troops using tanks and tear gas to drive five or six thousand hungry "bonus marchers" out of Washington in 1932.[34] Today, Soviet and Polish leaders are very nervous about the attitudes of their people toward perpetual food shortages and rising prices, food shortages traceable in part to the traditional Marxist disdain for agriculture and country people. Anyway, leaders like to keep food plentiful and cheap and employment high in the cities, and they design their policies accordingly. Needless to say, this doesn't help the farmers, who need a fair return on their efforts if they are to grow food for sale.

After independence, governments in Africa were naturally responsive to the demands of powerful—and multiplying— urban groups. They were also committed to a substantial expansion of public services and a drive to develop an industrial sector.[35] There was no place to look for the resources to accomplish the latter goals, except tax revenues from the agricultural sector.

The threat of insurrection has played an important role in shaping bad government policies toward agriculture in Africa. As one observer put it, in regard to West Africa:

The short-term preoccupation of West Africa's rulers is with the immediate danger of an unsatisfied urban mob. Long-term planning for the countryside is entirely incompatible with the siege mentality of politicians, soldiers, and bureaucrats who are literally counting the days before they lose their power (and lives) in the face of growing anger. . . . This anger means most in the major cities; it commands constant attention and the award of temporary palliatives, one after the other, all adding up to the relative impoverishment of farmers.[36]

The deepening problems of hunger in Africa are likely to have dramatic environmental consequences. There are already strong pressures toward population relocation, from the desertified lands bordering the Sahara to the "underpopulated" rain forests of the Congo, Zaire, Gabon, and the Ivory Coast.[37] Should massive transborder migrations occur, one can expect the same kind of disasters as those now afflicting the rain forests of Brazil (also in no small degree due to ill-advised government agricultural policies).

Establishing effective programs of population control is obviously an essential step in addressing the problem of hunger in poor nations on any long-term basis, simply because of the long lag time before such programs can have a significant effect. But other steps obviously should be under way now as well. The most important is to initiate programs to bolster agricultural economies, especially programs that reach the poorest farmers.

Exactly what those latter programs should be will vary from place to place, and what they should be in detail is beyond the scope of our discussion. But among the priorities should be arrangements for making credit available to poor farmers and giving them access to adequate markets. With credit, the farmers can decide for themselves the best production strategies.

► **BIOTECH FOR THE FARM** ◄

One can't leave a discussion about increasing global food production without considering the potential impact of biotechnology, especially genetic engineering.[38] The first thing that must be understood is that biotechnology has already vastly increased the amount of food available to us. The high-yielding strains of wheat, corn, and rice that formed the basis of the Green Revolution are products of it. Those strains were engineered by plant evolutionary geneticists, primarily by artificial selection (directing evolution by choosing parents with desired characteristics generation after generation).

Of course, "genetic engineering" now ordinarily means using recombinant-DNA techniques to manipulate the genetic endowment of organisms, transplanting genes from one strain to another or from one species to another. There is no question that these techniques eventually may speed the directed evolution of strains of crops or domestic animals and produce combinations that would be practically impossible using classic methods. In theory, plants can be created more readily with these techniques to produce higher yields, grow with less water, tolerate saltier water, be more resistant to pests, or more conveniently cultivated, and so on. And speed may be of the essence for changing old crops and developing new ones on a planet facing unprecedentedly rapid environmental changes.

There are no agricultural "free lunches" even with genetic engineering, however. One often-discussed project is to transfer genes that permit nitrogen fixation from legumes (where they occur naturally) to grains (where they don't). The prospect of nitrogen-fixing grains, eliminating much of the need for nitrogen fertilizer, is attractive indeed. But the task appears difficult, and the result, if successful, uncertain.[39] Grains are already more productive (in calories produced per acre) than legumes, and nitrogen fixation carries a cost, since energy that could go into edible parts is diverted into nitrogen fixing. Careful evaluation of trade-offs and extensive field testing will be required to determine whether future nitrogen-fixing grains can fulfill the dreams of some biotechnologists.

Overall, the potential of genetic engineering for improving crops is a long way from being realized, and the direction in which much biotechnological development is going does not hold very much promise for the agriculture of poor nations. For instance, much of the research is aimed at improving the interactions between crops and agricultural chemicals. But if strains are produced with seeds resistant to herbicides (one of today's goals, since it would allow chemical weed control in seeded fields), it won't be much help to peasant farmers in poor countries, who have little access to either specially developed seeds or herbicides.

Neither will the development of male sterility in new grains, which would bring the sort of vigor found in hybrid corn to other cereals.[40] These innovations are best adapted to large-scale agriculture, where farmers can afford the expensive seed, since they can't produce their own in the field. But large-scale agriculture invites increased pest problems, especially in the tropics, problems that would be exacerbated by the genetic uniformity of hybrid crops.

Poor nations appear likely to face severe difficulties created by the *successes* of biotechnology. For instance, efforts are now under way to use the new techniques to produce natural vanilla flavor in the laboratory. Success is just around the corner; but it threatens the livelihood of some 70,000 farmers in Madagascar, the world's biggest producer of vanilla beans. Laboratory production of cocoa butter and thaumatin protein, a substance several thousand times sweeter than sugar, could put out of business more than 10 million cultivators of cacao and sugarcane in poor countries.[41]

The complexity of the food problem is highlighted by these difficulties, since one reason there are so many hungry people in developing countries is that governments have concentrated on supporting production of cash crops for export, rather than food for local markets. The cash crops earn foreign exchange, which helps the relatively well-off, especially in the cities, but gives little benefit to subsistence farmers in the countryside or to the urban poor.

Foreign-aid programs for developing countries often follow the same course. In the famine-stricken Sahel, for instance, almost 30 percent of the limited aid for agriculture and forestry went to cash crops, mostly cotton and peanuts. As a result, production of these crops for export often rose as overall food production dropped.[42]

Unless institutional arrangements are made to prevent it, biotechnology seems likely to bring agriculture in the industrial nations even more under the control of large corporations, with ecological and economic results that are difficult to predict. Unless the rich give high priority to helping the agricultural sectors of the economies of poor nations in ways that provide food for hungry people and direct biotechnology research to that purpose, its achievements won't do much to improve their lot.

And, even with the best of planning, the research, development, and deployment required to establish new crops or crop varieties are time-consuming processes. Just establishing a new variety of a familiar crop can call for overcoming a series of social, political, and economic problems before the new variety is integrated into a nation's food system. That process can take as much as ten years. The development and wide adoption of an entirely new crop, however productive and otherwise useful, may take several decades.

So biotechnology, whatever its long-term promise, is very unlikely to improve agriculture fast enough to help humanity through the next few critical decades. It is no immediate panacea for the food problem, and no justification for complacency about population growth.

► **THE NEXT ASSIGNMENT** ◄

As you can see, supplying people with food is a complex process, made all the more difficult by the explosive growth of the human population. As Lester Brown, president of Worldwatch Institute, recently noted, every year farmers have to grow food for 95 million more people, using some 26 billion tons less topsoil—a loss about equal to the amount of topsoil that covers Australia's wheatlands.[43] Furthermore, he has estimated that world grain production will be increased by only 0.9 percent per year in the future—a horrifying prospect when one considers that the world population seems committed to a growth rate of closer to 2 percent per year for the next few decades.[44] While certainly no long-term solution to the problem of hunger is possible without population control, clearly population control is no short-term solution. Barring some catastrophe, the momentum built into world population growth assures that decades will pass before large reductions in population size of rich nations will be seen, and almost a century before populations of today's poor nations can show substantial shrinkage.

While it is essential that population-control programs be rapidly expanded and their goals made much more ambitious, humanity faces a long period of coping with high levels of overpopulation without destroying Earth's life-support systems. The need to bring birthrates well below death rates, increase food production while preserving the environment, and distribute food to all who need it is the greatest challenge our species has ever faced.

6

▲

Global Ecosystem
Health

▼

Population size influences our health, and thus our life expectancy, in two different ways. One is indirect, through its impact on "ecosystem health"—the integrity of Earth's life-support systems. The human population is supported by services received from Earth's natural ecosystems, which, among other things, control the mix of gases in the atmosphere, supply fresh water, control floods, supply food from the sea and products from forests, create soils, dispose of wastes, recycle essential nutrients, pollinate crops, and control the vast majority of pests that might attack them.[1] If those ecosystems collapse, the human economy will collapse as well, and *Homo sapiens* will undergo an unprecedented population crash. The larger our population, the more ecosystem services it demands. So it's therefore ironic that one of the greatest threats to the health of natural ecosystems is itself the growing number of human beings.

The other way population size influences health is direct, affecting what is classically known as "public health"—the health of the community one lives in as controlled by sanitation, preventive medicine, and social services.

Food is intimately involved in both kinds of health. Human attempts to produce more food more often than not reduce ecosystem health, which in turn undermines the ability of terrestrial and aquatic ecosystems to supply humanity with sustenance. Undernourished people are more susceptible to diseases and more likely to die from them. We have already discussed many of the local and regional impacts of people on ecosystems and the resultant loss of ecosystem services; in this chapter, we examine the health of ecosystems on a global scale. The population connection to global environmental problems is usually major and often obvious. In the next chapter, we look at public health, where the population connection is present, but often subordinate to other factors and sometimes difficult to demonstrate.

▶ **GREENHOUSE WARMING** ◀

One of the most important ecosystem services, maintaining the appropriate mix of trace gases in the atmosphere, is also among those most tightly connected to population growth. The connection is two-way. The growing human population is a major factor in the disruption of this service, and that disruption may well have exceedingly dire consequences for humanity. These connections are most evident in the case of global warming.

Our planet is kept habitable by the presence in the atmosphere of tiny amounts of "greenhouse gases" that, in essence, trap heat close to the surface.[2] The best known of these heat-holding gases are water vapor and carbon dioxide (CO_2), but there are more than twenty others, including methane, nitrous oxide, and ozone. Were there too little of these, Earth would be a frozen sphere rather like Mars. With too much, Earth, like Venus, would be too hot to support life. In short, we benefit from just the right level of "greenhouse effect."

Since the start of the Industrial Revolution, however, humanity has been adding CO_2 to the atmosphere, primarily by burning fossil fuels and secondarily by cutting down and burning forests. Carbon dioxide is released when anything organic (containing carbon) is burned; and CO_2 is removed from the atmosphere by plants in the process of photosynthesis on land and in the sea. It is also removed by a number of chemical and nonphotosynthetic biological processes, mainly in the oceans. Cutting and burning forests thus adds CO_2 to the atmosphere, unless the forest is replanted and can reabsorb carbon from the air, sequestering it in leaves, branches, trunks, and roots. As Peter Raven, director of the Missouri Botanical Garden and home secretary of the U.S. National Academy of Sciences, recently pointed out, the fires in the Brazilian Amazon in 1987 (which covered 77,000 square miles) contributed about a fifth of all the CO_2 that flowed into the atmosphere that year.[3]

All this CO_2 flowing into the atmosphere, in combination with increasing releases of other greenhouse gases, is gradually warming the entire planet, turning up the heat on the atmospheric system. It now appears that the heating may be detectable in climatic records; one of the most compelling bits of evidence is that, globally, the six hottest years of this century were in the 1980s. Furthermore, scientists examining satellite data have recently concluded that the oceans have been heating up by nearly 0.2 degrees Fahrenheit per year,[4] and at the same time evidence of an annual one-twelfth-inch rise in sea level as a result of warming has been reported by other scientists.[5]

Whether or not the warming has yet had a detectable influence on the weather is hotly debated. Detecting a subtle warming trend is one thing; identifying its effects on weather is another. For example, the 1988 drought was precisely the sort of event that computer models predict will become *more frequent* as the warming continues. So were the near-record-size hurricanes in the Gulf of Mexico the same year and the West Indies and South Carolina in 1989. In October 1989, the Philippines were struck by *three* powerful typhoons. Hurricanes can be thought of as devices for transferring enormous amounts of heat and moisture from equatorial regions toward the poles.

Still, observation of events of a sort predicted to become more frequent with global warming does not demonstrate that they were caused by a warming. We may never know whether the drought or the hurricanes were a result of the buildup of greenhouse gases or merely events that are part of normal climatic variability. Unless the climate slips over an unpredicted threshold, it will be extremely difficult to identify the start of climatic change due to the warming. If that change has started, it could be a decade or so before scientists have the data to be certain they have detected it. Several years of cool, wet summers and bumper grain crops in the United States could easily occur, even if the computer models of the impacts of global warming are correct. Such a stretch of favorable *weather* would very likely cause a relaxation of concern about the possibility of catastrophic change in *climate*. But the long-term environmental trends matter more than the transient events to which we more often pay attention.[6]

The role of population size and growth in generating the excess greenhouse gases can be seen with a few simple calculations. It is widely recognized that industrialized countries, with less than a quarter of the world's population, are responsible for roughly three quarters of the CO_2 released by burning fossil fuels—in automobiles, power plants, and other industrial apparatus used mainly by the rich. Coal is the worst offender among fossil fuels in terms of carbon dioxide per unit of energy generated; natural gas releases only a little more than half as much as coal, and petroleum is in between.

Suppose the United States decided to take the dramatic step of cutting its contribution to the CO_2 component of the global warming by terminating all burning of coal. That would necessitate substantial readjustments in our economy, since coal now supplies almost a quarter of U.S. annual energy consumption. Replacing coal with energy sources that don't release CO_2 (conservation, wind power, solar-voltaic panels, passive solar, hydroelectric, geothermal, nuclear fission) would require considerable effort and would carry other environmental costs.[7]

Suppose also that China's population remained at 1.1 billion—a very optimistic assumption, since demographers project it to rise at least to 1.4 or 1.5 billion, and some Chinese experts claim it has already exceeded 1.2 billion.[8] Suppose further that China scaled back its development plans so that it only doubled its per-capita consumption of commercial energy (it presently plans to *more than double* its use of coal by 2000).[9] That would raise Chinese per-capita energy use to some 14 percent of the U.S. level, about on a par with Algeria. Assume further that China produced that energy by using its vast stocks of coal. This modest development advance by China, certainly a legitimate goal by any standard, would more than offset the reduction of CO_2 emissions achieved by America's abandonment of coal.

Even without considering the *growth* of populations of either rich or poor countries, the huge populations we *already* have can magnify small and reasonable per-person changes into gigantic impacts. Small per-person changes can have very large effects when multiplied by enormous numbers of persons![10] The P factor in the I = PAT equation is critical here.

Accounting for projected population growth makes the situation look even bleaker. What if, in the course of development, India's per-capita energy consumption rose only to about the level of China's today—about 7 percent of U.S. per-capita consumption? That, combined with India's projected population growth, by the end of the next century would inject as much additional CO_2 into the atmosphere as would result from doubling China's per-capita energy use with no increase in China's population. That calculation is based on the projection we made earlier that India's population will reach two billion near the end of the next century, assuming success in family planning.[11] The dilemmas of both China and India underline the latent problems the world must face because of previous uncurbed population growth and demographic momentum.

Poor nations are now relatively minor contributors to the CO_2 load generated by burning fossil fuels, but a significant realization of their legitimate aspirations to develop, multiplied by their population growth, will change that very quickly. While the United States might manage its energy use in a way that would compensate for the per-capita increases just discussed for either China or India, it certainly would be hard pressed to compensate for both without dramatic changes in

lifestyle. Western Europe and Japan use their energy much
more efficiently than we do and so have considerably less potential for energy conservation. Likelier sources of compensa-
tion through conservation are the Soviet Union and Eastern
Europe, whose per-capita level of fossil-fuel use is high, but
whose energy technology is very inefficient. The USSR uses
roughly two thirds as much energy as the United States does
with a modestly larger population, and has a standard of living
less than half of ours. Poland's energy use is equivalent to
Sweden's and higher than that of Switzerland or France; but
since it's much less efficient, the standard of living is much
lower.

It is clear that significant changes in energy patterns will
be required in all rich countries in order to slow the injection
of CO_2 into the atmosphere if poor nations are to enjoy even
moderate levels of development. But the changes are technically feasible, and fast becoming more so. The political deter-
mination to make the changes has yet to become widespread,
however.

Other contributions of population growth to the CO_2 problem are also very substantial, but more difficult to measure.
Plants take up carbon dioxide in the process of photosynthesis;
when they die and decay or are burned, they release it again.
When trees are cut, carbon stored over decades or centuries
is released. In the tropics, much clearing of forests is for agriculture (often unsustainable) to meet the food needs of increasing populations. The amount of carbon dioxide being added to
the atmosphere in this way is uncertain—on the order of a fifth
to a half as much as that contributed by fossil fuels.[12]

One obvious long-term measure that would help mitigate
the greenhouse problem, therefore, is to regenerate forests.[13]
For this purpose, trees whose wood would be preserved even
after cutting rather than burned should be favored as much as
possible—ideally, high-quality hardwoods in the tropics.
These woods are preferred for construction and furniture.

But, unfortunately, it is precisely in the tropics that expanding human populations are contributing most heavily to
the destruction of forests. The relationship is complex. As described earlier, industrialization of agriculture in southern Bra-

zil has created an army of landless people whom the government funnels toward the "frontier" of the Amazon. The government also has tried to encourage migration into the Amazon from the desperately poor, famine-afflicted northeast.[14] Once in Amazonia, the migrants clear and burn the forests in an attempt, usually unsuccessful,[15] to make a living by farming.

Brazil's high rate of population growth is an important factor in the destruction of its rainforest riches, stimulating the government's promotion of migration to the Amazon. But projects sponsored by various international "aid" agencies, which have facilitated the destruction by financing roads and dams to support settlement, have been at least as important.

On the Indian subcontinent, the destruction of forests is even more directly tied to overpopulation, as timber-cutters respond to the needs of cities for firewood and lumber. In the foothills of the Himalayas, nocturnal tree-cutters, called "owl men," sneak out to harvest the last of a dwindling lumber supply.[16] A countervailing force in India and Nepal is the Chipko movement—"tree huggers." These are men and women who understand the critical role trees play in the local economy and attempt to save trees by education and, if necessary, blocking axmen with their bodies.[17]

Similarly, in China, the original destruction of the forest cover also had close connections with that nation's enormous population growth.[18] And, in spite of much propaganda about reforestation, the loss of China's forests continues. One of China's leading environmentalists, He Bochuan, estimates that since the Communists took over in 1949, forest cover has *declined* from 12 percent to less than 11 percent, despite massive attempts at reforestation, and that it will fall to 8.3 percent by 2000.[19] In a quarter of a century, forest fires have consumed the equivalent of a third of all the surviving saplings from China's reforestation programs. Exact figures are difficult to determine, since it seems that about half of the trees planted in official statistics are in fact imaginary, and only 40 percent of those actually planted survive. The Chinese forestry situation is obviously rather grim. *The People's Daily* reported that annual consumption of wood for building, paper, and fuel was

50 percent higher than regrowth, and that if this overdraft on the forests continued, "state timber enterprises would have nothing to log by the end of the century."[20]

China is only one developing nation facing this problem. A major source of the assault on forests and woodlots, especially in the arid and semiarid subtropics, is the dependence of more than 2 billion people on firewood for fuel.[21] As Peter Raven put it, "The basic reason this [assault] is happening is population growth, brought into intense focus in the warmer parts of the world by extreme poverty."[22]

Overconsumption and overpopulation in rich nations are also responsible for deforestation in the tropics. Demand for cheap beef in fast-food outlets has created the "hamburger connection." In much of Central America and Amazonia, forests have been cut down to provide temporary pasture for cattle raising—at least 10,000 square miles annually.[23] For a few years, those pastures can produce cattle destined to be devoured by citizens of developed nations. Then the pastures are abandoned as wasteland, and other pieces of forest are cut down to replace them. The immediate economic yield from destroying the forests is greater than it would be from using them in any sustainable way, and immediate yield is the main goal of the present economic system.[24]

Similar stories could be told about Japanese woodchipping of forests in Papua New Guinea, Thailand, Malaysia, Colombia, and Cameroon and elsewhere,[25] grinding them up to make cardboard for packing around new electronic equipment, or about the destruction caused by demand in rich nations for tropical hardwoods. In each case, the consumption and technological parts of the $I = PAT$ equation are important, but so is the population factor. Everything else being equal, if there were only half as many people in the rich world, they would be responsible for only half as much tropical deforestation.

Some rich countries are destroying their own forests as well. In Australia, some of the most interesting of all tropical forests, those in the politically backward northern state of Queensland,[26] are being destroyed simply because the timber industry wants to prove it can do it—regardless of what the rest of the world thinks.[27] In British Columbia, the Ministry of

Forestry is cooperating in the unsustainable destruction of that province's precious virgin forests. The rape of U.S. forests, especially old-growth forests, in Alaska and the Pacific Northwest (largely at taxpayers' expense) is a continuing disgrace— one only partially hidden from the public by the practice of leaving a narrow band of trees lining main highways. The forests of those areas are being destroyed by large corporations which care nothing about either the environment or long-term employment for local people in the timber industry.[28]

Again, this destruction, all of which contributes to global warming, can be partly assigned to faulty harvesting and inadequate reforestation, as well as to overconsumption of paper and other forest products. But population plays its inevitable multiplicative role: large (and still growing) numbers of Americans, Canadians, Europeans, and Japanese want homes, furniture, paper, and other products in which wood is used.[29]

In the next few decades, methane could almost equal CO_2 in importance as a trace gas in causing greenhouse warming. A molecule of methane traps roughly twenty-five times as much of the sun's heat as a molecule of carbon dioxide, and the concentrations are rising in the atmosphere twice as fast. The population connection with methane emissions is very clear, because the principal known sources of methane include rice paddies,[30] the flatus of cattle,[31] and soils of forests and fields that are cleared and burned by farmers. Another major source of methane appears to be the putrefying contents of garbage dumps, and it has been suggested that sun-baked asphalt is yet another.[32] All of these sources are intimately tied to the size of the burgeoning human population, so substantial reductions in methane emissions will not be easily achieved without substantial success at population control.

If the climatologists are correct, and the vast weight of the evidence indicates they are, global warming means much more than simply a few degrees Fahrenheit increase in average temperature between now and the middle of the next century.[33] The need for more air-conditioning to deal with more and hotter heat waves, some rise in sea level, and more frequent and destructive hurricanes could be the least of our problems. The worst consequence of global warming is likely to be alterations of climatic patterns caused by the rising temperatures, changes that will occur at a rate unprecedented in history.

► **CLIMATE CHANGE AND FOOD SECURITY** ◄

While the causes of global warming can be traced through various paths to the activities of a growing human population, the climatic effects of global warming on producing food for that population cannot be predicted with certainty. Computer models, however, suggest that climatic change from greenhouse warming will be rapid—possibly ten to sixty times faster than the average natural rates of change since the last ice age.[34] Those models also suggest that one of the more likely results will be a decrease in water availability in the world's principal grain belts.[35] This pace and kind of change will inevitably cause large-scale disruptions in world agriculture. As climate belts shift rapidly, major adjustments in irrigation and drainage systems will be required at a cost that could be as high as $200 billion worldwide.[36] Farmers in many areas will have to switch to drought-resistant crops, and will be forced to accept the lower yields that such crops produce. Drought-reduced harvests, like those of 1988, can be expected to occur with increasing frequency and severity.

A northward migration of climatic belts favorable to grain production might at first glance appear beneficial to agriculture in regions like Canada and much of the Soviet Union, where low temperatures and growing-season frosts are limiting factors. But if grain production is shifted to those areas, their often thin, infertile soils will limit yields.

Because CO_2 is an essential raw material for photosynthesis, it has been speculated that an increase in CO_2 concentration would enhance productivity. In our view, it is doubtful that this will yield a net benefit in the face of so many other limitations. Higher temperatures and increased CO_2 may unfavorably change relationships between crops and their pollinators, competitors, or pests.[37] For instance, crop plants might grow larger, but supply proportionately less nutritive value per unit of produce, as the ratio of carbon to nitrogen in the tissues increases. Moreover, insect pests may well eat more of the crop to compensate.[38] No one has any idea what shifts might occur in which pest attacks what crop. At the very least, depending on beneficial effects on crops from higher concentrations of CO_2 to compensate for the climatic impacts of warming would be an extremely dangerous gamble.

Finally, the conservatism of governments will result in considerable delay and exacerbate the problems involved in making adjustments. For instance, the United States Congress had only begun to discuss taking steps to prepare for or to delay the possible effects of global warming a year after the magnitude of the 1988 harvest disaster was apparent. The administrative branch had not taken any initiatives by mid-1989. Even though it was not certain that the drought was caused by the warming, the hot, dry summer did elicit more than enough scientific testimony to make a prudent government take out some "insurance."[39]

Food security will be influenced by global warming in ways other than through change of climate. The rise in sea level will cause losses in food production through flooding of coastal agricultural land and damage to fisheries by inundating coastal wetlands that support them.[40] Low-lying, fertile, and heavily populated deltas such as those of the Nile and the Brahmaputra/Ganges (Bangladesh) will be submerged first. Developed countries, though more capable of resisting the rising seas, will not be immune. Holland may have to flood some of its reclaimed agricultural land with Rhine River water to prevent saltwater intrusion into groundwater supplies.[41] Florida and its citrus industry may eventually disappear.

►   **MODELING GLOBAL CHANGE AND FOOD**   ◄
SECURITY

To examine the possible effects of climate change on food production, our group at Stanford constructed a simple global model that simulated population growth, annual agricultural output, annual food consumption, and the effects of unfavorable weather patterns such as those that occurred in 1988.[42] The model determines the amount of food available for consumption (production plus carryover stocks) in each year over a twenty-year period. For all runs of the model, it was assumed that average increases in grain production in years with favorable weather would keep up with population growth (1.7 percent annually). In those years, a surplus of 50 million metric tons of grain was stored. The model then was used to examine the effects of different frequencies and severities of widespread unfavorable weather patterns.

Under the most "optimistic" scenario, unfavorable climatic events occurred on average once every five years and caused a 5 percent reduction in global grain harvest, roughly the size of the drought-caused drop in 1988. Under the most "pessimistic" scenario, the average time between unfavorable climatic events was set at 3.3 years, and each event was assumed to cause a 10 percent drop in grain production below the trend.

In order to simulate the feedback between availability of food and population size, it was assumed that a food deficit of one ton of grain resulted in two deaths. Roughly three people are supported by each ton of grain produced now, but about one third of all grain is fed to animals; so theoretically some of the shortfall could be made up by feeding people the grain directly. Even so, actual death rates from starvation might be raised further than the model indicates. Undernutrition occurs mainly among the poorest people, say the bottom quarter or fifth of the population. This group bears the brunt of any deficits, while the rest usually maintain adequate diets, albeit at higher prices. Because of the disproportionate burden on the poor, diseases and hunger may take a heavier toll on them than our all-or-nothing simplification suggests.[43]

Results of the model suggest that the optimistic scenario (a 5 percent reduction in grain harvest on average twice per decade) would not lead to complete depletion of world grain stocks, although world food security (adequate carryover supplies to compensate for unexpected crop failures) would be threatened. These reductions would have little effect on overall population growth. Under the pessimistic scenario (10 percent reductions on average three times per decade), however, severe deficits in grain stocks occur about twice per decade, each causing the deaths of between 50 and 400 million people.

Weather patterns that might cause such drops include, for instance, repeats of the 1988 North American/Chinese/Soviet drought, equally or more severe, and totally different weather patterns involving other areas. In short, the model ignored the question of the *pattern* of crop failures that would lead to large declines in grain production. It also did not consider compensatory actions such as bringing set-aside land in the United States back into production, conversion from animal feed to food crops, or the general intensification of agricultural activity that would result from increased demand for food, except to the degree they are included in our "constant average increase" assumption. The model may also have been pessimistic in not incorporating increases in production that might result from technical innovations stimulated by famines.

On the other hand, some of the assumptions about carrying capacity were optimistic. It did not, for example, incorporate additional drops in harvest due to social breakdown related to famines, the spread of disease through malnourished populations, or inappropriate aid programs that damage the agricultural sectors of recipient nations. Indeed, the basic assumption of food production keeping pace with population growth in the absence of unfavorable climatic events should be considered *very* optimistic, since this is no longer the case in Africa or Latin America, and it is almost twice the rate of production increase projected as the maximum by Lester Brown.

Such a model, of course, is simply an aid to thinking about the possible consequences if short-term climatic change were to cause drops in grain production roughly comparable to those known to have occurred before, and considering the rest of the system to be essentially "surprise free." The results were not predictions, simply indications of the nature of problems that may occur if the global warming leads to more frequent and more severe climatic events that are deleterious to agriculture. They show that, if global warming progresses as many climatic models suggest it might, there is a risk of serious famines, each of which could kill more people than any war in human history. The results also indicate that climate change at the very least would reduce the margin of safety in the global food system.

The population–food system has no "fail-safe" backup mechanisms designed into it, even if climates should remain favorable to food production. The world depends upon the statistical "cushion" that adverse weather and unusual pest outbreaks do not occur everywhere at once.[44] To the degree that global food production becomes more concentrated (as in North America), humanity becomes more vulnerable.

▶   ACID RAIN   ◀

Whereas the greenhouse warming represents an impending catastrophe, serious damage from acid rain[45] is already upon us. Across North America and Europe, loss of life in lakes, streams, and forests—and of the services of those ecosystems —originates in the sulfur and nitrogen oxides that emanate from smokestacks and vehicle exhaust pipes.[46] Too many automobiles, too many industrial products, and too much energy use per person inflate the consumption factor of the Impact = Population × Affluence × Technology $(I = PAT)$ equation. Failure to invest in smaller, more energy-efficient cars and a refusal to pay for adequate pollution controls in factory and power-plant stacks make the ecologically damaging technology (T) factor substantial as well. But the P factor is important here, too. If there were only half as many Americans driving cars, using manufactured devices, and consuming electric power, acid-rain problems would be comparatively negligible, even if levels of per-capita consumption and pollution control were identical.[47]

The problem is becoming truly global. Vast areas of the world have precipitation substantially more acidic than preindustrial natural levels, including nonindustrial regions. Very acid precipitation has been recorded in remote, nonindustrial parts of China, due to coal burning for heating, cooking, and water purification.[48] Recent reports of acid precipitation have come from tropical Africa, produced there by agricultural burning to clear shrubland and encourage the growth of grass.[49] One does not have to await more detailed studies of the impact of increased acidity on living systems to be very apprehensive about this. Biologists know from first principles that rapidly changing the acidity of an ecosystem is a good way to disrupt its functioning.[50]

In the African case, the population element of the $I = PAT$ equation obviously dominates. As atmospheric scientist Paul Crutzen pointed out, there will be increased air pollution from the tropics as the population grows and more forests and savannas are turned into fields and grasslands that are burned more frequently.[51] It is not yet known how sensitive the African rain forest will prove to be to acid deposition, which in this case is combined with an assault from toxic ozone, also generated by the fires.

The prospects of nearly worldwide damage to vulnerable forests and tree crops in the future is not a cheering one in a world in which both forest and agricultural ecosystems are likely to be badly stressed from climate change—and many forests will be under a multitude of other population-related assaults. Furthermore, forest damage may itself contribute to climate change by putting still more CO_2 into the atmosphere, reducing the amount of moisture recycled through vegetation, and changing the reflectivity of the land surface.[52]

►   **DEPLETION OF THE OZONE LAYER**   ◄

The global environmental problem that has the loosest population connection is depletion of the ozone layer in the upper atmosphere which shields people, other animals, and plants from dangerous ultraviolet-B (UV-B) radiation. Without the ozone layer, life on land would be transformed into something like life under an ultraviolet sterilizer on an old-time roadhouse toilet seat—it would essentially be impossible. Depletion of the ozone layer threatens the flow of services from terrestrial ecosystems by damaging or destroying the ecosystems themselves.

For every 5 percent decrease in the ozone layer, there is a 10 percent increase in the UV-B reaching Earth's surface. That increment of radiation would produce roughly twenty thousand additional skin cancers per year in the United States, of which about one thousand would be fatal. So far the ozone layer over the United States has thinned 2 to 3 percent.

Everyone by now is aware of the danger of increased skin

cancers from exposure to UV-B, and most know that it increases the chances of cataracts. But the public is less aware that the impacts of increased UV-B are far broader than these risks suggest; we hear about them because scientists know more about them. But UV-B is widely injurious to virtually all forms of life. It damages DNA (the genetic material), impairs the immune systems of human beings, and inhibits photosynthesis. Algae, the base of marine food chains, are extremely sensitive to UV-B, and their populations in surface waters (which are penetrated by UV-B) could be reduced, with deleterious effects on fisheries dependent on them. More UV-B exposure also could make human populations more susceptible to disease and have damaging effects on fisheries, natural ecosystems, and crops. Broad-leaved crops such as soybeans appear especially susceptible. Exactly what the total biological impacts will be at various levels of exposure are unknown; all we can say is that as the ozone shield thins, life on Earth's land surfaces will become more difficult, and more skin cancers could be the least of our problems.

The threat to the ozone layer comes largely from the synthetic compounds known as chlorofluorocarbons (CFCs), which are used as refrigerants, foaming agents in plastics, and aerosol propellants—and are potent greenhouse gases to boot.[53] CFCs in aerosol spray cans have been banned for most uses in the United States since 1977, but are still widely used elsewhere.

Substitutes can be found for CFCs in all these uses; some may cost more to produce or will require changes in refrigerator design that will make them more expensive. Some substitutes will cause refrigerators to be less efficient.

The CFC threat to the ozone layer can be abated by operating only on the affluence and technology factors of the $I = PAT$ equation. But even here the job would be eased if there were fewer people—especially in poor countries such as China. That nation has the goal of providing refrigeration for its entire population. China had planned to use CFCs rather than more expensive substitutes, since it must strive to minimize the costs of development, which are already enormous because of its huge population.

Nonetheless, the ozone situation is a bellwether, because

eliminating the threat to the ozone shield is simple compared to the efforts that will be required to slow the global warming, abate acid precipitation, arrest the general toxification of the planet, or save a substantial portion of biodiversity. A first international protocol on reducing CFC production was reached in Montreal in 1987. Then it was found that ozone depletion was occurring faster than thought earlier. Negotiations for a necessary strengthening of that protocol with the goal of ending all production and use by 2000 have proceeded rapidly. An agreement to that end was signed in Helsinki in May 1989 by eighty nations, including the U.S.A., China, and India. The nations also agreed to establish a fund to help poor nations to develop alternates.[54] We hope that complete elimination of these compounds will occur, and that the rich will honor their commitments to help the poor with the inevitable costs. Most of all, we hope that the ozone protocols will serve as a model for dealing with other global environmental problems.

►   **DESERTIFICATION**   ◄

One of the most widespread population-related environmental problems is the ecological degradation of Earth's land surface in a process called "desertification." Desertification is caused by destruction of vegetation by woodcutting, burning, and overgrazing, by erosion by water and wind as a result of poor land-management, by salinization and waterlogging of irrigated fields, and by soil compaction (by cattle hoofs, tractors, drying, and the impact of raindrops on denuded soil surfaces).[55] Its terminal stage is easily recognizable—a barren wasteland, virtually devoid of vegetation, familiar to those who have seen TV stories of famine in the Sahel. A functional ecosystem is degraded to the point where it can provide few, if any, services to humanity.

But in its earlier stages, desertification can go unrecognized by most people. For instance, overgrazing has ruined much of the grasslands of the western United States. Nonetheless the average citizen of, say, Albuquerque, New Mexico, does not realize that he or she lives in an area desertified by human action—that the upper Rio Grande Valley was once a rich grassland.[56]

The United Nations has estimated that globally about 13 million square miles (almost four times the area of the fifty United States) of arid and semiarid land have lost about a quarter of their potential productivity due to desertification classified as "moderate." Almost 6 million square miles have lost over half of their potential productivity, and are severely desertified. Over 80,000 square miles have been reduced to zero economic productivity annually.[57] The areas most affected include the margins of the Sahara, eastern and southern Africa, much of south-central Asia, Australia, the western United States, and southern South America. Desertification even threatens relatively humid tropical areas where deforestation can change local climates and turn an area previously rich with life into a wasteland.[58] Approximately 230 million people, mostly in poor nations, are said to be directly and deleteriously affected by desertification.[59]

Unfortunately, these numbers are but rough estimates, and present a picture of "deserts on the march" that greatly understates the complexity of the situation. For instance, the image of the Sahara moving inexorably southward may well be inaccurate. Satellite studies in the 1980s show "a generally southward retreating vegetation front in the Sahel in 1982 to 1984 and a generally northward advancing vegetation front in 1985, 1986, and 1987."[60] It is probably more accurate to view desertification as a process of repeated pulses of land deterioration "from centres of excessive population pressure"[61] than as a process originating from edges of established deserts.

While understanding the precise pattern of land deterioration is necessary to reversing that deterioration, we must not let disagreements over that pattern or over estimates of the amount of desertification obscure the basics of the situation. It is a huge global problem; too many people is one of its major causes; and population growth interacts with bad land-use policies and changing socioeconomic conditions to produce it.

It is no accident that the most serious desertification is found in areas where burgeoning human populations are contributing to rapidly changing land-use patterns. For instance,

the 1950s and 1960s were a period of unusually favorable rainfall in the Sahel. As a result, cash-crop agriculture expanded
along with the human population. Specifically, the population
of Niger increased from 2.5 to 3.8 million from 1954 to 1968,
and peanut farming expanded from just over 500 square miles
to some 1700 square miles. Nomadic herders of the Sahel, who
previously grazed animals on land that had disappeared under
cash crops, were displaced to the north. They stocked new
lands (which tribal traditions taught were undependable for the
long term), and their herds increased during the moist phase.
Then, as tradition predicted, the climate turned dry again. The
vegetation was completely removed by cattle, camels, and
goats, and millions of animals died. An unknown number of
people, probably around 100,000, perished in the resulting
famine.[62]

Overpopulation of grazing animals and the people who depend on them in the Sahel often resulted from the drilling of
tube wells. The wells allowed herds to build up beyond the
long-term carrying capacity of an area. Cattle must trek daily
to water in order to survive, and their movements destroy vegetation and compact the soil. They concentrate around the well
sites, eating and trampling vegetation, and degrading the soil
of an ever-increasing area. Even the droppings of cattle add to
the process. "Cowpats" dry rapidly in the sun, heating up and
killing the bacteria and fungi that otherwise would speed their
decomposition. The dried cowpats form a "fecal pavement"
that discourages the sprouting of fresh grass.[63] The drilling of
even more wells is often seen as the solution to this problem,
but clearly it is much more likely simply to exacerbate it.[64]

The Sahel tragedy is just an extreme example of a general
trend on Earth's grasslands. As human populations expand, so
do those of the livestock that supply food, draft power, and
dung used as fertilizer or (in extremis) fuel. Not only in the
developing world but in much of the intermountain United
States,[65] herds now exceed the carrying capacity of the land.
The animals eat the grass faster than it can grow. In each of
nine nations in southern Africa, cattle exceed the carrying
capacity of the range by 50 to 100 percent.[66] In desertified
Indian states such as Karnataka and Rajasthan, the range can

carry only 50 to 80 percent of the cattle herds now on them. Many of the animals are emaciated, and droughts kill hundreds of thousands.[67]

In China, between 1949, when the Communist government took over, and 2000, it is estimated that the total area of desert will have doubled. At the moment, about one sixth of the nation is desert. In Inner Mongolia, some 33,000 square miles are threatened with desertification, and in northern China 15,000 square miles of farmland and 20,000 square miles of grasslands are also threatened. Between 1983 and 2000, an increase of almost 30,000 square miles of desert is expected in northern semiarid and arid areas.[68]

▶ **ENVIRONMENTAL DISASTER IN THE UNITED STATES: AN EXAMPLE** ◀

If one wants to see blatant evidence of the squandering of the human inheritance in the United States, perhaps the best way to do so is to travel to one of our most grossly overpopulated areas: south Florida. South Florida is an ideal real-life laboratory in which to observe the impacts of overpopulation on the quality of life in general and on ecosystem services in particular. If Florida were an independent nation, it would be one of the fastest growing in the world. Its population growth rate is about that of Bangladesh, 2.8 percent per year, which if continued unchanged would increase its 1987 population of 12 million to 17.5 million by 2010. A major difference, however, is that Florida's growth is not the result of a high birthrate but of immigration, about a quarter of which is of elderly people choosing to retire in a benign climate.

The signs of explosive growth are everywhere evident in south Florida. Lake Okeechobee is heavily polluted, and groundwater tables are dropping. Suburban developments are marching steadily into the once-wildlife-rich Everglades,[69] their invasion made possible by the draining of the marshes and the termination of the ecosystem services they once provided. Over this scene looms the highest point in south Florida, majestic "Mount Garbage," the Miami sanitary landfill. Mount Garbage doesn't get the job done, though. Informal dumps line

the area's back roads. Plastic garbage bags and derelict refrigerators decorate those roads and complement the plastic-bot-
tle-festooned shorelines of the Florida Keys, accented by old
fishing nets and floats, six-pack wrappers, and other colorful
debris made from processed petroleum. Mixed in with this are
the globs, cakes, and stains of unprocessed petroleum, washed
from the holds of passing tankers. All this and the generally
sleazy development are the most obvious symptoms of a population already too large, growing too fast, and overconsuming
nonrenewable resources.

Those superficial symptoms tend to distract attention from
much more fundamental problems, most of which are connected to the freshwater flows through the marshes of the
southern peninsula. Before European settlement, water
drained southward along a gentle gradient from the northern
part of the state into Lake Okeechobee. From there it flowed
as a sheet, many miles wide and a few inches deep, to Florida
Bay, the body of water between the Keys and the mainland.
That sheet flow is the famous "river of grass"—the central
part of the Everglades. The rich estuarine waters of Florida
Bay and the vast Everglades marshes supported a diverse flora
and fauna, including deer, cougars, and millions of nesting
wading birds. The influx of people and their agriculture and
industry has put heavy demands upon this water supply, in
terms of both its use and the course of its flow. The result has
been a disaster for the area's wildlife. Only remnants of the
previous bird populations—about 10 percent—now occupy the
Everglades. As they so often do, the bird populations signal
difficulties within the ecosystem.

The most poignant indicators of distress are the "panhan-
dling" great white herons.[70] Many of these 3-feet-tall, long-
legged birds now patrol regular territories on docks and in the
backyards of local human residences, begging for fish. The
birds nest on mangrove islets in Florida Bay, where they are
secure from raccoons and other mammalian nest-robbers.
Once the herons supported themselves and raised their young
on the fish of Florida Bay. But, as Audubon Society biologist
George Powell and his colleagues have shown, the herons can
no longer find enough of their natural food to raise enough

young to maintain their populations. Only the panhandlers are sufficiently successful reproductively to fledge enough young to replace themselves.[71] They are dependent on the kindly retirees of the Keys.

The human-population-related changes in the Everglades wetlands apparently have reduced the productivity of Florida Bay, something that bodes ill for the commercial and sport fisheries that are critical to the economy of the Florida Keys. In addition, subtle changes in coastal waters are suspected of causing a decline in the coral reefs, a major tourist attraction in the area. And, unless effective steps are taken to restore the wetlands ecosystem, Everglades National Park, a major tourist attraction important to the local economy, may close its doors in a decade or so.

Florida not only has serious difficulties created by human intervention in its freshwater flows, but also is the state most at risk from a sea-level rise resulting from global warming. The state is low and flat; the bottom of Lake Okeechobee is at sea level. The 2- or 3-foot rise in sea level that may occur in the next half century would flood a substantial portion of the state. A big chunk of the southwestern Everglades will disappear as salt water intrudes at rates that neither mangroves nor marsh grasses can adjust to. More serious, the porous limestone shelf on which most of the state rests will permit salt to penetrate aquifers far inland as sea level rises. It has been estimated that for every foot of rise in sea level, there will be about a 40-foot reduction in the depth of fresh water in Florida aquifers.[72] Indeed, the threat of salinization of aquifers is already present because of human manipulation of surface water flows even without rising seas.[73]

Most frightening of all, however, is the prospect of a higher sea level combined with the predicted increase in both the frequency and intensity of hurricanes. Storm surges will be carried far inland. It is likely, if the greenhouse warming continues as projected, that many acres of Florida now seemingly remote from the sea will, in the next century, find themselves swept by a fathom or two of fast-moving salt water.

Florida, even more than California, appears to be at the "edge of history." Growth is rampant, and human and natural values are being lost in a development mania in many areas. Environmental groups are working hard to prevent development in critical parts of the Everglades ecosystem and pushing attempts to restore something resembling the original hydrologic regime. But, as in much of the rest of the world, their chances of success depend on curing both local and global problems.

Population growth and "development" in Florida must be halted, and the lifestyles and attitudes of Floridians changed. But that won't save the state if the world doesn't solve its global problems. Ozone depletion could make sunbathing lethal and help kill the state's agriculture (both directly and by contributing to climate change). Climate change due to greenhouse warming also could greatly exacerbate Florida's freshwater-supply problems. If that warming continues unabated, most of the state may disappear beneath the sea in a few centuries or less.

▶   **COMPARATIVE IMPACTS**   ◀

Overpopulation in rich nations obviously represents a much greater threat to the health of Earth's ecosystems than does population growth in poor nations. The rich contribute disproportionately to the problem of global warming, being responsible today for about 80 percent of the injection of carbon dioxide into the atmosphere from burning fossil fuels, and sharing responsibility for tropical deforestation, which also adds to the CO_2 load. The developed nations probably also contribute more than their share of methane emissions, the second-most-important greenhouse gas. Similarly, most of the responsibility for ozone depletion, acid precipitation, and oceanic pollution can be laid at the doorstep of the rich. So can the local and regional environmental consequences of much of the cash-crop agriculture, tropical deforestation, and mining operations carried out worldwide.

Unfortunately, nations do not even attempt to keep statistics on average per-capita environmental impact of their citizens—which, of course, is simply the combined A and T factors of the $I = PAT$ equation. So, in order to make reason-

able comparisons, we must use a surrogate statistic for A ×
T: per-capita use of commercial energy. Much environmental
damage is done in the mobilization of energy, and even more
is done by its use. Energy use is central to many things we
consider affluence (A), and lack of energy efficiency in the
devices that provide affluence is a major cause of environmental damage (T).

Hundreds of thousands of fishes, sea birds, and mammals
killed at Prince William Sound in Alaska, the death of lakes in
the Northeast from acid precipitation, originating largely in
midwestern power plants, and a contribution to global warming
and acidification of ecosystems (CO_2 and nitrogen oxides from
vehicles and hundreds of power plants) all follow from mobilization of energy to power American society.

Energy is also used to pave over natural ecosystems to
create airports and parking lots; energy is required to produce
the plastic and paper and aluminum cans that clog our landfills
and decorate our highways and seashores; energy powers the
boats that slaughter the manatees in Florida lakes; energy was
used to produce the pesticides and to mobilize the selenium
from soils that kills birds in California's Kesterson National
Wildlife Refuge; energy cools the offices of Arizona developers
as they plan the further unsustainable suburbanization of the
American southwestern deserts; energy warms the offices of
oil-company officials in Anchorage as they plan the exploitation of the Alaskan National Wildlife Refuge.

Energy is being used to pump the Ogallala aquifer dry, and
energy lets us fly in jet airplanes 30,000 feet above the circular
irrigation patterns created by the pumping—energy that did
environmental damage when oil was pumped out of the ground
and now is causing environmental damage as jet exhausts are
spewed into the atmosphere. And, of course, energy damages
when it is used to mine ores, win metals from those ores, and
use those metals and other energy-intensive materials to manufacture automobiles, airplanes, TVs, refrigerators, and all the
other paraphernalia of our civilization.

Poor people don't use much energy, so they don't contribute much to the damage caused by mobilizing it. The average
Bangladeshi is not surrounded by plastic gadgets, the average

Colombian does not fly in jet airplanes, the average Kenyan farmer does not have a tractor or a pickup, and the average Chinese does not have air-conditioning or central heating in his apartment. In 1980, of some 400 million motor vehicles in the world, 150 million were in the United States, 36 million in Japan, 24 million in West Germany, 1.7 million each in India and China, and 181,000 in Nigeria.[74]

So statistics on per-capita commercial energy use are a reasonable index of AT—of the responsibility for damage to the environment and consumption of resources of an average citizen of a nation. According to that index of AT, a baby born in the United States represents twice the destructive impact on Earth's ecosystems and the services they provide as one born in Sweden, 3 times one born in Italy, 13 times one born in Brazil, 35 times one in India, 140 times one in Bangladesh or Kenya, and 280 times one in Chad, Rwanda, Haiti, or Nepal.[75]

These statistics should lay to rest the myth that population problems arise primarily from rapid growth in poor nations— although their impact is nontrivial and increasing very rapidly. They remind us that population shrinkage is essential among the rich, since each birth forgone relieves on average much more of the pressure on Earth's resources and environment than a birth forgone in a poor nation.

▶   **CONCLUSION**   ◀

In summary, overpopulation is rapidly degrading Earth's eco-systems in both rich and poor nations. The future of humanity probably depends much more heavily on the health of global ecosystems than on public health in the classic sense. Civilization can't persist without ecosystem services, and these are threatened in innumerable ways by the expanding scale of human activities. Curing cancer, for example, would increase the life expectancy of Americans by only a year or so; a collapse of ecosystem services will lower life expectancy by decades.

Perhaps the best way to end this discussion of the human environment is with a quote from *The Population Bomb:*

How well are we treating these symptoms of the Earth's disease of overpopulation? Are we getting ahead of the filth, corruption, and noise? Are we guarding the natural cycles on which our lives depend? Are we protecting ourselves from subtle and chronic poisoning? The answer is obvious—the palliatives are too few and too weak. The patient continues to get sicker.[76]

7

▲

Population and
Public Health

▼

The role of population size in public health is often very subtle and not as easily measured as it is for ecosystem health. Twice as many people clearly add twice as much CO_2 to the atmosphere, everything else being equal; twice as many people in a city will not double the chances of an epidemic. Of course, environmental degradation tied to population growth poses quite direct threats to human health; the well-known consequences of urban air pollution and contamination of food and water are obvious cases in point.[1]

▶　　　　　　**POPULATION AND POLLUTION**　　　　　◀

If there are only a few thousand automobiles in a city, natural air movements may carry away the cars' noxious effluents and rainfall may cleanse the air so that there is little or no health hazard. A few hundred thousand motor vehicles, however, may easily overwhelm these natural dispersal and cleaning functions and produce life-threatening smog.

A few thousand people living along a river may be able to put their sewage into it without causing it to become generally polluted. Dilution and the action of sunlight and microorganisms may keep the water pure enough to drink. A few hundred thousand people dumping their sewage into the same river may create a stew of disease-causing bacteria that only a fool would imbibe.

A few thousand people residing in a state may all be able to live on self-sufficient organic farms and enjoy fresh, uncontaminated produce. A few million in the same state will have to leave the farming to a relatively few large-scale, "efficient" industrial agricultural operations. Their food will often be leavened by pesticide residues and preservatives.

The more people there are in an area, all else being equal, the more effort they will have to expend to avoid various types of "pollution." Once a certain threshold is passed, each additional person added will create disproportionately more. The ores mined to supply the new person will, on average, be of lower grade and have to be hauled farther. The oil that is refined into gasoline for his or her car will come from deeper and farther away. Water will have to be moved farther to slake his or her thirst. The garbage he or she produces will have to be moved to a more distant point or be treated more extensively.[2]

This situation is simply an example of the economists' "law of diminishing returns."[3] Beyond a certain population size, if the per-capita affluence (A) of a population is held constant while the population grows, the environmental impact per unit of affluence (that arising from the technology factor, T) will nevertheless inevitably increase.[4] More people require more resources, and the richest and closest supplies will be consumed first. Then it becomes necessary to drill deeper for groundwater or oil, to separate metals from poorer ores, and to extend supply networks. These activities all require the use of more energy per person, and that generates more pollution per person (as well as other kinds of environmental disruption).

Diminishing returns hit poor countries even harder, since those countries often lack the capital required to apply technological fixes to pollution problems. There are no catalytic converters on the multitudes of cars in Mexico City, for example, and that contributes to one of the worst air-pollution problems on the planet.[5] Perhaps the most poignant case of diminishing returns in such nations, however, has no immediate connection to pollution. As fuelwood near expanding villages is exhausted, women must walk farther and farther for it, sometimes spending most of every day at the task.[6]

And the experience of both rich and poor countries indicates that pollution-abatement efforts are doomed to some degree of failure, especially in the absence of population control.

The United States, for example, is famous for suffering a glut of automobiles. Since 1970, while the population of the nation has increased by 25 percent, the number of passenger cars sold in the United States increased by 50 percent.[7] One result of that is continuing, unacceptably high levels of air pollution, causing as many as thirty thousand premature deaths annually, especially among those individuals with asthma and other respiratory problems. Perhaps 75 million Americans live where national air-quality standards for ozone, particulates, and carbon monoxide are not met.

All of this is *in spite of* the success of the Clean Air Act of 1970, which by 1989 did manage to reduce air pollution to two thirds of its 1970 level, even in the face of substantial population growth. If the population had not grown, however, air pollution would now be only a little more than *half* the 1970 level.[8]

The Office of Technology Assessment is not sanguine about the prospects for clean air by 2000, as projected in 1989 by the Bush administration in connection with its proposed new Clean Air Act.[9] The Bush proposals deliberately avoided tightening controls on vehicles, saying that the American love affair with cars made further restrictions on automobiles unacceptable to the public! Of course, the further clogging of freeways and the increased smog might dim the luster of that love affair.

What no one is suggesting is any effort to reduce the P factor to help with the struggle to give the nation healthy air. We are not, of course, arguing that population size should be reduced so far that everyone can "go back to nature" and live free of pollutants. Many benefits have accrued to those who live with some pollution. Cars provide the convenience of personal transportation (although, with increasing population densities, this is more and more an inconvenience). To many that convenience may be an ample benefit to exchange for the cost of a higher risk of dying young of heart disease or lung cancer. Having lots of people living along a river can provide the opportunity for lively cities with universities, concerts, a wide variety of industries to provide high-paying jobs, and a diversity of stores and restaurants in which to spend the money. Water-treatment plants, or even a slightly higher chance of getting cancer, may seem a small cost to pay for such benefits. Modern agriculture and global transport have provided an abundance and variety of food unknown in the past, and there is little evidence that, overall, the various residues that may be present in the food available in the United States have caused serious health problems.[10]

What we are arguing here is that pollution generally increases with population density, and that there is every reason to believe that after the population is dense enough to provide all the benefits one could wish, additional growth simply exacerbates the pollution problems and makes their solution much more difficult and expensive. Further, we would contend that in many cases pollution could be greatly abated by organizing ourselves differently—by reducing the A factor as well as the T factor. For example, smaller cars, more car-pooling, and good mass transport could greatly reduce smog problems (as well as making commuting more pleasant). Better yet would be reorganizing our cities so more people could walk to work. Catalytic converters and methanol are not the only ways to skin the smog cat. But if our focus is only on A and T, the P factor will always get us in the end.

The population connection to pollution, like that to ecosystem health, is thus pretty clear-cut. But what is the effect of doubling the number of people on the chances of an epidemic propagating? How does doubling the size of a city affect its livability? It is to such issues that we now turn.

▶   **EPIDEMICS AND HISTORY**   ◀

Few people realize that epidemic disease and population size have interacted in important ways in human history. Indeed, William McNeill has argued that epidemics have played a key role in the rise and fall of many civilizations.[11] For example, it is very difficult to explain the conquest of some 100 million Native Americans, many with advanced, well-organized societies, by a handful of Spaniards—except by invoking the incredible impact of the European diseases they brought to the New World. Native Americans had essentially no resistance to the common diseases of the Old World, diseases that largely afflicted children in European populations which had been regularly exposed to them long enough to evolve natural immunity.

Less than fifty years after Cortez landed, the population of central Mexico had been reduced to about one-tenth the size it had been before contact. The viruses of smallpox, measles, influenza, and mumps, and the bacteria that cause whooping cough, diphtheria, scarlet fever, and a variety of other nasty ills, introduced by the invaders, were much more effective than the primitive guns of the Spaniards. Indeed, only a raging smallpox epidemic prevented the Aztecs from destroying the last of the Spaniards after forcing them out of the Aztec capital of Tenochtitlán (the predecessor of Mexico City). The epidemic was traceable to a soldier in the Spaniards' ranks, one of the few invaders not immune, who contracted the disease and spread it to the Aztecs. Many Aztecs were killed, including their leaders, making possible the Spanish reconquest of the city (which had some sixty thousand homes and a population estimated to be a few hundred thousand). Overall, pestilence brought by the Conquistadors may have killed something on the order of a third to half of all the Aztecs and Incas,[12] and imported diseases continued to kill Native Americans in similar proportions into the mid-nineteenth century.

The destruction of Native American civilizations was apparently aided by the psychological impact of pestilence that differentially struck down the natives and allowed the Spaniards to escape virtually unscathed. Both the newcomers and the Aztecs assumed that this was a sign of heavenly displeasure, and it broke the spirit of the Aztecs. Whatever the details, there can be no doubt that diseases, especially smallpox, were by far the greatest and most effective allies of the Conquistadors.[13]

The thesis that disease has often shaped human history can be applied persuasively to the rise of Western Europe as the dominant world culture and to many other events. But whether or not one accepts all of his arguments, McNeill highlights another element that is even less widely appreciated than the overall historical role of pestilence. That is the role of population size and density in determining the vulnerability of a community to epidemics. Many bacterial and viral diseases that pass directly from person to person depend on cities—densely packed communities of thousands of people—for their persistence. Otherwise they run out of susceptible individuals to infect, and they die out. Measles, for example, cannot persist in populations of fewer than about 300,000 people.[14] Such diseases were not problems for our hunter-gatherer ancestors.

People have complex relationships with the tiny parasitic organisms that feed on them from the inside. Individuals gain protection by fighting off an invader with their immune systems; populations apparently gain protection by evolving resistance—that is, individuals of a resistant population on the average are better equipped to fend off a particular disease.[15] Populations that have no recent experience with a parasitic disease are susceptible to having a huge proportion of individuals infected.

As shown by the Native American experience with smallpox, those who contract the disease in such susceptible populations may suffer very heavy mortality. Moreover, the Native American tragedies are not the most extreme examples of die-offs. In an unidentified epidemic in northwestern China in the early fourth century, mortality was reported to be over 95 percent. The death of half or more of populations suffering novel epidemics was frequently reported before Columbus landed in America. Even the modern world has not proven immune. A new strain of influenza killed some 20 million people after infecting most of Earth's population at the end of World War I.

These episodes should not be dismissed as problems of the past. There is no finite number of diseases that, once conquered, will leave *Homo sapiens* free of the attack of microparasites. Novel human diseases come primarily from transfers from other animals. Pigs get influenza. Measles may be a form of the rinderpest virus (which causes an often fatal disease of cattle and their relatives) or of canine distemper viruses. It must have been transferred from an animal source within the last six thousand years or so, since human communities large enough to support the virus didn't exist before then.[16]

Smallpox was likely a gift from cattle or their relatives, as suggested by the close similarity of the smallpox virus to the cowpox virus. Smallpox has close relatives that attack many other organisms. Presumably, then, even if the historic human smallpox strain has been exterminated, another mutation and transfer might someday restore it. Syphilis is believed by some to be an evolutionary development of the spirochete that once caused a serious disease called yaws in the European population,[17] having evolved the venereal method of transmission when more clothing and less personal contact made simple skin-to-skin transmission much more difficult. And the influenza virus frequently evolves nasty new strains.

The details of these relationships between human beings and their parasites are not entirely understood and needn't concern us here. The key point is that, for decades now, *Homo sapiens* has been setting itself up as an increasingly ideal target for a worldwide epidemic—a pandemic—as we and others have pointed out repeatedly. The rising numbers of malnourished people living in conditions of poor sanitation and unclean water supply are rapidly increasing the pool of potential disease victims. In addition, ever faster transportation systems have made the pool of susceptible people essentially global.

Increases in the speed of transport can extend chains of infection to previously inaccessible areas. For instance, at the end of the last century, an outbreak of bubonic plague that began in the interior of China spread throughout the world after reaching the seaport of Hong Kong in 1894. In earlier plague outbreaks, the disease would not have reached many distant areas by sea, because on small, slow-moving sailing ships the supply of susceptible people usually would be exhausted before the voyage was over. But the development of steamship fleets after 1870 had changed all that, and within a decade after the Hong Kong outbreak the plague reached all of the world's important seaports. Modern sanitation and knowledge of the role of rats and fleas in disseminating the disease led to its rapid containment in most areas. In India, however, about 6 million people perished before the outbreak was controlled.

►   **TODAY'S EPIDEMIOLOGICAL ENVIRONMENT**   ◄

Of course, modern air transport means that a person carrying an infectious disease usually can reach anyplace in the world within a day or so. The dangers of rapid transport of smallpox (until its recent eradication) and yellow fever viruses by passengers on jet aircraft have been well recognized by public-health authorities.[18] Fast transcontinental transport adds considerably to the threat of diseases that ordinarily produce symptoms in a short time, greatly compounding the problems of quarantine and essentially binding all of *Homo sapiens* into one gigantic, potentially susceptible pool of hosts for infectious diseases. As Nobel laureate virologist Howard Temin wrote of AIDS in the light of post–World War II social changes, "If anything, the surprise might be that there has been only one major new epidemic." [19]

In short, the human epidemiological environment has become ever more precarious. We are creating a giant, crowded "monoculture" [20] of human beings, which would be at high risk in epidemics even if there weren't millions of people who were especially vulnerable to disease because of their debilitated condition, and even if carriers couldn't zoom around the globe with unprecedented speed. The major barrier between humanity and such disasters is the global public-health system, and it provides the least protection to those who are most vulnerable. The United Nations Children's Fund (UNICEF), however, in recent years has been making heroic efforts to extend immunization for the main childhood diseases to children in poor countries everywhere.

It is true, nonetheless, that humanity has made gigantic strides in its ability to deal with microparasites, and ordinary people in developed nations are certainly much less likely to succumb to a communicable disease than were royalty in the middle of the last century. Yet the likelihood is far from zero even for the richest members of society, as the AIDS epidemic has clearly demonstrated. Malaria, long in decline, is resurgent today among the poor, who have inadequate access to modern medicine and are not able to protect themselves (with screens and repellents) against the mosquitoes that carry the malarial organisms.

At a special meeting, virologists have recently gone public with their concerns about the possibility of viral epidemics made difficult or impossible to control because of "population growth and the fact that millions now live in crowded squalor . . . and jet travel allow[ing] infected people to spread a virus even before they are aware they are carrying it . . . [and] various environmental changes [that] could also influence the emergence of viruses."[21] They are worried not just about epidemics caused by known viruses, but about viruses that have not previously infected large numbers of people. Dr. Donald A. Henderson, dean of the Johns Hopkins University School of Public Health, "called for development of an international early warning system to detect newly evolving viruses quickly." He suggested establishment of monitoring stations "near rain forests where unknown viruses are thought to lurk, and in densely populated areas to which people have migrated from rural areas, where viruses may have infected only isolated groups."[22]

There is ample reason to heed their concerns. The vulnerability of human society to viruses that transfer from other animals, especially primates, was demonstrated by the appearance in Uganda in 1959 of a "new" virus disease, O'nyong-nyong fever.[23] An epidemic of O'nyong-nyong swept through much of East Africa, but remained nonlethal. It suggested, however, the potential that a new lethal virus could have for assaulting humanity—a potential that has been compared to the impact of the myxomatosis virus on the European rabbit populations in Australia, which it virtually exterminated. Richard Fiennes, in his book on diseases that can transfer from primates to human beings,[24] asked rhetorically what would happen if such a disease should appear "in packed human communities," and concluded that mortality could be 90 percent.[25]

Not all new virus diseases appearing in the human population have been as benign as O'nyong-nyong. The AIDS virus (HIV) is one of several new *lethal* viruses to threaten us in recent decades,[26] and the first to cause a large-scale epidemic, one that will almost certainly kill millions of people. The first new lethal virus to be recognized caused Marburg disease. African vervet monkeys were the original hosts of that virus, a relative of the one that causes rabies. In 1967, a consignment of monkeys carrying the virus passed through London's airport on their way to a laboratory in Marburg, Germany. In the laboratory, twenty-five people in contact with the monkeys or their tissues were infected by the virus, and seven died almost immediately. They passed it on to a few additional people, all of whom survived.[27]

Humanity had two strokes of luck in this case. First, the incubation period of the virus was short—only four to seven days. Victims had little chance to contact others and pass on the virus before they became sick and died. This allowed epidemiologists to trace the course of the infection and quickly limit it by isolating carriers. Second, people were not infected by the virus until after the monkeys reached Marburg. If the disease had been passed to people handling the shipment at the London airport, it might have been disseminated around the globe before anything could be done to stop it. Marburg virus is an excellent example of a disease-causing agent which rapid transport could play a key role in spreading, because of its short incubation time.

Marburg virus disease has subsequently been seen outside laboratories and has caused several hundred deaths in Africa.[28] There, as the human populations expand, pathogens are more frequently transferring from animal reservoirs into the human population and causing life-threatening infections.

A second serious disease also originated in Africa. That was Lassa fever, caused by another virus that originated in nonhuman mammals, in this case a rat. It first appeared in the Nigerian village of Lassa in 1969 as a highly virulent, contagious hemorrhagic disease. A small but deadly outbreak ensued, and the virus was imported into the United States when sick medical-missionary workers were evacuated. But human luck held again. The originally lethal virus became less virulent as it passed from person to person, and a serum containing survivors' antibodies has helped cure victims. The virus still causes hundreds of cases and many deaths each year in central Africa. In 1989, a forty-three-year-old mechanical engineer died of it in Chicago after flying to the funeral of his parents in Nigeria—again highlighting the speed with which potential carriers can now move around.

▶   **AIDS**   ◀

AIDS is caused by a special kind of virus, known as a retrovirus. It invades white blood cells, which play a crucial role in providing immunity to disease.

The original source of AIDS is thought to have been an African monkey, a close relative of the vervets that gave us Marburg virus; but the African origin of this disease has not been conclusively demonstrated, and the suggestion has been highly controversial because of connotations of responsibility. Nonetheless, human populations are exploding at record rates in Africa, ecological situations have been changing dramatically, malnutrition (and thus impairment of immune systems)[29] is widespread, and contact with our primate relatives there is more extensive than on any other continent. In addition, close relatives of the AIDS viruses[30] have been isolated from various African monkeys but not from wild monkeys living on other continents.[31] So the opportunity for transfer from an animal host was probably higher there than anywhere else, and the inference is not unreasonable.[32] The question of whether the virus transferred long ago and only "broke out" in response to recent deleterious changes in the human ecology of Africa, or whether the virus only invaded human beings in the last few decades, is much more in doubt.

If AIDS, like humanity, did originate in Africa, that is certainly no reason to blame Africans. It is the virus that causes the disease, not people, and people had nothing to do consciously with the appearance of the virus. Assigning blame simply makes dealing with this massive public-health problem much more difficult—and it is also wrong and unfair.[33]

Fringe groups have demanded that AIDS victims be quarantined, and blood tests are now required of immigrants into some nations. If the epidemic is not controlled, disruption of trade and international recriminations are possible outcomes because of irrational fears and the desire to blame others, especially foreigners or other scapegoats. Remember, transport systems are a key part of agricultural systems; anything that disrupts them will seriously compromise humanity's ability to feed itself. Should some American cities be seen as hotbeds of disease, one could imagine truckers, confused about actual risks, refusing to enter them. Under such circumstances, local food shortages could become acute, even if overall food production were maintained. Remember that much less complex and interdependent societies than the United States have virtually collapsed when confronted by epidemics like bubonic plague.[34] Nothing in the rules says that AIDS or some other epidemic could not have a similar effect, since the more effective public-health organizations of modern societies could be counterbalanced by the increased vulnerability inherent in modern distribution systems.

Whether or not AIDS can be contained will depend primarily on how rapidly the spread of HIV can be slowed through public education and other measures, on when *and if* the medical community can find satisfactory preventatives or treatments, and to a large extent on luck. The virus has already shown itself to be highly mutable,[35] and laboratory strains resistant to the one drug, AZT, that seems to slow its lethal course have already been reported.[36]

A virus that infects many millions of novel hosts, in this case people, might evolve new transmission characteristics. To do so, however, would almost certainly involve changes in its lethality. If, for instance, the virus became more common in the blood (permitting insects to transmit it readily), the very process would almost certainly make it more lethal.[37] Unlike the current version of AIDS, which can take ten years or more to kill its victims, the new strain might cause death in days or weeks. Infected individuals then would have less time to spread the virus to others, and there would be strong selection in favor of less lethal strains (as happened in the case of myxomatosis).[38] What this would mean epidemiologically is not clear, but it could temporarily increase the transmission rate and reduce the life expectancy of infected persons until the system once again equilibrated.

If the ability of the AIDS virus to grow in the cells of the skin or the membranes of the mouth, the lungs, or the intestines were increased, the virus might be spread by casual contact, by inhalation, or through eating contaminated food. But it is likely, as Temin points out, that acquiring those abilities would so change the virus that it no longer efficiently infected the kinds of cells it now does and so would no longer cause AIDS. In effect it would produce an entirely different disease. We hope Temin is correct, but another Nobel laureate, Joshua Lederberg, is worried that a relatively minor mutation could lead to the virus infecting a type of white blood cell commonly present in the lungs. If so, it might be transmissable through coughs.

In the United States and Europe, most AIDS patients are members of "high-risk" groups—promiscuous male homosexuals, intravenous drug users, and hemophiliacs. In central Africa, where the virus may have been in the human population the longest, it appears to infect men and women about equally.[39] Reliable statistics from that continent are scarce, but in some localized areas as much as one quarter of the population is claimed to be carrying the virus. The Centers for Disease Control in Atlanta more conservatively estimates for central Africa a still horrifying rate of 7 percent. In any case, it seems certain that the death rate from AIDS in nations like Rwanda and Uganda will move rapidly upward.[40]

The demographic impact of AIDS in Africa and elsewhere is uncertain—too little is known about patterns of transmission of current strains of HIV and about the potential for the virus to evolve a more efficient mode of infection and higher survival times. Computer projections suggest that, even in Africa, mortality from the disease alone (as opposed to social breakdown or economic effects) is unlikely to bring an end to population growth.[41] While AIDS *could* turn out to be the global epidemic that brutally controls the population explosion by raising death rates, the strains of the virus that have so far been observed seem not to have that capacity. In truth, it is impossible at the moment to predict what will happen.

Whatever the outcome of the coevolutionary battle between *Homo sapiens* and the AIDS virus, we can be confident that our species will face other deadly microparasites in the future. Until the size of the human population is diminished and the proportion of people without adequate diets, clean water supplies, and medical care is reduced, the danger will remain that one of those parasites could cause a devastating global epidemic that could threaten everyone's future.

▶   **ECOLOGICAL CHANGE AND DISEASE**   ◀

We want to mention briefly the conviction of ecologists that a growing human population is making subtle changes in the environment that are bringing more people into contact with old disease-causing organisms, and permitting some organisms that never before had a chance to cause problems for people the opportunity to do so.

An example of the latter is a previously nonparasitic soil amoeba (a protozoan related to the ones often studied in high-school biology classes) which has been allowed by nitrate pollution to invade lakes in the southeastern United States. There it has invaded the bodies of a few swimmers and caused a fatal inflammation of their brains.[42] Of course, no one knows precisely what environmental changes may have opened the door for the much more serious transfers of viruses from animals to previously uninfected human populations, but the suspicion is that they involve expanding human populations coming into closer contact with formerly isolated virus carriers.

In the United States, two "ecological" diseases have become widespread in recent years. One is caused by *Giardia lamblia*, which causes serious diarrhea, weight loss, and abdominal pain. It has made drinking the water from lakes and streams in the mountains of the western states a risky game, even at very high altitudes. *Giardia*'s emergence as a major problem appears related to the greatly increased density of hikers in those mountains.

The other is Lyme disease, a tick-borne infection related to syphilis which has as reservoirs deer and most other warm-blooded wildlife, from birds to squirrels and raccoons. The disease was only identified in the United States in 1975, but is spreading rapidly and is now considered to be, after AIDS, the most important "new" infectious disease in the nation.[43] An initial rash and flulike symptoms can be followed (as can the initial chancre and secondary rash of syphilis) by serious later complications, including recurrent arthritis, abnormal heart rhythms, and nervous-system problems. What triggered the epidemic is unclear. The spirochete that causes the disease may have been accidentally introduced from Europe. Its spread may have been facilitated by a combination of expanding deer populations in the Northeast (as woodlands invaded abandoned farm fields) mixed with human population growth and suburbanization (which brought people, ticks, and woodland animals into close proximity). Connecticut, where the disease was discovered, increased in population size from 2 million to 3 million people between 1950 and 1970.

Finally, in the subtropics and the tropics, irrigation projects that help to keep food production ahead of population growth have contributed to the spread of the parasites that cause schistosomiasis (called bilharzia in Africa).[44] It is second only to malaria as a serious disease afflicting large numbers of human beings. Like most forms of malaria, unless fairly drastic medical treatment is taken, the disease becomes one of chronic debilitation, although it also can kill.

In sum, as human populations grow they inevitably alter their environments, and that, not unexpectedly, will change relationships with parasites. Some may be able to attack us more readily, others may find the job more difficult.

▶   **THE HEALTH OF THE POOR**   ◀

There is, of course, another epidemic already upon us that threatens the health of billions of people. That is the epidemic of poverty. Looking at the crude division of the world into rich and poor nations produces striking statistics on the root causes of this epidemic. Over 80 percent of the world's wealth is held in the industrialized nations (which have about 23 percent of the people), and they have some 94 percent of the scientists and technologists. With all those handicaps the poor are deeply in debt to the rich, and suffering greatly in their attempts to service that debt. In 1987, $38 billion was paid, in 1988 $45 billion—a flow that former Chancellor of West Germany Willy Brandt called "a blood transfusion from the sick to the healthy."[45]

The poverty epidemic results in reduced health, and thus reduced life expectancy, for most people in poor nations (as well as many poor people in rich nations). This epidemic shows up clearly even in aggregated statistics. The fifth of the world's people in rich nations live an average of seventy-three years; the four fifths in the poor nations live an average of sixty. These differences do not represent differences in the remaining life expectancy of twenty-year-olds; they reflect very high infant and child mortalities among the poor. Of each 1,000 babies born to the rich, only about 15 die before they reach the age of one; in the poor countries an average of 84 die.

The numbers are even more dramatic if the very poor are examined separately. In Pakistan, life expectancy is fifty-four years and infant mortality 120 per 1,000. In Mali, life expectancy is forty-three years, and infant mortality 175 per 1,000 (or almost one in every five babies). Contrast these statistics with those of Japan, where a child at birth today can expect to survive seventy-eight years, and infant mortality is less than 5 per 1,000.

This poverty epidemic has many population-related causes, especially malnutrition, contaminated water supplies, lack of adequate medical care, and lack of education. These conditions often lead poor women to use "formula" instead of breast-feeding, a choice that, under crowded conditions with poor sanitation, seriously threatens the health of their infants. Not only are the babies exposed to a multitude of germs in the water used to mix the formula, they are denied the immunizational and other benefits of mother's milk. And some poor mothers dilute the formula to save money, starving their infants as a result.

Because of the scale of the problem—it involves at least a billion people—it would not be unfair to call poverty the greatest public-health problem today. And there is no question that rapid population growth among the poorest people is a major factor in keeping them impoverished. Instead of being able to put aside surplus physical and financial resources for use in raising the average individual's standard of living, less-developed nations must keep plowing much of their capital back into providing subsistence for ever-growing numbers of people. It is a sad treadmill: the more people there are in those nations, the more difficult it is for them to escape from poverty.

It is sometimes said, of course, that rather than population growth being a contributing cause of poverty, poverty is the cause of population growth.[46] There is some truth in this thesis. Poor people often are malnourished and suffer higher infant and child mortality rates than the well-off. Since they also lack social security and therefore need surviving sons to care for them in their old age, they have larger families. But the problem is partly circular, since high fertility also contributes to those high death rates.[47]

But the argument is almost moot. First of all, prosperity has not brought birthrates down to the necessary level even in rich nations such as the United States, and family sizes remain much too high even in Costa Rica, that most exemplary of developing nations (which has little severe poverty and an infant mortality rate comparable to eastern-European countries). Second, bringing the poor up to the levels of affluence of today's rich nations will produce unsupportable stresses on Earth's ecosystems unless the rich decide to engage in a massive redistribution of wealth. Third, there is no sign that the rich would seriously consider such a step. Fourth, whatever "charitable" steps are taken to help the poor will be more beneficial if the numbers of poor are smaller. And, fifth, population growth itself is a major barrier in preventing the poor from helping themselves. In short, the "does population growth cause poverty or vice versa" argument is counterproductive if the goal is to provide everyone with a decent life. If that is the goal, then all of us should be working very hard to end both poverty and population growth, not wasting our efforts trying to determine which causes which.

► **HOW DENSE CAN WE BE?** ◄

It has long been realized that high densities in human populations made them—all else being equal—subject to high rates of disease.[48] Indeed, it was only about a century ago that cities stopped being, in McNeill's term, "population sumps."[49] Until then, most cities had such high death rates from diseases that they could not maintain themselves without a constant flow of immigrants from relatively healthier rural areas. But today cities tend to be centers of the best medical care, even in poor nations, and disease is now a relatively minor factor in urban death rates. This does not mean, however, that cities are free of population-related problems—problems that should properly be considered part of "public health."

In rapidly growing, less-developed nations, migration to cities is going on at unprecedented rates. In 1920, about 100 million people lived in Third World cities; by 1980, ten times as many, about a billion, did so. Furthermore, if current trends continue, by the turn of the century there will be over 1.9 billion urban dwellers in poor nations, or about as many people as occupied the entire planet during World War I. In 1950, only three cities, New York, London, and Shanghai, were inhabited by over 10 million people. In 2000, there are projected to be twenty cities of more than 10 million, seventeen of them in developing nations. Overall, about half of humanity will be living in cities before 2010—more than 3 billion people.[50] While developed countries have been overwhelmingly urbanized for many decades, the change is dramatic for developing countries, which until the last decade or two have been mainly agrarian. Now, clearly, the promise of the city, no matter how unlikely to be fulfilled, is more attractive than the poverty of the countryside.

But the cities in poor countries are growing at staggering

rates. The largest, Mexico City, held some 17 million souls in 1985 and, barring disaster, will have over 25 million (about equal to the present populations of Ireland, Denmark, Norway, Sweden, and Finland combined) by 2000. São Paulo will be around 21 million;[51] and Calcutta and Greater Bombay will each have over 15 million and Delhi over 13 million.

The prospects for these gigantic agglomerations are not bright. They have grown so fast that they have far outstripped their ability to care for their inhabitants. Lack of sewage systems, inadequate water supplies laced with pathogens, air pollution, and gigantic garbage dumps (often occupied and "mined" by the poorest of the poor) plague these overgrown metropolises. Although their water supplies are generally superior to those of rural areas, a very optimistic estimate is that at least a quarter of the people living in Third World cities lack safe drinking water—over 250 million people, comparable to the entire population of the United States.[52]

Half of the population of Delhi are now slum dwellers, and according to the Delhi Planning Authority that fraction will be more like 85 percent at the end of the century.[53] In the summer of 1988, millions in Delhi went without water during the drought; when the rains finally arrived, wells were polluted by the human feces that are everywhere (because of the inadequate sewage system), and a cholera epidemic broke out among the poor. In Bombay, shantytowns make up half the housing, and social workers estimate that 200,000 to 500,000 people sleep in the streets.[54]

Mexico City has so many people without sanitary facilities that a "fecal snow" often falls on the city as winds pick up dried excrement. Its air pollution is rated the worst on the planet. São Paulo, Brazil, in the state of the same name, has been gathering problems in spite of its relative wealth. São Paulo State once was described as a "rich country plunked down in the middle of an India," but now "India" is creeping in. In the narrow verges of huge freeways, naked children now play among the cardboard shacks of *favelas* (shantytowns) within inches of eight lanes of roaring traffic. About a million people now live in the *favelas* (which first appeared in the mid-1970s), and about 4 million more in hideous slums.[55]

Many attempts are being made to resolve urban problems in poor nations, including the encouragement of industry to locate in secondary cities to divert some of the people fleeing from the countryside and reduce pressure on the megacities. Most migrants are peasants displaced by industrialized agriculture. Ironically, that industrialization is one of the strategies that have helped keep food production up with population growth globally. But, as long as population growth continues at anything like current rates, trying to solve those urban problems is like trying to bail out the ocean with a thimble.

Even rich nations are having trouble maintaining the livability of their giant cities. In New York City, the waiting time for a vacancy in public housing is eighteen years, and thousands of people are homeless. In most American cities, the need for shelters has doubled or tripled since Ronald Reagan moved into the White House.[56] In Britain, which is sliding downhill compared to the rest of the European Economic Community, over $40 billion is needed to rebuild crumbling sewer systems, $8 billion to repair gas mains, and many billions more to restore disintegrating government housing.

There are many other problems that appear at least partially traceable to the cramming of more and more people into cities. Recently, an "urban stress test" was applied to all 192 U.S. cities with populations of over 100,000 people.[57] The test scored each city on a scale of one (a model city) to five (highly stressed) on eleven criteria: population change, crowding, education, violent crime, community economics, individual economics, births to women under age twenty, air quality, hazardous wastes, water quality, and sewage treatment.[58]

The results of the survey showed a strong relationship with population. Cities with fewer than 100,000 people had an average score of 2.5; those over one million, 3.8; with those in between generally having intermediate scores. Cedar Rapids, Iowa (population 109,000), Madison, Wisconsin (176,000), and Ann Arbor, Michigan (108,000) had the best scores with 1.6, 1.7, and 1.8 respectively; Gary, Indiana (137,000), Baltimore, Maryland (753,000), and Chicago, Illinois (3 million) had the worst with 4.2, 4.1, and 4.1. The twenty-two cities with the best scores (1.6 to 2.3) averaged 116,000 people, with about

3700 per square mile. The twenty worst (scoring 3.8 to 4.2) averaged 1,154,000, with 8200 per square mile. Only two cities with populations over half a million scored below 3.0: Columbus, Ohio (2.6), and San Francisco (2.8).

The results, when the four environmental measures alone were considered, were similar. The nineteen cities with the best scores had an average population size of about 120,000; the thirteen worst averaged about 786,000. The message seems clear: measured either by social and environmental indicators together or by environmental indicators alone, more people mean more problems in American cities. Of course, one could argue that "correlation is not causation." The other possible explanation of the association of large cities with signs of stress —that crime, poverty, lack of education, and environmental deterioration cause cities to get larger—is more complex and we think less likely.[59]

These results, naturally, came as no particular surprise. Large American cities fill the evening news with their problems: Washington, D.C., as the "murder capital of the U.S.A.," New York City and Seattle having to ship their garbage out of state (or even overseas), Miami's drug wars, San Francisco's high rate of infection with AIDS, Los Angeles's choking smog. Almost two decades ago, the report of the United States Commission on Population Growth and the American Future stated: "Population growth in the United States has multiplied and intensified many of our domestic problems and made their solution more difficult." The commission explicitly included the problems of the cities, including those of law enforcement.[60]

Of course, some of these problems are more clearly tied to population size and density than others. The connection with smog and demand for water is obvious. That with sewage treatment is less direct: proper treatment costs money, and larger cities tend to be poorer per capita (the rich have moved to the suburbs).

While the incidence of violent crime is higher in large cities than in small ones, experimental studies of people under crowded and uncrowded conditions suggest that high density *per se* is not the cause.[61] Crowding merely seems to intensify each individual's reaction to a given situation, whether that reaction is helpful or harmful. Crime rates have long been thought to be tied to rates of city growth, which in turn often are connected with size and density.[62] High crime rates in rapidly growing cities may result from the associated lack of community feeling and coherence. And there doubtless is an "anonymity factor": in larger cities, the chance of being recognized while committing a crime is smaller. But doubtless also crime rates are tied in complex ways to employment rates, education, racial prejudice, teenage pregnancy, and other factors that themselves have connections to population size, density, and age composition. Much more research is needed to sort out what causes what in American cities, and final answers may elude us permanently. That American cities generally have much higher crime rates than those of similar size in Europe indicates that numbers *per se* must be a minor factor when compared with social and cultural factors.

We must emphasize again that in the area of public health the population connection is often relatively weak. People can live at very high densities, as in Tokyo, and still largely avoid many of the problems that are often associated with crowding. It would be a mistake to expect that simply reducing population densities would eradicate the problems considered in this chapter. It would surely ameliorate many of them, though, and in so doing add to the quality of our lives. But ending population growth and starting a slow decline is not a panacea; it would primarily provide humanity with the opportunity of solving its other problems.

8

▲

Population, Growthism, and National Security

▼

For a long time, population growth and economic growth were uniformly considered good. More people in the tribe, city, state, or nation meant more security. More people allowed the divisions of labor and economies of scale by which modern economies advance. Growth in those economies has raised the standard of living of a significant minority of human beings to heights unimagined by anyone before this century.

The tandem growth of populations and standards of living in the West over the last few centuries has led people to believe that population growth would always be an essential stimulant to economic growth. The idea traces back at least to Henry George, who at the end of the last century wrote:

. . . a greater number of people can collectively be better provided for than a smaller . . . the new mouths which an increasing population calls into existence require no more food than the old ones, while the hands they bring with them can in the natural order of things produce more . . . I assert that in a

state of equality the natural increase of population would con-
stantly tend to make every individual richer instead of poorer.[1]

At the extreme, this idea resulted in an announcement by economist Colin Clark in 1969 that India would within a decade be the most powerful country in the world because of its growing population![2]

The vast majority of economists no longer believe that population growth inevitably leads to prosperity, although many still think it is necessary. As Kenneth Boulding commented, "Anyone who believes exponential growth can go on forever in a finite world is either a madman or an economist."[3] Let's take a look at some of the arguments for perpetual growth raised by madmen and economists.

One major "economic" argument that is made for keeping the American population growing is that if we don't our population will grow older, and that will cause major economic and social problems.[4] The first part of the statement is undeniable. Whenever a growing population reduces its birthrate and gradually stops expanding, the age composition of that population shifts toward the older age classes. In other words, there will be proportionately fewer young people and more old people. This is simple arithmetic; there is nothing whatever that can be done about it. We are told that this disastrous change should be avoided at all costs. It will lessen innovation, send baby-food manufacturers to the poorhouse, and, above all, burden working people with an army of unproductive oldsters to take care of—letting ourselves in for a perpetual "Medicare crisis."

None of these arguments is particularly cogent. First of all, unless birthrates drop precipitously, there will be plenty of time for various parts of the social and industrial system to adjust to the changing age composition. Second, although there will be proportionately more old people who need care, there also will be proportionately fewer children. Higher costs in Social Security will be largely balanced by reduced costs for the care and especially the education of children. The ratio of productive to dependent people in the population will not change much.[5]

Furthermore, while it is unlikely that in the future children will need less care, it *is* *likely* that in the future old people will need less care. The health of the American population as a whole is improving, and there is a growing recognition that there is no reason whatsoever to remove people arbitrarily from the economic system at the age of sixty-five. People who remain active live longer and remain healthier and don't need to be supported by younger people. (This does not mean that we'll be able to avoid some difficult social choices, as medical science continues creating ever more expensive life-prolonging treatments.)

As former Deputy Assistant Secretary of State for Environment and Population Lindsey Grant has pointed out, those worrying about too few workers to support too many old people "may be worrying about precisely the wrong problem. Now and in the foreseeable future, the problem seems to be, not a shortage of labor, but rather a redundancy of labor of the wrong types and in the wrong places."[6]

Recently capital has been moving around the world in search of the cheapest available labor, and population growth has ensured that there is plenty of that. The huge size and resource consumption of the world population today also necessitate increasing trade between nations and regions. The day of the resource-self-sufficient nation is over. But one result of the increasing economic interdependency of nations is a rising mobility of capital. The easy transfer of capital between nations could, under a policy of maximally free trade, lead to the pauperization of America, since the wealth of our nation has been partly based on the ability of workers to make a decent wage.[7] As economist Herman Daly noted, "The equilibrium wage under free trade will be the third world level."[8]

A bonus of the U.S. population's changing age structure is that people in the age class that provides us with most of our criminals, 16–30, will be proportionately fewer in our population. Considering the enormous social and economic costs of criminal activities and of maintaining the courts and the penal system, those savings alone might more than offset any additional expenses of taking care of older people.

The innovation issue is more difficult to deal with. In some academic disciplines, such as mathematics, the most innovative steps are made by young people. In science as a whole, innovation may be more concentrated in the middle years, when a balance between new thinking and experience is of value. But whatever the loss in innovation, if any, in a somewhat older population, it may be more than made up for by an increase in experience. There are, of course, additional ways to assure that levels of innovation do not drop. One is to start taking advantage of the potential for innovation in young minds when they are found in women, members of minority groups, or the desperately poor.[9] We should be doing that regardless of society's demographic status. Others include changing both the educational system and society as a whole in ways that encourage innovation. There is no evidence that brute numbers of young minds are the wellsprings of innovation. Otherwise, there would have been no Golden Age for Athens, and China and India would be the world leaders in innovation.

The absurdity of the "don't stop growing because we'll grow old" view is that soon or later America (like every other nation) *must* stop growing. So the "problems" of an older population will have to be faced sooner or later. By pushing that moment off to "later," we are simply condemning our children or grandchildren to dealing with problems of age composition in a world that is much more overcrowded and much more resource-depleted and has a much more malign environment. By not working to stop growth now, we may be mortgaging any chance at all for the next few generations to lead decent lives.

With these exceptions, direct connections between population growth and economic issues are rarely heard. But policy-makers cling to the dogma that economic growth itself is essential to the health of society, and that such growth can cure population problems—on one hand, by providing materially for an indefinitely large population, and, on the other, by leading to a halt in population growth via a demographic transition, a topic to which we will return.

►   **ECONOMIC BLINDERS**   ◄

It has long been clear to ecologists that the extreme growth orientation of mainstream economics is a major reason that politicians, businessmen, and others advised by economists, as well as the public at large, fail to recognize the increasing seriousness of the population crisis in particular, and the deepening predicament of *Homo sapiens* in general. *Most people do not recognize that, at least in rich nations, economic growth is the disease, not the cure.* They are infected with a blind faith in the efficacy of growth to solve all problems and lead them to the promised land; they have put their faith in what may be terminal growthism. They do not recognize that "perpetual growth is the creed of the cancer cell,"[10] that growth must cease at maturity.

Some farsighted economists have attempted to swim against the tide of dogma in this area; Herman Daly is the outstanding contemporary example.[11] But Daly's cogent analyses have been largely ignored by the economic establishment, although they are attracting the attention of some bright young economists.[12] One group at World Resources Institute has pioneered in developing a new method for measuring a nation's economic performance that includes accounting for the depletion of natural resources such as wildlife, forests, fisheries, groundwater, and soils, as well as minerals, in national-income reports.[13] This sort of accounting, if widely adopted, would provide a far more accurate picture of economic progress and the outlook for all nations. Much of what today is considered "production" causes ecological destruction, which never appears in conventional national balance sheets. The result is a false impression of wealth.

These ideas are still foreign to most economists, however. The failure of conventional economics to contribute to a resolution of the human predicament is understandable from a cursory examination of what economists are taught. All one need do is look at the circular-flow diagram that "explains" the generation of gross national product in any standard economics text. There are no inputs into the circular flow; it is simply a diagram of a perpetual-motion machine, an impossibility except in the minds of economists. Economics texts, of course, give no coverage at all to what is now the central question of economics: How big can the economic system be before it irretrievably damages the ecological systems that support it?[14]

The majority of economists have never been taught that ecosystems provide humanity with an absolutely indispensable array of services, services that are "free," but would, of course, be infinitely costly to replace. They are ignorant of the role that natural ecosystems play in regulating trace gases in the atmosphere, providing fresh water, generating soils, and preventing floods and droughts.

Since they are unaware of the stress that natural systems are now under, most economists believe that the scale of economic activity can be increased indefinitely (or at least so far into the future that limits to growth need be of no concern today). Many share with British economist Wilfred Beckerman the notions that economic growth has gone on "since the time of Pericles" and that there is "no reason to suppose that it cannot continue for another 2500 years."[15]

Both ideas are straightforward nonsense, as a few simple calculations by social scientist Jack Parsons showed.[16] He calculated what the income of the average English household would have been at the time of Pericles (490–424 B.C.) *if* growth had gone on since that time at the rate of one percent a year.[17] Note that that rate would be considered disastrously low by today's typical economist. But even at that conservative figure, the English family (if there had been "English families" in those days!) at the beginning would have been poor indeed. It would have had the buying power for an entire year, in 1970 money, of less than a millionth of a penny.

In fact, the state of the economy over most of the sweep of human history was, by the standards of economists today, stagnation.[18] As one might expect from this, Beckerman's prediction about the future turns out, if anything, to be sillier than his misrepresentation of the past. Parsons applied the same conservative one percent annual growth rate to the English economy into the future from 1970. At one percent per year, the per-capita gross national product (GNP)[19] would double about once in a lifetime (seventy years). At that rate, it would take only about fifteen hundred years for the *hourly* wage in Britain to hit a million dollars (that's not inflation, that's in 1970 dollars). In A.D. 4470, or 2500 years in the future from 1970, an English child's weekly allowance (about one half of one percent of the weekly per-capita GNP) would have the purchasing power of about ten billion 1970 dollars.

The absurdity of the idea of perpetual economic growth is

highlighted by Parsons' notion of the "millionaire barrier."
After less than seven hundred years of one percent growth,
the average person in England (or the United States) would
have an income of over a million 1970 dollars annually. Who
then would do the work to produce what all the millionaires
would consume, and who would clean up after them? Presumably, economists would expect the populations of the poor nations to avoid growth and dedicate themselves to the task of
supporting and serving the idle rich nations whose economies
would miraculously keep growing!

One important relationship today between economic
growthism and population growth is that the growthism keeps
economists from becoming influential advocates of population
control. As long as economists and those who listen to them
believe there are no limits to growth, the pressing need for
population control will not be obvious to them. Their failure to
recognize those limits is partly rooted in two related axioms of
mainstream economics: that there is an infinite number of resources, and that a satisfactory substitute can be found for
every resource.

▶   **DESTROYING THE WORLD FOR PROFIT**   ◀

Biologists unfamiliar with economic theory are often shocked
when they discover an industry that appears to be deliberately
destroying its resource base. The problem first came to our
attention when it became clear that the whaling industry was
knowingly harvesting whales at a rate that would lead to their
extinction. Until then, it had not dawned on us that industries
dealing with biological resources were not necessarily concerned with achieving long-term maximum sustainable yields
from them, but were concerned primarily with maximizing the
current return on their capital. If exterminating the resource
(pumping aquifers dry, wiping out the whales, clear-cutting
tropical rain forests, exhausting the soils on factory farms)
brought the maximum return, then the resource would be destroyed.

This behavior is based in part on the first axiom of mainstream economics:[20] since an infinite array of resources is be-

lieved to exist, once one resource has been utterly destroyed there will always be another that can profitably be exploited to extinction, then another, and another, and another.[21] People a decade hence will be dealing with an entirely new set of resources!

These attitudes have led to many unwise decisions for the long term, such as ignoring the need for worldwide conservation of topsoil or petroleum, rapidly depleting aquifers, and building large dams and then deforesting the watersheds above them.

But even if the first axiom were true, and there were an infinity of resources to plunder, that would not necessarily solve our problems. There *could* (in an unreal world) be an infinity of resources, but each having dramatically different properties. Then, even though the opportunities to profit from their exhaustion might be infinite, some resources would be irreplaceable in terms of the function they can serve in the human economy (fresh water is a good example). Depletion of one key resource in the spectrum therefore could limit the scale of the human enterprise.

Since such a proposition would cast doubt on the "grow forever" central dogma, economists have resorted to assuming the problem away through the second "infinite substitutability" axiom. They justify it by a total misinterpretation of the fundamental physical, chemical, and biological rules that govern the real world.

▶   **THE LIMITS TO SUBSTITUTION**   ◄

Economists Harold Barnett and Chandler Morse most clearly expressed the second axiom:

Advances in fundamental science have made it possible to take advantage of the uniformity of energy/matter—a uniformity that makes it feasible without preassignable limit, to escape the quantitative constraints imposed by the character of the earth's crust. . . . Nature imposes particular scarcities, not an inescapable general scarcity. Man is therefore able, and free, to choose among an indefinitely large number of alternatives.

There is no reason to believe that these alternatives will eventually reduce to one that entails increasing cost—that it must sometime prove impossible to escape diminishing quantitative returns. Science, by making the resource base more homogeneous, erases the restrictions once thought to reside in the lack of homogeneity. In a neo-Ricardian world, it seems, the particular resources with which one starts increasingly become a matter of indifference.[22]

Of course, Barnett and Morse had the laws of physics exactly backwards—since it is the *lack* of homogeneity that makes "resources" possible. If Earth were homogenized, there would be no coal, petroleum, iron ore, etc., just a uniform mixture of the atoms that now constitute the planet.[23] Energy and matter are not "uniform" just because, in some circumstances, matter can be converted into energy (and in theory the reverse can take place), any more than a fine goblet and a pile of broken glass are "uniform."

But even ignorance of physics is not sufficient excuse for the faith of economists in infinite substitutability. All that should be needed to destroy that faith is casual observation of the practical difficulties commonly encountered in making substitutions. Nuclear power has not exactly been a roaring success as a substitute for fossil fuels; aluminum wire is, in many applications, a very inferior substitute for copper wire. Some substitutions, such as plastics for other structural materials, petroleum for coal, and small computers for gigantic machines and even entire libraries, appear to be very successful. Indeed, the success of the computer industry in sharply reducing the materials and energy required in processing information is viewed by some as the ultimate proof that humanity can do anything it sets its collective mind to and improve its environment in the process.[24]

Unfortunately, there is plenty of evidence that the real opportunities for adequate substitution are limited, and that even quite "successful" substitutions in nonliving resources can have their drawbacks. As a single example, plastic cannot now substitute for metals or other materials in many applications, but disposal of plastics (and the toxic wastes generated in their manufacture) creates extremely serious environmental problems. In the long run, the plastics industry will suffer from the depletion of (and competition for) petroleum and other fossil fuels from which plastics are made, or of wood, from which they can be made. Plastics are a prime example of a substitution that has pushed the T factor in the $I = PAT$ equation in precisely the wrong direction.

Economists are even less aware, by the way, that there are more severe problems in making substitutions among living resources than among nonliving ones. Dams are not usually a satisfactory substitute for the flood-control services of forest ecosystems when the latter are destroyed, and insecticides are poor substitutes for the pest-control services of natural predators when the predators are killed off.[25] And, of course, there are no substitutes for clean air, topsoil, or fresh water.

There are several conclusions to be drawn from the problem of "meta-resource depletion"[26]—that is, the reduction of the total number of Earth's exploitable resources through the extermination of populations and species, the destruction of forests, the poisoning and depletion of aquifers, the erosion of soils, the using up of high-grade ores, and so on. As that capital is used up in an attempt to support continual increases in population and per-capita affluence, industrial civilization will gradually grind to a halt. Indeed, economic growth, as measured by change in real gross national product, has been slowing down in industrialized nations. Japan, which was growing at an average annual rate of 9.4 percent in 1965–73, dropped to 4.1 in 1973–86. In the same period, economic growth in the United States dropped from 3.1 to 2.6, and average growth rates in most European nations, Canada, South Africa, and Australia were cut about in half.[27] That, of course, is as it should be. Any more stuff in the world certainly should not go to the likes of us![28]

►   **EDUCATION FOR ECONOMISTS AND OTHERS**   ◄

In our opinion, whether humanity will be able to move toward a population size and an economic system sustainable largely on income will depend in no small degree on economists. The basic biological and physical science of the human dilemma is well enough understood to permit sound recommendations for immediate action.[29] But almost no work has been done on ways to make the needed conversions in economic systems so that scientific recommendations can be implemented with a minimum of disruption.

The discipline of economics will be a central one as humanity struggles to maintain Earth's habitability. And that is appropriate, for it was an economist, Thomas Malthus, who first recognized the key role played in human affairs by population growth. The seeds of change are there. A few economists have united with biologists to form the International Society of Ecological Economics and publish the journal *Ecological Economics*.[30] And it is already recognized by many economists that graduate education in the discipline focuses too little on important questions of policy and too much on learning to manipulate esoteric mathematical theory based on preposterous assumptions.[31]

Somehow the new interdiscipline of ecological economics seems a natural union, as the common origin of the words "ecology" and "economics" (referring to nature's housekeeping and society's housekeeping) implies. Today it consists of a group of farsighted economists (considered a fringe group by the rest of the discipline) and increasing numbers of ecologists who are becoming aware of the central role economics must play in solving the human predicament. If we are to escape our current predicament, it should become a major area of specialized education, and replace neoclassical economics as the central focus of economics departments.[32]

Those being trained in ecological economics would first be given the baseline understanding that society's first priority must be to keep nature's house in order. They would learn that the key to doing this is to reduce the number of people to a quantity that can be properly sheltered without destroying the house. Considerable instruction on the basics of how the physical-biological world works must be included in the training of all economists. Otherwise they will continue to whisper the wrong messages into the ears of politicians and businessmen. The latter, in turn, will continue to see growth of the global economy as the cure rather than the disease, and will remain unconcerned about the population explosion.

Of course, resistance to those fallacious messages could be much enhanced if material on the human predicament were woven into basic teaching in elementary and high school,[33] and if every college student in the nation were required to take at least one course that gave a basic overview of the "state of the planet." At Stanford University, there has been considerable uproar over the content of a required "Western Civilization" course. But most students (and most faculty) remain ignorant of the size and growth patterns of the human population, what is involved in producing food, how ecosystems provide essential services to society, the comparative deployment of U.S. and Soviet nuclear forces, how people's perceptual systems give them a biased and inadequate view of the modern world, the basic theory of evolution, and the laws of thermodynamics. All these are more important to the average citizen than what Plato or Richard Wright wrote or who was gathered at the Congress of Vienna (not that well-educated people shouldn't know those things also!). The complacency with which our education system at all levels accepts the production of citizens hopelessly unequipped to understand the population explosion and many other aspects of the modern world is a national disgrace.

Can economists unite with ecologists, reform their discipline, and help pull humanity through the crisis decades ahead? We hope so. You will know there is a chance when the President's Council of Economic Advisors recommends that it be subsumed in a new "Council of Demographic, Ecological, and Economic Advisors," when a central task of economics is seen to be devising an economic system with the proper scale and attributes to permit it to function permanently within environmental constraints, when economic growth is always discussed in a context of counterbalancing shrinkage and redistribution, and when GNP is replaced by some measure that takes into account resource depletion and ecosystem deterioration as minuses. When all economists realize that perpetual growth is both impossible and undesirable, economics as a profession will have become a force for survival rather than for destruction, as it all too often is now.

►   **DO WE NEED CANNON FODDER?**   ◄

Arguments in favor of population growth that are unconnected to issues of economic growth are sometimes made. One of the most imbecilic is that the safety of the nation demands large numbers of people to keep up military strength.[34] The basic idea appears to be that the more cannon fodder a nation has, the more security it has. By those standards, of course, neither China nor India has a worry in the world militarily. They should be the superpowers, and poor Israel with only 3 million people should be terrified by the threat posed by some 90 million enemies in nearby nations. By these lights, Russia (population then 170 million) should have handily defeated Germany (population 65 million) in the First World War,[35] and Japan (population 70 million) would never have had any success in taking on China (population 500 million) and then simultaneously the United States (population 140 million) in the Second World War.[36]

In fact, the notion that population size by itself provides military power is utter nonsense. In modern times victory has rarely gone to the possessor of the larger battalions for that reason alone. Leadership, morale, technological capabilities, and, in recent history, industrial strength above all have determined the eventual winners. Within wide bounds, population size has been irrelevant. In two world wars, a vastly outnumbered Germany very nearly defeated its enemies on the basis of industrial prowess, superior military organization and tactics, internal lines of communication, and the best infantry in the world. Israel has kept its larger neighbors at bay with a better-educated population, better-trained troops, a superior grasp of technology, and the benefit of drawing upon the industrial and technological resources of the United States. Israel's enemies have had to make do largely with the inferior and limited industrial/technological support of the Soviet Union. Similarly, the Vietnamese beat first the French and then the Americans even though they were outnumbered in the latter instance by more than four to one.[37]

► **ENVIRONMENTAL THREATS TO NATIONAL** ◄
SECURITY

Most of the world's other rich nations realize that there is now an unparalleled nonmilitary threat to their security. It has been created by rapid depletion of Earth's nonrenewable resources, deterioration of the global environment, and the widening of the economic gap between rich nations of the industrialized North and poor nations of the South—all contributed to mightily by exploding human populations. That threat not only portends a continual deterioration of living standards virtually everywhere in time of peace, but also contributes to conflict between nations [38] and thus increases the chances of nuclear war.

An end to civilization caused by overpopulation and environmental collapse would amount to a gigantic "tragedy of the commons"—to use the phrase made famous by Garrett Hardin.[39] Individuals (or nations) acting independently for their short-term gain create situations that, in the long term, destroy common resources ("the commons").[40] As Hardin wrote, "Ruin is the destination toward which all men rush, each pursuing his own best interest in a society that believes in the freedom of the commons. Freedom in a commons brings ruin to all." His reference is to overgrazing of a village's common pasture; civilization's ruin will stem from treatment of the global ecosystem as a "commons" that can be exploited by every nation without thought for their common security.

Perhaps no feature of Earth is more a commons than the atmosphere. The atmosphere connects all nations and people, past and present, and it interacts intimately with oceans and land, including plants, animals, microorganisms, and soils, as a major component of ecosystems. Disruption of atmospheric ecosystem services can have grave international repercussions. For instance, the climate of the Soviet Union's wheat belt might deteriorate as a result of greenhouse warming. The United States might suffer similar agricultural problems and have no grain to sell abroad. If the Soviets were in need of imported grain, tension between the two nations could rise, and those tensions might be aggravated by agricultural problems in other regions, which could no longer obtain food imports. We have become so interdependent that each nation's security increasingly depends on the security of others.

Altered rainfall patterns, which are virtually certain to accompany a global atmospheric warming, could also exacerbate tensions over increasingly scarce water supplies in places as disparate as the Middle East and along the U.S.–Mexico border. Egypt, whose population is projected to increase from 55 million in 1989 to 71 million in 2000 and 103 million in 2020, is already tottering on the brink of chaos. A significant reduction in the Nile's flow would push it over the edge. If rainfall became sparser in the Middle East or demand for water increased significantly, an explosive situation would become much worse. The waters of the Jordan, Yarmuk, and Litani rivers have been sources of tension for years, and the 1967 Arab–Israeli war was fought in part over them. It is sobering to consider that Israel, which consumes five times as much water per capita as its neighbors, may have a serious water shortage in the 1990s, even without climate change.[41] The hard-nosed Israeli stand on the West Bank and Gaza since 1988 may be just a foretaste of what is to come, since Israel is now using about 95 percent of its renewable water supplies.[42]

International tensions also could be heightened by reduced river flows between Pakistan and India (over the Indus) and India and Bangladesh (the Ganges). Disputes over water have occurred in those regions and in the basins of the Tigris/Euphrates, Amur, Mekong, and Nile rivers, and the Río de la Plata. The waters of 120 of the world's 200 major river systems are shared by two or more countries.[43] With the entire planet overpopulated and serious regional water shortages already widespread, the potential for drought-induced conflict is enormous.

These are not distant problems for Americans. A significant decline in the dependable supply of water available from the Colorado River could lead to further trouble between Mexico and the United States. Such a conflict could be greatly intensified by more Mexicans seeking to enter the United States in order to make a living.[44] Agricultural conditions in many regions are deteriorating as productivity declines because of soil erosion, failing irrigation systems, desertification, or changes in climate. The inevitable result is an increase in the worldwide flow of ecological refugees.

Transnational air-pollution problems also will be affected by global warming, but in ways that are virtually impossible to predict. Forest systems, already stressed by air pollution and acid precipitation, are not likely to respond well to abrupt changes in temperature and rainfall regimes. Indeed, there is evidence that some forests in the northeastern United States are already being degraded by the combined stresses of pollutants and climatic change.[45]

In the longer term, changes in ocean temperatures, rising sea levels, and changed freshwater flows could affect the dynamics of oceanic fish populations and, temporarily at least, depress productivity. World fishery harvests have been barely keeping up with population growth for the last two decades, and are now thought to be approaching, if not beyond, maximum sustainable yields. Per-capita declines seem to be in store in the near future (drops over short periods have already occurred), even without changes in oceanic environments that are (in terms of evolutionary time) very rapid. Shots have already been fired over fishing rights; that may be only a hint of things to come unless cooperative and sustainable management of the fisheries commons can be achieved.

Other large-scale problems with the atmospheric commons facing humanity include increased ultraviolet-B radiation as a consequence of stratospheric ozone depletion, acid deposition, and other forms of air pollution. But serious though these are, climate change, with its clear population connection, has the greatest potential for contributing to international conflict and for diminishing the economic security of all nations.

9

▲

The Bang, the Whimper, and the Alternative

▼

This is the way the world ends
Not with a bang but a whimper.

T. S. ELIOT, *The Hollow Men*

By now it should be clear to you that humanity is quickly breeding itself into a corner. We do not want to dwell on the possible endings for civilization, since they are implicit in much of what has gone before. But it seems appropriate to give a brief summary of the possible ends of the road we're now on, and of the new route humanity might take, before turning to the question of solutions.

► **THE BANG** ◄

The population explosion contributes to international tensions and therefore makes a nuclear holocaust more likely. Most people in our society can visualize the horrors of a large-scale nuclear war followed by a nuclear winter.[1] We call that possible end to our civilization "the Bang." Hundreds of millions of people would be killed outright, and billions more would follow from the disruption of agricultural systems and other indirect effects largely caused by the disruption of ecosystem services. It would be the ultimate "death-rate solution" to the population problem—a stunning contrast to the humane solution of lowering the global birthrate to slightly below the death rate for a few centuries.

As this is written (mid-1989), it fortunately seems that the chances of the Bang have lessened. New-minded leadership in the Soviet Union is for the moment in the ascendancy. President Mikhail Gorbachev, along with a few other world leaders, seems to be aware that environmental security is at least as important as military strength in providing security to nations, and appears to be doing everything possible to damp down the arms race between the United States and the Soviet Union. An apparently more pragmatic government also is in place in the United States, although it is still too soon to tell whether the superpowers are on the road toward massive nuclear-arms reduction and true reconciliation. What is certain is that the structure of military forces around the world still provides plenty of chances for local conflicts to escalate into Armageddon even in the face of growing East–West rapprochement.

There remains the problem that, as the world gets further and further out of control, crazies on both the left and the right may exert increasingly xenophobic pressures on national governments. The rise of fundamentalism in both East and West is a completely understandable but not at all encouraging sample of what the future may hold in terms of conflict. Those struggling to achieve a permanently peaceful world still have much work to do, especially as growing and already overpopulated nations struggle to divide up dwindling resources in a deteriorating global environment.

▶   **THE WHIMPER**   ◀

But for now, after forty years of worrying about it, the Bang seems to be getting less likely. The same can't be said about "the Whimper." The Whimper is simply the way that civilization will end if current population/resource/environment trends continue. Such a continuation could bring us essentially to the same sort of world as would be left after a nuclear war and a nuclear winter—just more slowly, on a time scale of years rather than weeks.

The exact sequence of events in the Whimper is impossible to predict. If population growth continues on its current path, both ecosystems and social systems will be subjected to greater and greater stresses of many kinds. It seems likely that hunger, already affecting a billion or so people more or less chronically, will become acute in more places. That, in turn, will make the epidemiological environment ever more precarious and increase both intranational and international sociopolitical tensions. People in rich nations may be able to ignore starvation in the poorest nations for a while, but increasing hunger and disaffection among the poor within rich nations will be more difficult for elites to overlook.

Unless emissions of greenhouse gases, of chlorofluorocarbons and nitrogen oxides and other ozone-depleting gases, and the precursors of acid precipitation are strongly curtailed, the breakdown of both natural and agricultural ecosystems will accelerate. Agricultural systems, under current practices, will continue to deteriorate anyway from massive erosion, faulty irrigation, and depletion of groundwater supplies.

Most likely, some crucial system that we don't understand in detail, such as the global climate system, holds the key to the overall downhill slide. If, by some miracle, the climatic system returned to the relatively stable, favorable conditions of 1930–70, it might take three decades or more for the food-production system to come apart unless its repair became a top priority of all humanity. If, on the other hand, recent climatic events were not part of "normal variability," but rather were caused by atmospheric warming, we will be plagued by very difficult problems in this decade or the next.

If a large-scale nuclear war (followed by a nuclear winter) can be avoided, and if societies continue to behave much as they do now, we can expect an uneven but relatively continuous deterioration of the human condition over the next four to six decades. The pace of the downward slide is exceedingly hard to predict. The workings of the climate, the epidemiology of virus diseases, the success of technological fixes now being sought, and the resilience of various societies under severe stress are among the important factors that simply are not well enough understood. Furthermore, many scientists studying the human predicament are apprehensive that problems totally unanticipated today will arise. They realize that luck will be involved as well.

We don't live in a surprise-free world. When *The Population Bomb* was written, we and our colleagues were enormously worried about the course that humanity was on. Yet it is sobering to recall that the book appeared *before* depletion of the ozone layer had been discovered, *before* acid precipitation had been recognized as a major problem, *before* the current rate of tropical-forest destruction had been achieved, let alone recognized, *before* the true dimensions of the extinction crisis had been perceived, *before* most of the scientific community had recognized the possibility of a nuclear winter, and *before* the AIDS epidemic.

At that time, too, the greenhouse warming seemed at worst a distant threat that might never materialize, not something that could cause serious difficulties within a few years. On the latter, we wrote in *The Population Bomb*:

The greenhouse effect today is being countered by low-level clouds generated by contrails, dust, and other contaminants that tend to keep the energy of the sun from warming the Earth in the first place. At the moment we cannot predict what the overall climatic results will be of our using the atmosphere as a garbage dump. We do know that very small changes in either direction in the average temperature of the Earth could be serious. . . . In short, when we pollute, we tamper with the energy balance of the Earth. The results in terms of global climate and in terms of local weather could be catastrophic. Do we want to keep it up and find out what will happen? What do we gain by playing "environmental roulette"?[2]

What indeed? The lesson is clear: bigger and nastier surprises pop up as humanity stresses its life-support systems to the limit. The atmosphere seems especially capable of providing such surprises. Climatologists tell us that relatively minor changes in such factors as the concentration of greenhouse gases could possibly push the system from one relatively steady state over a threshold into a quite different steady state —one for which humanity is quite unprepared. Suppose, for example, warming caused the floating outer fringes of the West Antarctic ice sheet to break up and come loose from anchor points on islands and the shallow seabed. That would allow a more rapid flow of ice from land to sea, adding an enormous volume of water to the oceans. The consequences would be appalling. Sea level would rise 16 to 26 feet,[3] causing massive flooding of coastal areas around the world. Vast expanses of additional land would be exposed to destructive storm surges and saltwater intrusions into many freshwater aquifers. A wise civilization would give itself a wide margin of safety to deal with such hazards.

We can't foretell precisely where the "if current trends continue" scenario will lead us. But one thing seems safe to predict: starvation and epidemic disease will raise death rates over most of the planet. Another is that social problems will proliferate with population growth, and that democracy as a form of government will be at risk. A recent study by former Ambassador Marshall Green and Patricia Barnett compared measures of population pressures and the political stability of nations. They found that, in general, rapid population growth, particularly in nations with sharp ethnic divisions, "places enormous strains on political institutions." It threatens political stability by promoting rapid urbanization, increasing the proportion of youths in the population, and expanding labor forces more rapidly than jobs are created.[4] The study found that "only a handful of countries with serious demographic pressures managed to maintain stable constitutional governments with good records on civil and political rights."

Since social systems are so little understood, we can only make informed guesses about other social trends. One is that religious fundamentalism may become rapidly ascendant. People, rightly feeling betrayed by political leaders, by science, and by secular society in general, will seek intellectual shelter in a set of "eternal values" and the promise of a better life in the next world. Xenophobia and rancor may increase as people search for scapegoats and as international conflict over natural resources such as water heightens. Truly new-minded leaders like Gorbachev may be overwhelmed by those who are unable to grasp humanity's plight or simply don't care.

It also seems possible that breakdowns will be most severe in overdeveloped nations. Not only do people have farther to fall, but those societies also rely much more on nation-scale cooperative ventures for their continuation and well-being. Very few Americans, Argentinians, Europeans, Australians, or Japanese live on farms; most depend utterly on complex transport systems to supply their food, and on complex systems of energy distribution to preserve and prepare that food. In turn, the farming enterprise requires energy subsidies and transport systems to maintain production. In short, while a Bangladeshi farmer may subsist through hell and high water on the produce from his own plot, a Stanford University professor can keep eating only if railroads and trucks keep running and electricity and natural gas continue to be distributed.

Even if large-scale war can be avoided, it seems likely that regional conflicts will become more frequent as disputes over land, dwindling water and energy sources, environmental refugees, and "who's to blame" become more frequent.

Whatever form it ultimately took, the Whimper would destroy civilization just as effectively as a large-scale war. The changes in our environment seen over the last fifty years will be dwarfed by those of the next fifty, and those changes are likely to be accompanied by an enormous rise in death rates. That's the rub. The world is ill-equipped to handle a massive escalation in death rates. The deaths of many hundreds of millions of people in famines, for example, will present utterly unprecedented problems—especially when the nations in which they are dying have the capability of threatening nuclear terrorism.

The richest countries, those with the technological resources to assist the rest of the world and to develop more benign technologies, are also the nations most vulnerable to disruption from terrorism, epidemics, water shortages, and ecological breakdown. Because these societies are highly centralized and interconnected, local disasters would tend to propagate. Food riots or epidemics leading to a breakdown of transport systems, for instance, could kill a large number of Americans who otherwise could still buy food even at highly inflated prices. Local conflicts over floods of environmental refugees or transnational pollution problems leading to breakdowns of international trade could add to the problems of keeping societies functioning.[5]

The Whimper thus could lead to a collapse of civilization just as surely as the Bang. Populations of human beings could be greatly reduced, and national governments could be so weakened that they would be replaced by something resembling feudalism with a strong overlay of tribalism. Large cities with ethnically mixed populations could suffer fates similar to that of Beirut, made all the more difficult by severe shortages of food and the nearly total breakdown of centralized services.

Attempts would be made to keep high technology going, but it might prove impossible. As the "standing crop" of automobiles, trucks, railroad engines and cars, refrigerators, power-plant turbines, and the like were destroyed or fell into disrepair, society could revert to the sort of conditions that prevailed in the Dark Ages, with fundamentalist religions and local despots playing a greater and greater role in human affairs. This precipitous decline would be most noticeable to those living in the now rich nations and to the very poorest people who now depend on aid for survival. The adjustment might be less severe for survivors in less-developed regions, and hundreds of millions of people might hardly notice at all, since they are living at a subsistence level now.

▶   **THE ALTERNATIVE**   ◀

Of course, both the Bang and the Whimper could be averted. The basic outline of how to do so is very short:

1. Halt human population growth as quickly and humanely as possible, and embark on a slow population shrinkage toward a size that can be sustained over the long term while allowing every person the opportunity to lead a decent, productive life.

2. Convert the economic system from one of growthism to one of sustainability, lowering per-capita consumption so as to reduce pressures on both resources and the environment.

3. Wherever possible, convert to more environmentally benign technologies.

In other words, we must simultaneously reduce all three multiplicative factors in the $I = PAT$ equation (population, affluence/consumption, and the use of environmentally malign technologies).

Needless to say, doing this would require a transformation of society. The cost would include giving up many things that we now consider to be essential freedoms: the freedom not to consider society's needs when planning a family, freedom to drive gas-guzzling cars, freedom to own and use an off-road vehicle, freedom to use and discard huge amounts of nonbiodegradable plastics, and, perhaps most important, the freedom (if not an obligation!) to consume more and more. We would also need to give up our "freedom" to deny rights and opportunities to women and members of other races and religions and to exploit the citizens of other nations without concern for the consequences to them. All in all, it would be a big change for Americans, but the benefits would be enormous.

The first benefit is avoiding the total collapse of civilization and the disappearance of the United States as we know it—a modest reward! But the benefits could extend far beyond that.

On the positive side, Americans in a new world could enjoy longer, more relaxed, more enjoyable lives. We could have less air pollution, fewer toxic compounds in drinking water, reduced levels of stress, and access to crime-free public transportation systems. Especially if accompanied by more healthful diets, these benefits all would help increase health and life expectancies. A less crowded, less frantic society in which all children were wanted and cared for could offer a safer, more peaceful life. If the transition to a sustainable society could be made globally, the threat of war would recede.

The inevitable aging of the population as growth slows, stops, and begins to shrink would reduce the portion of the population in the high-crime-rate and -drug-use years and help alleviate those problems. Once the scramble for acquisition was damped down, more social effort could be put into education and into dealing with social ills such as sexism, racism, and religious prejudice. It would be the ultimate test of whether human society is even remotely "perfectable." More people could learn to value cultural diversity, a trend already detectable in nations like the United States.[6] At the same time, society could evolve in ways that took advantage of the natural human tendency to be a "small-group" animal—now seen in the tendency for ethnic groups, rather than nations, to be the focus of loyalty.[7] In a sustainable world, with a carefully maintained environment and reasonable equity, ethnic fragmentation would not necessarily be a bad thing.

All that halting growth and starting a slow population decline could do is give us an *opportunity* to solve the myriad other dilemmas that plague society. It is our guess, doubtless colored by our own histories and predilections, that any resolution of the human dilemma that might lead to *stability* over even the medium term (say, a few centuries) would have to be based on democratic decisions acceptable to most of the world's people—a mutually agreed-upon system, the major features of which were somehow mutually enforced by social pressures or other sanctions. To establish civilization on such a path will require inspired leadership, something that has been absent in the United States for some time. But there is hope in that area: world leaders like Prince Philip of Great Britain,[8] Prime Minister Gro Harlem Brundtland of Norway, and the late Indira Gandhi of India have taken courageous stands on the population issue and its connection to environmental problems; and Mikhail Gorbachev of the Soviet Union shows promise of revising that nation's backward views on global problems and international cooperation.

No doubt this sounds like a Utopian pipe dream. There is, however, nothing whatever in "human nature" to make unattainable most of the features of what many of us would consider to be a Utopia. At one time or another, human societies have gotten along without war, have largely suppressed racial prejudice, and have at least begun to equalize opportunity between the sexes. But the road to Utopia, we believe, can be traveled only in small steps, and there can be neither Utopia nor survival without population control.

Many of the objections to the helpful small steps are simply vigorous assertions: "People won't pay any attention to you—they won't have smaller families." But many did pay attention to *The Population Bomb*,[9] and Americans have been having smaller families for nearly twenty years. All that's needed now is for those families to shrink just a little more.

"You can't get Americans out of their cars!" Who says so? If there were clean, safe, and speedy mass transit, we suspect many people would prefer to have a relaxed time to read the newspaper on their way to work and a glass of beer or wine on the way home, rather than breathing poisonous gases in a traffic jam for an hour or so each way.[10]

"People won't go on mass-transit systems because they're not safe." This strikes us as a simple failure of imagination. For example, as international tensions slacken, many people now in the military could be assigned temporary duty as transit police. The organizational ability of the vast surplus of higher military officers that now runs up the cost of national defense (there are many times more generals per soldier at the present time than there were during the Second World War) could be employed in organizing the transit police. Furthermore, the excellent Metro in crime-ridden Washington, D.C., has been made very safe by the use of high technology—TV cameras are everywhere. So, even if we run out of surplus military officers, the problem is not insoluble.

"Mass transit would put too many autoworkers into unemployment lines." A lot of them are there already, thanks to Detroit's failure to anticipate changes in the 1970s and 1980s and its subsequent loss of market. Furthermore, increasing automation and budget constraints have led to reduction in white-collar staff as well. Even so, unemployment in the automobile industry could, at least temporarily, be offset by hiring the workers to build (or rebuild) mass-transit systems. Many additional jobs could be created to rebuild the nation's decaying infrastructure—highways, bridges, streets, water mains, etc.

There could be a return to more fine handwork and less mass production in both industry and agriculture, which would help solve environmental problems as well as unemployment problems. Small trends toward both can be seen in the popularity of craft fairs and in the growing interest in ecologically sound, more labor-intensive organic farming. And if a steady-state society can't maintain enough jobs to keep its citizens busy for forty hours per week, the work week could be cut to thirty-five or thirty hours. Unemployment then might be largely eliminated. We really can't see any truly insuperable barriers to reorganizing our society so that virtually everyone could lead a more pleasant, productive, satisfying life. Just because it's *possible* doesn't mean that society will actually get the job done, however.

Above all, no matter how daunting the problems of organizing a sustainable society may turn out to be, they are problems we must face unless we wish to follow our current path to either the Bang or the Whimper. And achieving a sustainable society depends absolutely upon the establishment of an effective worldwide program of population control—a topic to which we now turn.

10

▲

Connections and
Solutions: I

▼

Let's return now to questions we introduced in Chapter 1. Why haven't more people demanded action to end the population explosion? Why aren't newspapers filled with articles on demographics: how many people there are and where they are, birthrates, death rates, and age compositions? Why doesn't virtually every evening TV news program contain stories on these topics, or on the social determinants and consequences of childbearing decisions, or on the whys or wherefores of using contraceptives, as well as their availability and efforts to develop new and better ones? Why doesn't every schoolchild learn the history of the population explosion as the most important, astounding, and far-reaching event of the twentieth century? Why do even scientists like us, trained to deal with population/resource/environment issues, find it takes constant effort to realize that the habitability of Earth is rapidly decaying? Why is it so hard to see the connections between population pressures and other aspects of the human predicament?

▶   **OUR EVOLUTIONARY HANDICAP**   ◀

A major reason lies in the evolutionary history of our species, which has profoundly shaped every human being's general view of the world.[1] First of all, biological evolution made us primarily "sight animals." Thirty million years ago, our ancestors were jumping around in trees. Judging the distance to the next branch by sight is much more efficient than doing it by smell or hearing. Natural selection favored those of our ancestors with good vision, and sight is now our dominant sense. Our perceptual systems only take in perhaps a billionth of the possible stimuli that are "out there," and they give emphasis to those detectable with the eyes. Thus litter in the landscape impresses us much more than a thin film of (to us) odorless, flavorless poison on our fruit; if we had become primarily taste/smell animals like dogs, our concerns would be very different.

A second thing that our biological evolution did for our sensory systems was design them to respond strongly to "events": the charge of a lion, the snap of a breaking branch, the appearance of an attractive potential mate. In order to make these important occurrences stand out, evolution also seems to have made our minds perceive the environmental backdrop as constant.

Most of us have experienced a startling demonstration of the suppression of change in the environmental backdrop against which our lives are played out. If you see a friend regularly, he or she seems unchanging. So does the person you greet in the bathroom mirror every morning. But if you find a picture taken of yourself and your friend twenty years ago, what a shock you have. Can you ever have looked so young? What about those clothes!

These features of our nervous system were all very useful in the old world that humanity once inhabited. In that world, there was no reason to clutter the mind (which after all evolved as a tool for keeping us alive and maximizing our reproduction) with extraneous "meaningless" information. Why need an australopithecine or a Roman emperor notice whether the climate was changing? Neither could cause a change, and neither could do anything about one if it occurred. Better to keep one's mind clear to detect the stealthy approach of a leopard or the passing of an attractive individual who might prove to be a good mate.

Furthermore, our evolutionary history prepared us primarily to survive as individuals in small groups. If some members of a group behaved inappropriately, they were often the ones to suffer starvation or be killed by a predator. If inappropriate behavior by an individual threatened the group, he or she was eliminated.[2] The existence of other groups, except for nearby friends or enemies, was unknown.

In the last few decades, however, humanity has entered a brand-new world—one in which slow-developing changes such as climate alteration and population growth are much greater threats to most people than stalking predators. With its unprecedented increase in numbers, humanity has become the dominant organism on the planet, one capable of changing Earth dramatically. As a result, a survival premium has been placed on being able to detect "gradual" trends taking place on a time scale of decades. In addition, inappropriate behavior by groups now can threaten all of humanity—as exemplified by the assault on the global environment launched by the industrialized nations or Brazil's treatment of the Amazon rain forest.

But human beings, besides tuning out gradual trends, do not easily recognize the need to adjust their ways of life to accommodate the needs of more than five billion fellows, most living thousands of miles away. That all people must change their behavior to permit everyone on the planet to lead a decent life is not a notion evolution has prepared us to accept readily. It is not surprising that *Homo sapiens* has brought its old mind into the new world. After all, biological evolution would require many thousands of generations to adjust the old perceptual apparatus to new situations, and world-scale problems have appeared only in the last one or two generations.

So, if society is to come to grips with the population explosion and the other elements of the greatest crisis it has faced in historic times, it will have to do so through *cultural* evolution. Cultural evolution consists of changes in the body of nongenetic information that is passed from person to person and generation to generation. Cultural information, unlike the genetic information coded into the DNA of human beings, can be altered very rapidly—well within a single generation in the modern world, sometimes within a week.

Cultural evolution must be harnessed and directed so as to amplify people's awareness of the gradual environmental changes that so threaten our civilization. Somehow we've all got to learn that a fluctuating but continually climbing line on a graph measuring the concentration of a colorless, odorless gas in the atmosphere may represent an enormously greater threat to our children's security than all the world's terrorists put together. People must learn to perceive in columns of population statistics an increasingly certain death knell for their way of life.

It's tough to override a legacy of billions of years of biological evolution and tens of thousands of years of cultural evolution. We know that from personal experience. Our 1966 visit to India was featured at the opening of *The Population Bomb*, because it was in India that we most readily perceived the population problem *directly*. The seriousness of the problem in rich and poor nations was already clear to us from analysis of statistical trends, but in India the symptoms were acute enough to impress themselves directly on nervous systems specialized to respond to sight. (To say nothing of sounds and smells quite sufficient to register on our less well-developed auditory and olfactory apparatus.)

In short, India's overpopulation appeared to us, as first-time visitors, as "news." Visits to India, Bangladesh, or central Africa might give others a feel for the direction in which the world is moving, although people less accustomed to looking at graphs with squiggly lines might wrongly conclude that the locus of the population problem resides mainly with the poor.

Making the population connections therefore isn't all that easy, because people are basically designed not to pay attention to the factors that are related to population growth, or to that growth itself. Population growth, climate change, faltering food security, the loss of stratospheric ozone, increased acidity of rain, the extermination of populations and species of plants and animals, and various other signposts collectively pointing toward global collapse are all trends too gradual for human beings to perceive easily and are not obviously connected to one another. Worse yet, most of them are difficult or impossible to perceive directly, even when attention is called to them.

▶   **CHANGING MINDS**   ◀

So the first part of dealing with the human predicament must consist, quite literally, of changing our minds. By moving to a directed cultural evolution, to what has been called "conscious evolution,"[3] we believe that can be done. In schools and through the media, people should be taught or reminded of the selective nature of their perceptual systems and their inadequacy for registering many ominous trends. People can be trained to have "slow reflexes" as well as quick ones; they can learn to react to the continual expansion of human numbers as adaptively as to a car swerving into their lane.

Although getting these ideas incorporated into schools and the media would take a major effort initially, it could be done with relatively minor changes. In first grade, instead of reading "See Spot run," children might read "See the corn plant grow in the sun." Better yet, they can grow vegetables in the classroom and be shown what happens when the plants don't get enough water. This is one way to start building the background necessary to understand the world food situation and the threat to it inherent in global warming.

Population issues could be introduced early and often, with explanations of the limits to agriculture and the difficulty of feeding too many people. The importance of small families can be discussed, and happy, successful families in classroom stories and films should never be shown with more than two children.[4] It is critical that the importance of personal behavior in both creating and solving global dilemmas be shown early.

Newspapers already have business sections that contain graphs and columns of numbers that deal with the state of the economic system. Why shouldn't they also have an environment page, recording critical demographic statistics and the state of ecosystems on which the entire economy depends?

Carbon-dioxide and methane futures are a lot more important than financial and commodity futures (and clever entrepreneurs may even learn to make money on them!). Similarly, TV news programs could add reports on indicators of environmental health—just as they now have detailed reports on the Dow Jones averages. This has already started in the San Francisco Bay Area, where several local TV stations now have regular environmental reports.

►   **POPULATION CONTROL**   ◄

If our society wakes up to population–environment trends that now threaten civilization, what actions should be taken? The answer is embodied in the $I = PAT$ equation: we must reduce all three sources of impact. But because of the time lags involved, first priority must be given to achieving *population control*. We deliberately use the term "population control" rather than the more euphemistic "family planning." Family planning all too often means planning to have too many children, but spacing them more evenly. In Costa Rica, for example, all married women are informed about family-planning services, and 90 percent of them have used contraceptives at some time;[5] family planning clearly is available, as a result of excellent work by the Asociación Demográfica Costaricense, and yet the average completed family size is 3.5 children and the nation's growth rate is 2.5 percent (doubling time twenty-eight years). Similarly, in Rajasthan, which has the fastest-growing population in India, 97 percent of women who refuse birth control are well informed on family-planning programs. The trouble is that family planning focuses on the needs and desires of individuals and couples; population control focuses on the needs of societies as well. Of course, population control need not be coercive; indeed, it is probably more effective in the long run if it is not.

Redoubling existing efforts to bring population growth to a halt and begin a slow decline through humane programs is imperative. Overpopulation contributes directly to global problems such as climatic change and makes their potential consequences much more dire. Civilization must plan and carry out as rapidly as possible a population program that will result in a number of people that Earth can support in reasonable comfort primarily *on income*. The prospects of trying to deal with the dislocations caused by climatic change alone (to say nothing of other elements of the human predicament) in a world inhabited by 8 to 12 billion people are daunting indeed.

Remember what would happen if, by a birth-control miracle, India achieved replacement reproduction around 2025. In that case, India's population would continue to grow until almost the end of the next century, and when it stopped India would have about 2 billion people. Picture what monsoon failures would mean to 2 billion Indians! Imagine what might happen if they shared the Indian subcontinent with 300 million Pakistanis and 300 million Bangladeshis, and two of the three nations were well armed with thermonuclear weapons. There would be ten times as many people as now reside in the United States jammed into the subcontinent, which has an area slightly more than half the size of the "lower forty-eight" U.S. states. It would not be a situation conducive to international tranquillity.

In 1985, more than forty world leaders, representing more than half of Earth's people, signed a "Statement on Population Stabilization," which said in part:

Degradation of the world's environment, income inequality and the potential for conflict exist today because of over-consumption and overpopulation. If . . . unprecedented population growth continues, future generations of children will not have adequate food, housing, medical care, education, earth resources, and employment opportunities.

The group, which included the heads of state of China, India, Bangladesh, Egypt, and Kenya, implicitly urged the United States to turn away from the disastrous Reagan policies on population:

Recognizing that early population stabilization is in the interest of all nations, we earnestly hope that leaders around the

*world will share our views and join us in this great undertaking
for the well-being and happiness of people everywhere.*[6]

In a similar vein, in 1987 the report of the World Commission on Environment and Development, *Our Common Future*[7]
(often called the "Brundtland Report," after Gro Harlem
Brundtland, Prime Minister of Norway and chair of the commission) stated:

*Present rates of population growth cannot continue. They al-
ready compromise many governments' abilities to provide education, health care, and food security for people, much less
their abilities to raise living standards. This gap between numbers and resources is all the more compelling because so much
of the population growth is concentrated in low-income countries, ecologically disadvantaged regions, and poor house-
holds.*

While the need for population control is finally becoming
clearer to some of those in power, achieving it is as difficult as
ever. Indeed, the longer we dillydally, the harder it will be.
For one thing, limiting family size goes against the evolutionary
grain. We are products of four billion years of natural selection, descended from ancestors who, generation after generation for billions of generations, outreproduced other members
of their populations.[8]

The population problem is rooted in one of humanity's
greatest triumphs—overcoming natural controls on population
size: predators, starvation, and disease. Controlling death
went entirely with the evolutionary grain. But now we face a
crying need to pay heed to the other side of the demographic
equation, and to do it fast. We *know* it can be done, because
virtually no human population is reproducing up to its biological potential today, and many are stringently restricting their
reproduction. To one degree or another, most couples limit
their childbearing—they pay less and less heed to the "maximize your reproduction" message engraved in their genes—in
part because there's much less danger that their children won't
survive to reproduce.[9] Cultural evolution clearly can override

biological evolution: a population explosion to the point of a population crash—a catastrophic decline caused by high death rates—is not humanity's inevitable destiny.

▶   **POPULATION SHRINKAGE IN RICH NATIONS**   ◀

The first task is to convince people in both rich and poor nations of the need to have fewer children—and then help them to follow through. In most rich nations, changing attitudes on family size isn't such a formidable challenge. Average birthrates in those nations are only slightly above death rates (15 and 9 per 1,000 respectively), and most populations, like that of the United States, are already below replacement reproduction. In Europe and Japan, completed family sizes average 1.7 children, and many European nations are in the 1.3 to 1.5 range. Indeed, a few nations—Denmark, Austria, Italy, West and East Germany, and Hungary—have reached ZPG and are slowly shrinking. So once the significance of the $I = PAT$ equation is understood, things could progress rather rapidly.

Nearly all European nations are below replacement reproduction, despite some of them having "family allowances," small income supplements for families with dependent children. Canada also has a family allowance, yet its fertility is virtually identical to that in the United States. All that's needed to bring average family sizes down to 1.5 or below in most rich countries—so as to speed population shrinkage—is a slight reduction in current birthrates.[10]

Probably the desired changes could be accomplished by simply establishing public education programs explaining the reasons for a goal of "stop at two." Ultimately, of course, an ideal society would have a population-size goal that could be achieved by small adjustments in *average* family sizes. Merely expressing on news programs the sort of concern commonly shown when rates of inflation or unemployment go up might be sufficient. It would also be helpful if the President and other prominent politicians frequently showed awareness of demographic trends—and expressed concern if birthrates didn't remain satisfactorily low.

In the United States today, the goal ought to be a completed family size of about 1.5 (that is, a reduction of 0.4 from the current 1.9). That would take us to the level of many European nations, hardly an impossible goal. Ideally, some people who do not particularly want to have children would remain childless, a few couples who are especially good at nurturing offspring might have as many as four, and the majority would have one or two.

For the moment, however, the need is so severe that a "stop at two" program should be launched for simplicity's sake —and because too many couples might decide that they are especially good at nurturing offspring! A little leadership two decades ago probably could have moved the nation further toward that goal. But Richard Nixon largely ignored the findings and recommendations of the National Commission on Population Growth; he, Gerald Ford, and Jimmy Carter all supported family-planning assistance to poor nations, but neglected the overpopulation of the United States. Ronald Reagan not only undermined America's security by dismantling much of the laboriously built apparatus for environmental protection, he also turned back the clock on progress in population control.

In 1984, the Reagan administration made the United States a laughingstock at the United Nations' Population Conference by taking a Maoist position on population control. Chairman Mao's famous phrase "Of all things, people are the most precious," widely used at the first Population Conference in 1974, is usually misinterpreted as a call to maximize the numbers of the precious. And the old-time Communist position was that what counted was the economic system; if that was right, population size would take care of itself. Ronald Reagan, with his usual grasp of reality, had our delegation take the same position in 1984 (except, of course, for his choice of economic system!). Fortunately, that position was ignored by everyone else, including the Chinese—who had long since done their arithmetic and instituted strong measures of population control.

But Reagan's irrational position was translated into action when his administration withdrew funding from the International Planned Parenthood Federation in 1985 and in 1986

ended all American support of the United Nations Fund for
Population Activities (UNFPA), because those organizations
supported the right of women to have abortions, even though,
because of the American government's concerns, they didn't
fund abortion activities directly.

Eight years of Ronald Reagan did untold (and still largely
unrecognized by Americans) damage to United States policies
and prestige. George Bush started out with much more promise, since unlike Reagan he is informed on population issues.[11]
Bush headed a special Republican Task Force on Population
and Earth Resources when he was a member of the House of
Representatives. In 1973 he wrote:

*Today, the population problem is no longer a private matter.
In a world of nearly four billion people increasing by 2 percent,
or 80 million more, every year, population growth and how to
restrain it are public concerns that command the attention of
national and international leaders. . . . It is quite clear that
one of the major challenges of the 1970s . . . will be to curb the
world's fertility.*[12]

Those words were penned when George Bush was U.S. Ambassador to the United Nations. Now the world is well over 5
billion people, there are 95 million more every year, the world's
fertility was not curbed in either the 1970s or the 1980s, and
Bush is a world leader. But there is no sign yet that the population problem will "command his attention." Ten months into
his administration, Bush vetoed a bill to restore U.S. population assistance programs, a sad capitulation to the Republican
lunatic fringe. Worse yet, Reagan's retrograde domestic population policies may be difficult to reverse entirely because of
his appointments to numerous federal benches and the Supreme Court—and George Bush himself encouraged that court
in its assault on *Roe v. Wade.*

So we face an uphill fight in the United States if the nation
is to move rapidly toward population shrinkage with government encouragement. A lot of citizen pressure will be required
to overcome the effective counterpressure of well-organized
groups fighting to end women's right to safe abortions and to

restrict the dissemination of contraceptive information and devices. (At the end of Chapter 12 we list some organizations that you might join to help keep this from happening.)

▶   **THE ABORTION DILEMMA**   ◀

That the United States can reduce its birthrate to below its death rate should not be doubted. One need only look at Italy, a Roman Catholic nation, which has an average completed family size of 1.3![13] Italy reduced its birthrate through illegal abortion when the importation and sale of contraceptives were prohibited. Now contraceptives are available, abortion is legal, and the abortion rate has fallen. But in the United States the abortion issue is one of the hottest and most politically divisive. It has also become counterproductively mixed up with issues of population size. For example, antiabortion groups have vigorously attacked Senator Timothy Wirth of Colorado, one of the most honest and knowledgeable politicians in the country, for including the need for population stabilization in his bill to deal with global warming. We therefore need to take a closer look at the abortion problem.

Let us say at the outset that we believe that the key to population control ultimately is contraception, not abortion. When safe, easy-to-use contraceptives are available to all sexually active people, abortion should become much less of an issue.[14] The best solution to the problem in the United States is to increase usage of contraceptives and reduce today's disgracefully high abortion rate. We say "disgracefully high" because abortion is a crude, relatively dangerous method of birth control, even when legal and conducted under medical auspices. Facing the decision can be difficult psychologically for a woman (although there are no data indicating any lasting effects for most women).

Most important, abortions are deeply offensive to a sizable minority of Americans. That offense is partly based on a belief that has no biological basis, the idea that "life begins at conception." Life, of course, is a continuum, and a sperm or an egg is not even a tiny bit more or less "alive" than a fetus or an adult human being.[15] If all forms of human life were entitled to equal protection under the law, then most teenage boys would be committing murder several times a week by killing large numbers of sperm. Society, fortunately, defines an individual's beginning legally, not biologically. In many ways, the historic legal definition of personhood beginning at birth serves society well, although advances in medical technology will continue to introduce complications.[16]

What would happen if the United States banned abortion but made no effort to increase people's knowledge of and access to contraception? Our sex-obsessed society might at first glance seem bound to condemn many poor women to death at the hands of quack abortionists and many more teenage children to bearing children of their own. Huge social costs then would be added to the environmental costs of not further lowering the birthrate. But a more dispassionate analysis casts some doubt on this view.[17]

Let's suppose for a moment that a series of Supreme Court decisions effectively reverses the historic 1973 decision in *Roe v. Wade*, the decision that in essence made abortion available nationally on demand.[18] First of all, that would not make abortion illegal; it would simply permit individual states to pass laws restricting or outlawing abortion. Since both pro- and antiabortion forces are morally committed to the battle, the conflict would simply be refocused on the fifty statehouses.

It is not clear what the results would be. When *Roe v. Wade* was passed, twenty-seven states already had liberal abortion laws; four essentially permitted abortion on demand, and California and a few others came close. At that time, only 15 percent of Americans favored an unrestricted right to abortion. Today, roughly half of all Americans feel that a woman has a right to an abortion if she wants one, and an overwhelming 80 percent think she has that right in the case of rape or incest, if there is a high probability that the baby has a birth defect, or if carrying the fetus to term would endanger her life. In other words, attempts to get antiabortion laws passed in state legislatures might be much less successful than it would appear at first. In states with initiative processes, pro-choice propositions might often prevail. Even in largely Catholic Massachusetts, a referendum to stop funding abortions for poor women with tax monies was trounced in 1986.

It seems most likely that battles at the state level, taking place over decades, would end up with a checkerboard of state laws ranging from complete prohibition to abortion on demand. But all in all, one might expect a return to the pattern of the late 1960s, in which women of means crossed state lines or went to Mexico, Europe, or Japan to have abortions, while poor women were left with riskier alternatives. Today, of course, Canada would also be an option.

But many other changes will have improved the chances even of poor women to obtain abortions if they are outlawed again. In the late 1960s, there were some eight hundred agencies involved in reproductive counseling and related activities; today there are 4,400. Most counseling agencies provide other services besides abortion. They would still be in business and, within the limits of state laws, continue providing support and advice to women with unwanted pregnancies. In states where abortion remained legal, many more agencies would probably be opened, offering inexpensive abortions to women who could afford the air or bus fare to reach them. In the reproductive field, they would fill the sort of niche that Nevada long filled for divorce and gambling. And, of course, women's groups almost certainly would give support to their sisters in need, even where it was illegal. Many of their members believe as fervently in the right of women to control their own bodies as "pro-life" people believe abortion is murder.

Furthermore, surreptitious abortion would be much simpler to do and more readily available than in the 1960s. It would be more acceptable (remember, half the population would approve), so both pregnant women and those who aid them would be less in fear of social ostracism, prosecution, conviction by juries if prosecuted, or condemnation by professional societies. Illegal abortions would be much less likely to come to the attention of even zealous authorities. The safer, easier vacuum method would greatly reduce the number of bungled abortions, which in the past often led to the exposure of illegal operations.

In addition, new home pregnancy-testing kits can alert women much earlier to their pregnancies and permit them to make use of abortifacient drugs such as RU 486, already approved in Catholic France. In combination with another drug,

RU 486 now is 96 percent effective in the first six weeks. If that drug (which can be used in the privacy of the home with no help) is not approved for sale in the United States or is made illegal, then the problem becomes another law-enforcement attempt to suppress an illegal drug—something our society has been notoriously unsuccessful in doing, even when most of the public approves of the attempt.

There is little doubt that if abortion is outlawed, everything else being equal, the abortion rate will drop a little and the birthrate will rise. The very fact of breaking a law or the trouble and expense of travel will deter some women. Similarly, there will be some rise in the death rate of women, partly because there will be more childbearing (and childbirth is more dangerous than abortion) and partly because there will be more bungled abortions and more risky postoperative bus rides. More children will be born with birth defects, since even if drugs more advanced than RU 486 came into common use, they still might not be useful in the later stages of pregnancy when various defects can be detected. And, finally, there will be the far-from-negligible added costs to society of both law enforcement and support of the additional unwanted children.

On the other hand, there would also be some lifting of the burden from the minds of those in the antiabortion movement who sincerely believe that, as long as the procedure is legal, they are made accomplices in murder. Although we disagree with that view, there is some benefit in giving more peace of mind to a substantial minority in our population. Sadly, though, that peace would be bought primarily by visiting hardship, suffering, and, in some cases, death on poor women—a trend that has already begun with the July 1989 Supreme Court decision allowing states to outlaw abortions with public funds or in public facilities.

It should be obvious that the only sensible solution to the abortion dilemma is to eliminate unwanted pregnancies. Accidents do happen, of course, and no doubt always will; half of the abortions occurring in the United States in the late 1980s apparently were results of contraceptive failures; the other half were necessitated by a failure to use birth control. Clearly, the U.S. abortion rate could be substantially reduced by wider use of contraceptives—as well as by many people switching to more effective contraceptives.[19] This is particularly true for the appalling rate of teenage pregnancy, which accounts for over a quarter of the abortions. Teenagers in many European countries are as sexually active as American kids, but their premarital pregnancy and abortion rates are much lower—because they have been informed about and use contraceptives.

Many people in the right-to-life movement unfortunately have also been active in preventing the teaching of sex education (including information on birth control) in public schools; some have even worked to restrict the availability of contraceptives to the public—tactics that surely are counterproductive to their stated goal of stopping abortions. Instead, we hope that at least some antiabortion activists will shift their efforts to ensuring that condoms are available in every high-school bathroom and that every American not only has access to contraceptives but knows how to use them.

►   **CONTRACEPTIVES**   ◄

The birth-control pill has been available in the United States since 1960; except for sterilization, it is the most effective contraceptive method available. Mechanical methods such as condoms and diaphragms are quite effective also, especially if used carefully. The use of condoms also is important in controlling the spread of sexually transmitted diseases, including AIDS; fortunately, their use has been rising among unmarried people in the United States. Less effective (but far better than nothing) means such as sponges and spermicidal jellies and foams are for sale in any drugstore (spermicides also appear to provide some protection against the AIDS virus).

Intrauterine devices (IUDs) must be emplaced by medical personnel, but they are very effective and can remain in place for years with only an occasional check. Unfortunately there is no doubt that some IUDs have been unacceptably risky, and the new generation of them should be used with great care until their safety can be properly evaluated.

Some newer contraceptives are being tested in other countries, and a few are being introduced in the United States. The most promising new methods are the long-term injectable steroids (essentially the same compounds as provided in the pill, but not requiring a daily dose) and the under-skin slow-release steroid implants. These long-term applications give protection against an unwanted pregnancy for periods of from six months to three years. Possibilities for the more distant future include "immunizations" against sperm and methods that suppress sperm production in men.

Feminists have sometimes complained that contraceptive research has been biased toward putting all the responsibility for birth control on women. Nevertheless, methods that seem to work on males (other than condoms) have been developed, but they have been plagued with very severe side effects. That is not the case, however, with sterilization. Vasectomies are safer procedures than tubal ligations, and thus allow the male to assume the risks (in this case minimal) of contraception.

Unfortunately, the prospects for developing new birth-control methods in the United States are not bright. Deaths and other serious problems associated with the use of some IUDs (notably the Dalkon shield) in our lawsuit-minded society have led to withdrawal of the challenged devices and others as well from the market, because the companies producing them were losing money on them—or feared they would lose money on them if new problems arose. Not only were the lawsuit settlements and awards costing millions, but use rates dropped in response to publicity about the problems. This occurred following news about linkages of the pill with heart attacks and cancers (the latter largely unfounded) in the 1970s, and again when the problems arose with the IUDs. The lawsuit threats and prolonged testing requirements have also had a chilling effect on research on new and better contraceptives in recent years, bringing it almost to a halt in this country. That RU 486 was developed in France was no accident.[20]

One should not take the difficulties with contraceptive devices lightly. There is a pressing need to develop safer, more convenient, more accident-proof methods of contraception. At the same time, the risks of using various forms of contraception must always be weighed against the costs of unwanted pregnancies (including the risk of death in childbirth). The calculations are not simple, especially because the psychological costs and benefits of having (or not having) children are subjective and difficult to account for.

Unquestionably, the public should be fully informed about the relative risks and costs of birth prevention and raising a child so that they can make sensible choices. The joys and satisfactions of parenthood are many; but the costs are also high in a modern society. Most people know that their choice of family size will directly affect the parenting rewards their *children* can look forward to.

In developed nations like the United States, dealing with the population component of the human predicament is largely a matter of providing adequate public education and access to the means for controlling reproduction. The greatest need today is for better understanding of the urgency of population reduction, as well as for reducing individual impacts on our battered planet. All of this could be facilitated by leadership at the top, which has been absent for almost a decade in the United States.

The challenge in developing countries is considerably more complex, as we'll see in the next chapter.

11

▲

Connections and
Solutions: II

▼

Halting population growth in less-developed countries will be much harder than in industrial nations, for several reasons. The most important is their age compositions. Because these populations contain huge numbers of young people, to end growth quickly (except through high death rates), completed family sizes must drop well below replacement—almost to the vicinity of one—for a period of time. That is what China embarked on with its one-child-family program, and it is no trivial task. Collectively, the developing nations (excluding China) now have an average family size of 4.8 children, so a decline of more than three offspring per family is required.

► **POPULATION POLICIES IN DEVELOPING** ◄
NATIONS

Children are highly valued for powerful economic reasons in peasant societies—a factor that has been a barrier to family-planning success in many developing nations. Children are needed as a source of labor or income while young and as social security for their parents' old age. In societies where as many as 25 percent of all children die before reaching their fifth birthday, large families are seen as necessary to ensure that some will survive to be adults.

Today, more children survive than in the past, but infant mortalities in the poorest nations are still high by our standards, and the compensating tradition persists. Poor farmers with large families end up with several sons among whom they must divide their land. A few generations of subdividing lead to farms that are marginal or submarginal in size or quality. Poor people don't have the luxury of long-range planning. Where food is going to come from today, this month, and this year are problems for *now*. The size of future farm plots is beyond today's planning horizon; the sons must worry about that later.[1]

Sons represent needed labor and potential support for parents in old age. They help work the farm or they go to the city to find work and, when possible, send money home. In the absence of a social-security system, sons are the principal hedge against starvation in one's declining years. Small wonder family planning has had little impact in much of the developing world, where both economic pressures and the traditions they have shaped (often codified in religions) are strongly pronatalist. The route to successful population control in less-developed countries is through changing these fundamental attitudes, and the best way to do that is to alter the conditions that created the attitudes in the first place. We'll return to this idea later.

Other problems, of course, must be overcome in addition to providing motivation for people to have small families. In nations with primitive medical, transport, and communications systems, simply extending family-planning programs to remote rural areas can be very difficult. In the past, the motives of aid donors wishing to provide population-control assistance have been suspect, and often with good reason when racism or other prejudices have been behind their actions.[2] On the other hand, corruption among local officials dispensing aid is also a serious problem.

► **CHINA AND INDIA: SUCCESS AND FAILURE** ◄

What, then, is the best strategy for achieving population control in poor nations? Perhaps the best way to answer that question is to examine the most successful population-control program in the world—that in the People's Republic of China. The Chinese have gone through many ups and downs in population policy, although since the late 1960s their domestic policy has been one of "planned population growth"—perhaps best summarized in an official statement in 1974: "Man must control nature, and he must also control his numbers."[3] By the late 1970s, even the official rhetoric (previously full of condemnations of the idea of overpopulation) had become frankly Malthusian. In short, the Chinese came to the need for population control late, but then their rigidly organized society allowed the government to implement steps that might well be impossible in a democracy.

Admitting that rapid population growth was hindering their development, the Chinese government established an intensive program of "birth planning." Through the extensive health-service system, "barefoot doctors" and family-planning workers distributed information, birth-control pills, IUDs, condoms, diaphragms, foams, and jellies. "Voluntary"[4] sterilization, for couples who were finished with childbearing, and abortion as a backup were provided at local clinics and hospitals. The vacuum technique for abortion, now used around the world, was developed by the Chinese in the 1960s.

The program's goal in the 1970s was for each couple to have two well-spaced children. Incentives to comply included paid maternity leave, time off the job for breast-feeding, free child care, essentially free contraceptives, and paid time off for abortions and sterilizations. Cooperative parents were rewarded with better housing and with educational opportunities for their children. Marriage and childbearing decisions were made through the governing council of the commune or the work brigade; pressure from one's peers was an essential facet of the program. One member of the council usually was responsible for the community's birth planning. In rural areas, respected older women with children were organized into "women's cadres" to promote the birth-planning program.

All this was in place when population surveys in the late 1970s shocked the national leadership by indicating that, instead of the earlier estimates of 900 million people in 1979, the Chinese population had already climbed to a billion. Among other problems, this cut the scale of China's per-capita economic growth by 10 percent.[5]

The government decided something must be done. Estimating that the basic carrying capacity of the nation was about 650–750 million people (a number still almost certainly too large for the long term),[6] China made a momentous decision. For the first time in history, a nation set as a goal *shrinking its population*. It resolved to stop growth at 1.2 billion and then start a decline toward the sustainable size. To accomplish this, the one-child family was promoted as an ideal, with the hope that the average family size would drop to 1.5 children.[7]

Key points to remember about the Chinese program include:

1. It is indigenous; no significant outside aid has been involved except technical assistance in conducting demographic surveys and censuses.
2. It is being carried out in a nation where the government has put substantial effort into providing equal rights and education for women.
3. It has been part and parcel of an extremely successful program to bring basic health care to the entire population, with emphasis on maximizing infant survival and maternal health.
4. It has used peer pressure as a major motivating tool, even though the basic policy was centrally designed and applied from above.
5. There has been considerable openness on the part of the central government about the successes and failures of the program, including abuses of human rights that have at times occurred. Whether such openness will continue following the recent bloody repression in China remains unclear.

China's population-control program has been the most successful on record: it reduced fertility by more than half in about a dozen years. In 1979, the one-child family was made an official goal to be achieved by half of all couples, with two children being the limit for the rest. By the mid-1980s, the average completed family size had dipped to 2.1, just about replacement level.

Despite its success, there are two sad things about the Chinese program. The first is that the nation waited so long that, when a serious attempt was made to bring down birthrates, the program had many elements of coercion that are offensive to those of us who believe reproductive behavior should basically remain in the control of the individual. The Chinese government, rightly or wrongly, concluded that there was too little time to change attitudes toward childbearing so that individual decisions would, collectively, produce a socially desirable result.

We must hope that our government doesn't wait until it too decides that only coercive measures can solve America's population problem.[8] One must always keep in mind that the price of personal freedom in making childbearing decisions may be the destruction of the world in which your children or grandchildren live. How many children a person has now has serious social consequences in all nations, and therefore is a legitimate concern of society as a whole.

The second sad thing about the Chinese population-control program is that it has not accomplished enough.[9] Resistance in traditional rural populations has prevented the one-child goal from being met in many areas and has led to many abuses. The resistance has been one reason for coerced abortions and sterilizations. The desire to have a son within the one-child limit led to an increase in female infanticide (a traditional but in recent decades largely suppressed response of Chinese parents wishing sons). Because of these difficulties, the one-child-family program was relaxed. In addition, the new capitalism in the farming sector has raised the perceived value of children and led to a rebound in the birthrate. In 1989, the average completed family size was about 2.4, and the growth rate appeared to have climbed from about one percent in the mid-1980s to some 1.4 percent.

China's population passed 1.1 billion in 1989, and now demographers believe it will reach 1.5 to 1.7 billion before attaining ZPG. That is, in absolute numbers China will add about the equivalent of double today's United States population before growth stops. For a nation that already has more than four times the population of, but no more arable land than, the United States, with severe pollution problems because of its dependency on coal for energy, with falling grain production, and with natural ecosystems already severely compromised by massive deforestation, destruction of wetlands, and desertification, *any* population increase is too much. Moreover, these population projections could be too optimistic if the birthrate continues to go back up. Perhaps the basic lesson from China's experience will turn out to be that even a very strong program of population control, pushed by a repressive government on a regimented society, can fail if a nation starts too late.

China's future is a big question mark despite its great and effective effort to overcome its overpopulation. Much will depend on whether the movement for more democracy is allowed to reemerge, how the nation's relations with the rest of the world unfold, and how population policies develop in the next few years.

India's population situation is increasingly ominous despite much earlier (but relatively ineffective) effort compared to China. India was the first nation to recognize its population problem and try to do something about it. In 1952, Margaret Sanger, the founder of Planned Parenthood in the United States, Mrs. Elise Ottesen-Jensen of Sweden, Lady Dhanvanthis Rama Rau of India, and some other advocates of family planning established the International Planned Parenthood Federation. That same year, India instituted the first official family-planning program in any less-developed nation.

For the first ten years, the effort made little progress, concentrating on surveys, pilot projects, and experiments with the rhythm method. Then, in 1965, with the nation's food situation deteriorating, India reorganized its family-planning program. The population then was some 480 million people, and birth and death rates were estimated at about 43 and 20 per 1,000 respectively.[10] The goal of the reorganized program was to reduce the birthrate to 25 by 1975.[11] No such luck. By 1975 there was some progress, since India's birthrate had dropped to 35, but the death rate had declined to 15. The growth rate had thus dropped only from 2.3 to 2.0 percent. The population, meanwhile, had reached 600 million. But the program had too little emphasis on needed social change and too much on distribution of birth-control technology. In 1989, the birthrate had inched down to 33, but the death rate had declined to 11, so the growth rate had only dipped slightly during two and a half decades, while the population rose to 835 million.

India's family-planning efforts suffered a major setback in 1976 when Indira Gandhi's government, recognizing that the population-control effort was floundering, stepped up pressure on government employees (who comprise a large fraction of the work force) to be sterilized after having a third child. The move was so unpopular that it was a major cause of Gandhi's being voted out of office in 1977. Since then, some progress seems to have been made in reducing birthrates in India's growing middle class, but little elsewhere. In 1989, Indian scientists told us the entire program was basically "on hold" because elections were coming up and family planning was considered too controversial.

To be fair, though, India is a democracy, and China is a dictatorship. China's ability to impose a unified policy on the populace from the top down doesn't exist in India. Moreover, Chinese society is relatively homogeneous, and, for the number of people involved, linguistically simple with a widespread common written language. India, by contrast, has dozens of languages and hundreds of dialects, a great hindrance to dissemination of information, a problem exacerbated by the caste system.

China has had other advantages that have arisen from other policies. Among these were the establishment of the "barefoot doctors" basic-health-care program, which focused strongly on maternal and child health, and a huge and successful effort to educate all young people. The opening of opportunities for education and employment of women no doubt was also important.

India has not given high priority to making these advances,

but has instead put its limited resources into such things as building of steel mills, huge energy projects, and the production of consumer goods.[12] This misallocation of resources is reflected in national statistics. India's infant mortality rate is twice as high as China's (96 per 1,000 live births as opposed to 44); 59 percent of India's adult population was illiterate in 1982, compared to just over a third of China's; and school enrollment of children in India is by no means universal.[13]

Clearly, India's demographic situation, combined with the bleak prospects for agricultural expansion on the subcontinent (and some prospect of declining production), darkens her future. Time has grown extremely short. Far more effective efforts both toward meeting people's basic needs and toward population control will be needed to give that overpopulated nation any chance of surviving intact to 2050. Mobilizing India's immense human resources to this end will be difficult, but the presence of an industrial "core" of the nation, including a sizable cadre of well-educated people, could help.

▶   **AFRICA: A DEMOGRAPHIC BASKET CASE**   ◀

Turning to sub-Saharan Africa, we find still more dismal prospects. Most African nations, unlike India, don't have the advantage of a "core" of development. Most have very few well-educated people and no heavy industry or high-tech capabilities.

Kenya's population numbers are grimmer than India's. In 1965, Kenya's population was about 9.5 million people, its birthrate about 50 per 1,000, its death rate 17, and its growth rate 3.3 percent (doubling time a little over twenty years). By 1985, Kenya's population had more than doubled, its birthrate had *climbed* to 54 (average completed family size about eight children!), its death rate dropped to 13, and its rate of natural increase was at a world record of 4.1 percent—a rate not matched by a national population for as long as demographic statistics have been kept. At that rate, Kenya's population would have doubled again in just seventeen years.

Readers of *The Population Bomb* were asked to consider the significance of doubling times then implied by vital statistics in developing nations. It was pointed out that in order for a nation like Kenya just to stay even, to maintain the inadequate living standards of 1968, it must in some sense double its production of food and other necessities in under two decades: "The amount of power must be doubled. The capacity of the transport system must be doubled. The number of trained doctors, nurses, teachers, and administrators must be doubled."[14]

Concern was expressed about Kenya at that time (1968), when its doubling time was twenty-four years. Now the population *has* doubled. But, in spite of substantial outside aid (hundreds of millions of dollars annually),[15] Kenya's per-capita standard of living has remained roughly the same, as measured by GNP. But even that is a very deceptive measure. Per-capita food production has dropped almost 30 percent since 1972, and the needed food has been imported, some as aid, some with borrowed money. Annual food aid in cereals went from 4,000 tons to 209,000 tons between 1975 and 1984.

The explosive growth of the population has led to the increasing subdivision of Kenya's farms, and their average size is already too small to absorb efficiently the efforts of a single family. Yet today the average family farmer faces the prospect of further dividing his little plot among four sons, since the average family size is about eight children. Deforestation and soil degradation have added to the woes of the poor, causing firewood to become increasingly scarce and making crop yields increasingly hard to maintain.

The situation is exacerbated because much of the best land is used for producing cash crops such as coffee and tea, which are exported—improving the balance of trade, but doing little to help the average Kenyan who does not get his or her share of the cash. Nairobi, the capital, has been growing at about 8 percent a year, twice the national rate. People forced off subdivided farms stream into the city, seeking employment and becoming enmeshed in an increasingly unpleasant, burgeoning, crime-ridden set of slums. In 1976 there were 400,000 unemployed Kenyans; today there are about 2 million (out of a work force of perhaps 10 million).[16]

There have been some important improvements in the

quality of life in Kenya, however. Infant mortality rates have dropped substantially, and literacy rates and school attendance have climbed. But, with too few jobs to offer to graduates and a deteriorating resource base, the nation teeters on the edge of disaster. It has not managed to maintain its quality of life through the last population doubling. Fortunately, since 1985 the birthrate has begun to fall and the growth rate has eased a little.[17] But the momentum of population growth guarantees at least another doubling and a continued flood of young people into schools and the labor market for the next few decades. Kenya has no choice but to continue its struggle for development, but it is further behind the eight ball than in 1968 and has even farther to go.

Kenya is hardly alone in Africa; it is merely an extreme example. The population of the entire continent is growing at almost 3 percent per year, with a doubling time of twenty-four years. The average death rate for the continent is still 15 (for West Africa, 18), as contrasted with an average of 10 in Asia and 8 in Latin America. Even more indicative of Africa's deteriorating condition, infant mortality in the poor nations of tropical Africa hovers around 120 per 1,000 live births[18]—a stunning contrast even to the average of 84 in poor nations as a whole, let alone the 10 in the United States and the 6 in Sweden. Thus there is still substantial room for death rates to drop—if the trends followed in poor nations on other continents are followed.

▶   **THE MOSLEM WORLD**   ◀

There are about a billion Moslems in the world, mostly concentrated in a narrow belt running from the Atlantic Ocean through North and Central Africa, the Middle East, and on through Pakistan. The belt is broken by India, but picks up again in Bangladesh and continues with little interruption through Southeast Asia to Indonesia and the southern Philippines. With an average completed family size of about six children, Moslems are reproducing faster than any other major religious group, despite death rates of almost 14 per 1,000 and tragically high infant mortality rates that reach about 150 per 1,000 live births in West Africa.[19]

There are differences of opinion on how much being Moslem in itself contributes to high birthrates. But the generally low status accorded to women in contemporary Islamic societies no doubt has much to do with both high birthrates and infant mortality rates. That low status deprives women of the control over their own lives and reproduction that demonstrably lowers both of those rates in other societies. Historically, Islam, while supporting a superior position of males, provided legal rights and security in society to women far beyond those of the animistic religions it replaced.[20] Unlike Catholicism and many other Christian sects, it has never offered any moral objection to contraception. Since there is no central Islamic religious leader, there is no official Moslem view on population control, but rather a diversity of views emanating from various officials and religious leaders. Some relatively modernized Moslem nations, indeed, have established strong and fairly successful family-planning programs, notably Tunisia, where both birth and death rates are significantly lower than in neighboring nations. It seems reasonable to accept the view of sociologist John Weeks that it is not Islam itself that is causing high population growth rates in Islamic nations, but poverty and the inferior status of women in these traditional patriarchal societies.

▶ **LATIN AMERICA: SOME HOPE, SOME HORROR** ◀

In Latin America, the situation is not as grim as in Africa, but it's bad enough. Population growth rates are high in Central America and tropical South America—an average 2.1 percent per year for both (doubling time thirty-three years). Some of the symptoms of overpopulation resemble those seen in Africa, especially the decline of per-capita agricultural production, the overemphasis on producing cash crops and beef for export (with the cash going mostly to a few rich people), the lack of concern for the nutritional needs of the people, and the burgeoning slums and overnight shantytowns surrounding major cities.

But, while the African nations have simply outstripped and seriously degraded their resource base, with little or no modernization of agriculture, Latin America's problems, for the moment, stem more from misallocation and inefficient use of resources. Continued population growth at present and projected rates, however, will soon enough put them in Africa's position, especially if deforestation and land degradation continue at current rates.

Latin America's advantages are many; it has relatively high literacy rates and at least the potential for developing good basic health-delivery systems; here again the problem has been one of misplaced priorities. In many countries, especially Mexico, Brazil, and Argentina, a modern developed sector exists, with the necessary cadre of educated people. But tradition (especially in regard to the status of women), political instability, and the influence of the Catholic hierarchy [21] have hindered social progress, especially in areas relevant to controlling population growth. Recent United States policies, particularly in Central America, have also been unhelpful in this respect.

▶ **WAITING FOR THE DEMOGRAPHIC TRANSITION** ◀

Remarkably little has been accomplished in population control in the twenty years since *The Population Bomb* appeared. Global population growth has slowed a little, but nearly all of that slowdown is due to fertility reductions in two principal regions: China and the industrialized nations, especially the West. A few other developing nations have achieved significant fertility declines, but most are growing as rapidly as before.

Far too much time has been wasted waiting for what was long believed to be an automatic demographic transition—a decline of birthrates as a result of industrial development. And far too many development advisers have grossly overestimated the carrying capacities of less-developed regions. While reducing birthrates seemed to them a worthy goal because it improved people's health and well-being, they assumed that limits to growth (including both population growth and economic expansion) would be encountered far in the future, if ever. Only now events are showing how wrong they were!

Faith in the demographic transition as an inevitable consequence of "development" has proven to be a snare and a delusion, in part because development was viewed as syn-

onymous with industrialization. Since fertility reductions occurred in Europe and North America more or less in tandem
with industrialization, it was blithely assumed that the latter
caused the former. More recently, a closer examination of both
processes revealed that in fact industry *per se* had little to do
with it.[22]

Indeed, the "just aim for development and the population
problem will automatically take care of itself" proposition will
not bear close scrutiny. Fertility rates generally are lower in
more developed nations, but so are rates of illiteracy and malnutrition.[23] Would those who recommend waiting for the demographic transition to solve the population problem also
advise taking no direct action to educate or feed people while
pressing for economic development? Of course not, because
they know that literacy and a satisfactory diet can be achieved
by appropriate programs in the absence of high levels of per-
capita income, and there are no taboos against such efforts (as
there often are in the case of programs to decrease fertility).

According to demographic-transition theory, as per-capita
incomes rise there is a tendency to substitute consumer dura-
bles (automobiles, refrigerators, TV sets, etc.) for children.
But if population growth among the poor prevents that rise in
income, the demographic transition simply wouldn't occur.
And if incomes rise in spite of population growth, what exactly
are the terms of exchange between goods and children? Will
the average Indian have to consume as much as an average
Canadian before Indian fertility rates will drop to the Canadian
level? The result, if a rich level of consumption were achieved
by the world's 4 billion poor, would be environmental catastrophe. We cannot escape from the iron grip of $I = PAT$.

In recent decades, those wed to demographic-transition
theory have had to ignore fertility declines that occurred in
some developing countries with little or no industrial development (Sri Lanka, Costa Rica, and China, for instance) and
failed to occur in others that had made progress in industrializing (Brazil and Mexico). The connection between per-capita
GNP and fertility was essentially nil, although development
experts had asserted for years that the way to reduce birthrates
was to increase the average income.[24]

Part of the answer was that the benefits of industry and

increased incomes had not been equitably distributed within the societies in question.[25] It turned out that other factors were much more important in the fertility equation and, not too surprisingly, they are related much more directly to women and families than to overall development. The critical prerequisites to reduced fertility are five: adequate nutrition, proper sanitation, basic health care, education of women, and equal rights for women.[26] The first four factors help to reduce infant mortality, allowing a reasonable expectation that a given child will survive to adulthood.

Female education is an especially interesting and in some ways the most unexpected finding. Women will apply even a few years of schooling to improving life for their families by providing more nutritious, balanced meals, better home health care and sanitation, while men usually use an education to earn a better income.[27] Improving the home situation reduces infant and child mortality, making women and men more receptive to the idea of smaller families. And the women's education makes them more open to contraception and better able to employ it properly. Finally, when women have sources of status other than children, family sizes decline.

These factors relating to women explain in part why China's "birth planning" met with greater success than India's family-planning program. They also provide welcome clues on how to improve other flagging population programs.

▶   CONTROLLING POPULATION IN DEVELOPING   ◀
                        NATIONS

Now we know that population growth in poor nations can be ended humanely, but is it too late? Despite the time that has been lost, the developing nations are ahead of the rich ones in at least one important respect: most of them have committed their societies to reducing birthrates. Nearly all developing nations now have family-planning programs, and many of them have set a goal of ending population growth (but, except for China, not shrinkage—yet).

There is, of course, great variation among nations in the degree of commitment to their family-planning programs. But in recent years the commitment has tended to deepen, especially as other countries have witnessed the proliferating environment/resource problems plaguing Africa south of the Sahara. Most important, government officials in the affected African nations have begun to shake off their deep-rooted traditions and take population control seriously.

Meanwhile the United States and most of the other developed countries remain in a demographic dream world, failing to recognize the impact of our gross overpopulation on our own nations' environments and resources, and on the planet as a whole. There is no hope whatever for saving civilization unless the rich quickly wake up to Earth's peril and begin to institute programs aimed at speeding population shrinkage and more sensible policies of resource utilization at home.

People in poor nations are very aware of our role in generating the global environmental threats that loom over us all— of our profligate use of energy and other resources. They can hardly be expected to listen to us telling them they must have fewer children if we still have no population policies whatsoever except to restrict immigration.

So rich nations need to establish population policies and make it clear that stopping growth is the first goal, followed by population shrinkage as soon as possible. They could also usefully launch a wide-ranging public discussion, with participation by scientists who are familiar with global problems and limitations, as well as social scientists who can contribute ideas on how effective social policy can be developed. The central question is what kind of society each should have one or two centuries from now.[28] These discussions could be a beginning of planning to realize those goals. The discussions should involve many countries, including at some stage the developing nations.

A model for this process might be the international effort to address the depletion of the stratospheric ozone layer, one of the simpler problems in the whole knotty complex connected to overpopulation. The discussion of ozone depletion began among scientists and widened to include the environmental community, and then policy-makers. At first it was limited to Western nations, then expanded to the Soviet Bloc, and finally to the developing countries.

Even when the developed nations put sensible population

policies in place, they will be obliged to expand their assistance to poor countries, both to help curb their population growth and to achieve sustainable development. As is surely clear from the foregoing, the poor can't do it without help; even the highly regimented Chinese require technological aid from rich countries if they are to have a chance for even moderate progress in development. And why should the poor go it alone? The rich played a major role in putting the poor in their present dilemma. Moreover, the rich stand to save their own hides by helping to resolve it. The flow of aid from rich to poor right now is disgustingly small. The record donor, Norway, gives just 1.12 percent of its GNP, the Netherlands 0.98, Denmark 0.89, and Sweden 0.87. Among Western nations the United States is tied with Ireland for most niggardly: we give only 0.2 percent of our GNP. [29]

In recent years, Japan's foreign-aid contributions have risen dramatically and have broadened in scope as well. Originally, most Japanese aid went to neighboring Asian nations and was targeted for industrial development. More recently, donations have gone to other poor countries and have included rising amounts for environmental protection. The Japanese now are way ahead of the United States in foreign-aid generosity in proportion to their wealth and may soon close the gap in dollar amounts.

In population assistance, the largest dollar amount given in 1989 was by the United States—$197.9 million. That's about one-third the cost of a single, militarily useless Stealth bomber. Nations like Norway and Sweden give proportionately much more population aid.[30] That aid, properly given and targeted, is the most necessary of all—although it is only a small percentage of all economic-aid donations. *Washington Post* columnist Hobart Rowan had the courage to say it right out: "It's time to face facts: Third World aid without birth control is like trying to pour water uphill . . . The reason for the absence of honesty on this issue is no secret: most officials panic at the thought of the political backlash from the Catholic Church in poverty stricken areas of the Third World."[31]

When industrialization began in Europe, obviously there was no competition from other regions, nor was Europe anyone else's source of raw materials or sump for surplus production. When the United States and Japan emerged as industrial powers a century ago, the world was still spacious enough for the newcomers to follow the European pattern. They therefore also sought to bottle up large pieces of the nonindustrial world as resource and marketing preserves. The "Third World" of today, by and large, consists of those formerly bottled-up lands whose infrastructures were formed not primarily for their national or regional benefit, but to serve the metropolitan industrial powers.

In short, citizens of rich nations will now have to pay for their greed and several centuries of their forebears' greed. But by paying the price, they will be buying a livable world for their children, grandchildren, and all their descendants.

▶   **REDUCING IMPACTS**   ◀

Although our basic focus in this book is on the population element of the $I = PAT$ equation, we must at least outline the most critical steps necessary to limit affluence (or at least those aspects of affluence that depend on material consumption) and to reduce the environmental impacts of the technologies that provide the goods consumed. These steps would help move rich nations like the United States toward sustainable development; fortunately, many of them could be implemented quickly.

Energy conservation should top the list in the United States and numerous other nations, especially in the Soviet Bloc (where there is less financial incentive for individuals or commercial enterprises to conserve). The West would certainly serve its own interests by sharing conservation technologies with the East.

Of course, stringent conservation of fossil fuels should be undertaken while humanity builds a bridge to a future that does not depend on burning them at all. That time is coming soon under any circumstances; to destroy much of the world to extract and burn every last available bit of fossil fuel would be insane. The United States could start by gradually imposing a higher gasoline tax—hiking it by one or two cents per month until gasoline costs $2.50 to $3.00 per gallon, comparable to prices in Europe and Japan. The higher fuel price would create a powerful incentive for people to buy and drive smaller, more fuel-efficient cars and use energy-efficient alternative forms of transportation. It would make driving safer once the majority of automobiles were smaller, help preserve crumbling highways and bridges, reduce air pollution and acid precipitation, and slow global warming—among other benefits.

Naturally, some adjustments would have to be made. For example, provision of more company-van pools, better bus service, and modern light rail transit systems could help get people to work who could no longer afford to commute by car.

Many other forms of energy conservation could be put in place as well—all of which should be familiar to anyone who remembers the energy "crisis" of the 1970s. Between 1974 and 1980, a series of incentives and programs were set up by the federal and many state governments to encourage conservation. Unfortunately, most of them lapsed or were terminated during President Reagan's tenure.

A good example of how small changes in technology could make large differences in environmental impacts can be seen by considering the Reagan administration's relaxation of automobile efficiency standards that had already been met by Chrysler. If the regulations had been left in place, in a decade or so the amount of gasoline saved would have been equivalent to the entire amount of oil estimated to underlie the Arctic National Wildlife Refuge. That single step could have made unnecessary the threatened desecration of one of the last truly wild places on our planet, part of a precious heritage that should be passed on unspoiled to future generations.

The incentives and programs for conservation and the development of renewable energy sources should be reinstated and strengthened with additional new policies to accelerate the switch to energy efficiency. Enormous opportunities still exist for better insulation and more efficient heating and cooling of homes and commercial buildings. Business travel can be minimized; electronic communications can be substituted in many situations (for example, conferences by satellite TV). Other opportunities are obvious: more durable and energy-efficient lighting fixtures, TV sets, cooking appliances, and refrigerators.[32] There is also enormous scope for recycling of materials.[33]

Another example of a broad-spectrum cure that requires changes in both consumption and technology is reversal of present trends of deforestation. Preserving forests, especially tropical forests, is essential to keeping Earth habitable. It would yield many other benefits, from supplying humanity with new foods and anticancer drugs to keeping flows of fresh water dependable.

Replanting forests would help remove carbon dioxide from the atmosphere and slow the global warming. Indeed, restoration of vegetative cover and regeneration of forests everywhere should be near the top of the human agenda. This move is needed for other important reasons besides retarding the buildup of CO_2. Halting and reversing desertification, slowing the horrendous global rate of agricultural soil erosion, protecting agricultural productivity, and providing sources of fuelwood for poor people are among the enormous benefits that would be realized.

But to reforest much of the planet would mean, among many other things, giving up the use of tropical hardwoods, eliminating oversized newspapers, finding some way to market and ship small items without using layers of plastic and cardboard, and decreasing the flood of paper that now issues from computer printers and copying machines.

Much more reading material could be delivered electronically, if problems of convenience and readability could be solved. Computers and electronic mail (E-mail) can avoid some paper use; fax machines may prove to be another paper/energy-conserving mechanism (no envelopes, no need to fly letters around). Perhaps some sort of "magic slate" device could be developed that could be repeatedly reused for preliminary drafts of documents that account for much paper consumption.

In developing nations, the fuelwood crisis can be ameliorated by the adoption of more fuel-efficient stoves, developed and introduced with local participation so that the stoves meet local needs (proper cooking temperatures for local dishes, light for evening gatherings, etc.).

Some cures must be employed even though they may involve the deployment of more expensive or less convenient technologies than those in use today. For instance, the development of energy-mobilizing technologies that do not deposit CO_2 in the atmosphere must be promoted. Especially promising are solar cells to produce electricity and its use to produce hydrogen as a portable fuel. A possibility that should remain in the *potential* "mix" is a future generation of nuclear-power reactors that are designed with safety as a primary consideration and that produce a minimum of nuclear waste.

To reduce emissions of methane (another greenhouse gas), cattle herds could be reduced, and the consumption of alternative foods to beef encouraged. Similarly, manufacture of the CFCs that cause destruction of stratospheric ozone should be phased out as fast as possible. Less damaging substitutes are available for most uses, though they may be a little more expensive. Research should be continued to find substitutes that have no effect on the ozone layer. The risks of continued damage to the ozone layer are too severe to allow minor cost considerations to cause the continued injection of the worst CFCs into the atmosphere.

▶   **IT CAN'T BE DONE WITHOUT COOPERATION**   ◀

Population control—let alone the alleviation of global environmental problems—will not be easily achieved in a world plagued by racism, religious prejudice, sexism, and gross economic inequality. The notion that numbers give strength is strongly ingrained—often leading to fear of being outreproduced by other groups. White racists rail against too many babies in black ghettos. In Northern Ireland, the Protestants worry about Catholic birthrates; in Israel, the Jews are concerned about burgeoning numbers of Arabs; and in South Africa, different racial groups worry about increases in the others.

To resolve virtually any element of the human predicament, xenophobia must be overcome. Worldwide cooperation will be required to address effectively the consumption and technology elements of the human environmental impact—of the $I = PAT$ equation. The list of tasks is daunting: the rate of climatic change must be slowed, its effects minimized, and general global environmental deterioration—especially the extinction of populations and species of other organisms—reversed. That is the only way that nations can find anything resembling security for the future.

In essence, the movement toward regulation of the global commons must be revitalized. Successful international regulation has historically been achieved by bringing it in through the back door—by creating agencies to regulate in areas where national governments had no jurisdiction, such as the Law of the Sea. The latter has had some success as individual nations have taken responsibility for managing resources in adjacent waters.[34]

Unwillingness to surrender national sovereignty has always been the main stumbling block to establishing a world government. But far more international regulation and management of international commons now take place than most people realize. Most of this is accomplished through a complex maze of trade, political, monetary, and other kinds of agreements and through the activities of the United Nations' many agencies and some other independent ones such as the World Bank. In addition, much is done, if not always for universal benefit, by private organizations ranging from multinational corporations and the global stock-market network to nongovernment organizations like Planned Parenthood, Oxfam, and CARE.

Through these, an incipient world government does exist, but it is radically different from national governments, since it lacks central administrative or legislative bodies. Administrative functions are carried out through a diffuse system of more or less separate agencies. These have only indirect power to influence nations, although international peer pressure often works, reinforced by retaliatory actions by other nations against recalcitrants.

A World Court also exists, but it too has no power to enforce its decisions. Unfortunately, the two superpowers, whose observance of decisions would have the most influence on other nations to do the same, have been among the worst scofflaws. Recently, though, the Soviets have announced their intention of abiding by the court's decisions, and the United States has been showing signs of being more cooperative. In time, a tradition of observing World Court decisions and international regulatory sanctions could be built into a true governing system worldwide. But it won't be easy; the level of social development and "internationalism" varies enormously among nations.

The population/environment/resource/economic superproblems that loom in humanity's future demand a stronger, better-recognized, and better-respected system for managing the global commons. It may not be possible—or desirable—to create a strong centralized world government patterned after national governments, but a great deal of scope exists to build on the present model of diffuse, semi-independent agencies with different (though often overlapping) responsibilities, which tend to solve problems through consensus and international agreement.

A Global Commons Regime, using the Law of the Sea as a model, might be established to regulate human interactions with the atmosphere. Such a regime would, of course, have to be given some authority over such diverse activities as agriculture, the clearing of tropical forests, the generation of power, the use of internal-combustion engines, the manufacture of chemicals, plastics, and hair sprays, and the disposal of toxic wastes.

There is no guarantee that an effective Global Commons Regime could pull humanity through the coming crises; but it seems certain that without such a broad-gauge effort to deal with global population/environment problems, civilization will collapse. In the face of the common threat to all nations and peoples, the political quarrels now expressed in minor wars and revolutions, and even the competition between the East and West blocs, pale by comparison. One could hope that the overwhelming need to collaborate in averting the worst consequences of these superproblems could impel nations to forge new alliances and find avenues of cooperation, and to find peace. What needs to be done will require an effort that is nothing less than monumental. But the benefits for all of humanity, if the atmosphere/ocean commons could be cooperatively monitored and protected, would also be monumental.

A central problem facing us now is finding ways to convince national and international leaders and the world's people that opportunities for action to assure global environmental security are fast slipping away. To repeat the old saying, it's the top of the ninth and humanity has been hitting nature hard. But we must always remember that nature bats last!

12

▲

What You Can Do

▼

Okay, you say. The whole thing is overwhelming. What can I possibly do about it? At first glance, it doesn't look easy for an individual to help solve the human predicament. We can't choose to drive a 75-mile-per-gallon safe car until they're available on the market. It's impossible to ride mass-transit systems that don't yet exist. Consumers of food and wood products have little direct control over patterns of pesticide use in agriculture or forestry practices in the United States (let alone in Mexico or Brazil). Many problems of resource use or environmental deterioration are most effectively addressed through political action—when large groups of people have decided that things are going in the wrong direction and use the political system to change that direction.

But there is one very important thing that each of us *can* do about the population explosion: not have too many children. Ideally, each couple should have only one or, at the very most, two.

Let's face it: bringing up kids these days isn't easy (not

that it ever really was), and it gets more expensive every year. The cost of supporting a child from birth to college for today's middle-income parents in the United States will average more than $150,000 in current dollars, and sending the kid to college could double that[1]—no small investment.

The recent fashion for single parenthood by choice, whether by adoption or not, seems very strange to us personally. We can't decide whether those who try it are brave or foolhardy—or whether we're just getting old-fashioned![2] In any case, it's certainly not in society's interest (or the children's) to encourage single parenthood, especially among low-income teenage girls where the trend seems most prevalent. It's hard enough for two reasonably congenial, mature parents to handle the hassles and sometimes exhausting demands of parenthood; the burdens for only one can be overwhelming—especially if, as is often the case, the family's income is low. Children from single-parent homes appear to contribute significantly to our increasing drug and crime problems. Such children may also grow up with subtler social and emotional problems stemming from the lack of a father or mother.

Raising children is probably the most important task most of us will ever undertake. Obviously, it's easier to raise one or two children well than three, six, or ten. Many scientific studies have confirmed that, even in fairly affluent societies, children in small families on average grow into healthier, better-educated, and more successful adults than do children of large families.[3] Of course, we can all point to exceptions—unusually dedicated and talented parents who have produced a flock of overachievers, but these are truly exceptions. Most people can't meet those standards.

Today, of course, considerations must go beyond the very real advantages for the children of being in a small family. Our society's future depends on almost everyone having a small family. Citizens of rich countries, especially the United States, have an extraordinary opportunity to influence the future course of civilization by restricting their reproduction. While such restrictions are badly needed in poor countries too, the age composition in most rich countries will let population shrinkage begin much sooner. Given the relatively enormous impact of the average baby in a rich nation on the resources and environment of Earth, the fewer there are, the better the children's chances will be to live in a habitable world. Every birth avoided in rich nations today may make possible the future births of thousands of babies with rich prospects in centuries to come—babies that can never be born if civilization collapses.

A reasonable goal for the United States for the next decade or two might be typical family sizes of one or two children, averaging 1.5, only a little less than the 1.9 we have now. With no change in family size (and a small reduction in immigration),[4] the Census Bureau projects that our population will stop growing and start shrinking gradually around 2040, when there will be over 300 million of us.[5] But if more Americans take the responsible step of having no children or only one, we could much sooner end growth, with a smaller peak population, and begin slow shrinkage. At the same time, we could reduce the chances that our children would face a draconian Chinese-style population-control program if and when the U.S. government awakens to the need.

There are also many things you can do as a consumer to operate on the A (affluence) and T (technology) factors in the all-important $I = PAT$ equation. The collective choices we make as consumers can accelerate or slow global warming, acid rain, the loss of biodiversity, and so on. Individuals have a responsibility not just to restrain their reproduction, but wherever possible to make choices that help to preserve Earth's habitability. Eating less beef (A) and more vegetables, wearing sweaters while keeping the thermostat lower in the winter (A), and driving a fuel-efficient car (A and T) are three obvious helpful choices. So are taking a Sunday bike ride (T) instead of a drive in the car, buying energy-efficient lighting fixtures (T), and using cloth rather than disposable diapers (A and T). Donating some of your leisure time to tree planting is another (A). Note that while we've indicated eating less beef and forgoing watching TV to plant trees are reductions in "affluence," this is misleading. Both *are* reductions in consumption but also are activities that may give you a longer life. A whole book could be written on the many things people can do

to lower consumption (A) and discourage the use of environmentally damaging technologies (T) while improving the quality of their lives, but our topic in this book is population.[6]

Of course, there are plenty of things you can do in your
personal life about the P factor, overpopulation, besides restricting your own reproduction. You can persuade friends and
relatives to do the same. If it's too late for you (you already
have five kids), you can still influence your children (and
grandchildren) not to follow your example. If you have older
friends or relatives who are urging their offspring to produce
mobs of grandchildren, you can tease them about trying to get
their children to repeat their own mistakes—or ask them
whether they are trying to prevent their bank accounts from
exploding in the future by keeping them drained to help pay
for college for their grandchildren. Give them a year's membership in ZPG (see page 246) or the National Audubon Society
as a gift. Above all, keep it light. Suggesting that their attitude
is irresponsible in this day and age may be direct, but you're
unlikely to change their minds.

With your contemporaries, a direct approach *may* be more
successful. You can emphasize that being a "good parent"
today should mean not only providing the best possible up-
bringing for one or two children—working toward quality, not
quantity—but helping to see that future population size is such
that those children have a chance for a good life. But don't be
too intense. Talking casually about the population explosion
with your friends will help; concentrate on the "Take-Home
Messages" suggested on pages 237–39. Showing at least mild
disapproval of irresponsible reproductive actions can also help
to influence others. We, for example, don't give baby presents
for any child past number two. And we emphasize that people
who care so much for children that they want to have more
than two can accomplish that through adoption or being foster
parents—unless what they really care about is their own egos
rather than what will happen to their children's world. We
should instill this ethic in our society's children from the very
youngest age.

More public education is needed to develop more awareness about population issues. People still graduate from uni-

versities and colleges without knowing the size or growth rate of the human population—information that should be in every schoolchild's head by the sixth grade. Still less have they been taught to appreciate the connections between population growth and the deterioration in the quality of life they see every day: traffic jams, smog, urban blight, disappearing natural areas and greenbelts.

Changes can be made in school curricula by individuals through local PTAs, teacher associations, or school boards. Students themselves can bring about changes in curricula in colleges and universities (they did so widely in the late 1960s and 1970s, and many changes became permanent); so can concerned faculty members. And people can directly inform their own and their friends' and relatives' children about these matters. Take heart from the much greater proportion of people who are now at least alerted to the population problem compared with nearly total ignorance a quarter century ago.

Perhaps the major remaining problem in the United States and other rich countries is to inform those who know there is a population problem but believe it is confined to developing countries. We have found that, given a little additional information, those folks quickly grasp the enormous contribution overpopulation among the rich makes to the human predicament. Related to this is the notion, fortunately fading, that people with wealth or "good genes" must have large families because otherwise we'll be overwhelmed by the unintelligent, the poor, or the "genetically defective" (that usually means a member of some other race, religion, or social class).[7]

The many fallacies inherent in this view are dealt with in detail elsewhere.[8] We'll only point out here that if there were natural selection against "intelligence," it would take hundreds of years for the average intelligence of the population to change significantly; meanwhile the future of humanity will be determined demographically in a few decades. Furthermore, if we need more brainpower to help solve the human predicament, it could be most readily generated by improving our shoddy educational system and seeing that women, blacks, Hispanics, Native Americans, other minority groups, and the poor had full opportunity to develop their talents.

Not only are notions about the rich and intelligent passing on their good genes scientific nonsense, they are dangerous because they promote overreproduction by those with the heaviest impact on the planet. The use of fossil fuels by poor ghetto children is negligible compared to that of the executive with three big cars, a 5,000-square-foot home, and airline tickets for a vacation in Paris. Rich kids are a much greater threat to our future than poor kids, especially when the rich kids are raised to think the highest human calling is to make more money and spend it on gadgets. Our society must evolve to the point where it would be disgraceful for one's daughter to marry a real-estate developer who has turned a piece of Arizona desert into a subdivision with an artificial lake, helping to increase southwestern water deficits—or a man who owns a "muscle car" and makes an extra contribution to global warming while needlessly wasting gasoline.

Efforts can also be made to encourage the media to cover population-related subjects, from children's programming on up. Population growth indeed doesn't get enough attention in the newspapers or on television; little happens from day to day, so it isn't "news." Although journalists now are much better informed about the connections between resources, environmental problems, and population changes than they were twenty years ago, they still miss numerous opportunities to point them out.

Citizens can write letters to editors and TV stations and networks—or telephone them—noting the omitted facts or ideas. Any time gridlock, garbage-disposal quandaries, global warming, AIDS, and other population-related problems are discussed without bringing in the population connection, a storm of letters and phone calls should follow. Some sample letters to the media are appended to this chapter. You can use the "Take-Home Messages" list to help compose them.

Collective action can be more effective than that of an individual, especially at the national level. Political pressure is needed to push the United States into developing rational population and environmental policies for the nation and seeing that they are implemented. We have a great advantage in the United States in that, while our nation may not be widely beloved elsewhere, it is widely emulated. We have the opportunity to set a positive example for the world, and too frequently we've been setting a negative one.

How can Americans complain to Brazilians about the destruction of Amazonia and its contribution to global warming while we drive fuel-inefficient cars and are busily cutting down the magnificent old-growth forest of the Pacific Northwest and are destroying the Tongass rain forest in Alaska at public expense? How could we offer aid and advice to India on population control when our own population problems are so extremely serious and India is forty years ahead of us in trying to solve the problem? We must get our own house in order.

Doing so often means pressuring politicians. While individuals often feel powerless to affect political events, in the United States they aren't. An American's most important privilege—and responsibility—is to vote. It is entirely legitimate to ask any candidate requesting your vote where he or she stands on population, resource management, and environmental problems. And it never hurts to let candidates or officials know when you approve or disapprove of their actions or positions. Letters to members of Congress urging them to support or initiate action count much more heavily than many people think. They also appreciate being thanked.

There are a number of things you should keep in mind when writing. Suppose, for example, you write a pleasant letter to a congressman, Joe Glotz, asking for his position on a population-related issue or requesting that he press for some action to promote smaller family sizes. Do not then be fobbed off with a reply that basically says only "Thank you for your views." Instead, write again, politely insisting on a straightforward answer. If that doesn't work, send a third letter, saying that you and your friends are getting weary of evasive answers (or of his lack of action). If possible, get some of your friends to write also. Mention that you are considering organizing a campaign to get rid of Joe Glotz in the next election.

If that doesn't work and you've got the time, organize the campaign. Tell Glotz that you're going to send him home, far from the perks and glory of Capitol Hill. If possible, try to have his local office or local appearances picketed—even if you're the only sign carrier. The media love that sort of thing, and politicians *hate* it. Nothing throws a bigger scare into the worst of them than the thought of going back to being a private citizen. Remember, you *can* make a difference!

Taking on bad politicians is not the only effective action you can take. You can encourage the good ones—and there are more of those than many people think. For example, if Claudine Schneider (Republican representative, Rhode Island) and Timothy E. Wirth (Democratic senator, Colorado) are still promoting bills to take action to slow global warming, write to them and let them know how grateful you are for their efforts. Do the same for Albert Gore (Democratic senator, Tennessee), John Heinz (Republican senator, Pennsylvania), Alan Cranston (Democratic senator, California), and others who have made the effort to become well informed on population/environment problems.

Best of all, if you are so inclined, get into politics yourself. You can work behind the scenes as a campaign worker or an official's aide, or even run for office yourself.

If politics isn't your cup of tea, you can add your voice to those of others by joining and supporting public-interest organizations that are working for population control and environmental sanity. These groups advance their goals by educating the public, lobbying, and/or suing to move policies in the right direction. As social animals, most of us enjoy participating in a community effort to do anything, including saving the world. And politicians listen to organizations with large memberships (as witness the success of the National Rifle Association!), so join any you think are doing good things, even if you can afford only the minimum membership fee.

Some national organizations that we think are doing good jobs and deserve support, whether financial or through volunteer work, are listed at the end of the chapter. The list is by no means exhaustive and doesn't include a multitude of effective local organizations with relevant goals, any of which you could join and support. In fact, if you are a member of a church, you may be able to make it more active on issues relating to the stewardship of our planet—including population limitation.

One of the pleasant social ways of staying well informed is

to organize your friends into an informal network and divide up the chores of keeping track of various issues.[9] A division of labor with your friends who are concerned citizens can lighten everyone's burden and add to social enjoyment. If you are particularly interested in demographic issues, you could become your group's population expert. One of your friends who is interested in recycling might take on the task of keeping up on waste-disposal problems. Another who is particularly bugged by smog might concentrate on atmospheric problems. The political activist in your group could keep track of the degree to which your local politicians are trying to deal intelligently with the human predicament.

Don't fall into the trap of deciding you can work only with those you can agree with 100 percent on all issues. Try to keep an open mind and be very skeptical of "authorities." When you're through reading this book, check it out. Skepticism is a virtue to be cultivated. After all, we might be paid members of the international ecological conspiracy! Read something by Richard Grossman, who will doubtless consider us too deeply involved with the capitalist "establishment."[10] Follow the comments on the editorial page of *The Wall Street Journal*, which probably will describe us as crazed Communist doomsayers (if it ever mentions us at all). You and your friends should try to check both facts and analysis in anything you read. Do your own "back of the envelope" calculations—you'll be amazed at what simple arithmetic can tell you. A diversity of views is one of the great advantages of a democracy and should be seen as a benefit that helps keep everyone thinking about the issues. Just relax and save the world by working with people you agree with only 70 or 80 percent of the time.

We are convinced that the world *can* be saved. Serious as the human predicament seems, there is a bright side to the picture. That predicament was not caused by cosmic events totally beyond the control of *Homo sapiens*. It is entirely the result of human mismanagement, much of it stemming from the mismatch of our old minds functioning in a new world—a new world our old minds largely created. Human beings got themselves into this fix, and human beings can get themselves out. Therefore, when people ask us whether we're pessimistic or optimistic we always say that we're optimistic about what could be done, but rather pessimistic about whether humanity will get its act together and do it.

The reason for our optimism is historical. Given the political and social will, recent history shows that societies can undergo dramatic and rapid transformations. When we were young, it was almost unimaginable that in the 1980s the highest-paid performer in the United States would be black, that black athletes would dominate most professional sports, that there would be black airline pilots and generals, and that a black candidate would be a serious contender for the presidency of the United States. Although there is still a long way to go in expunging racism from American society and in improving the economic condition of the black community, enormous strides in opening opportunities have been made since our youth, and the most critical changes took place in little more than a decade in the late 1950s and early 1960s.[11] At the same time, the status of women changed dramatically, and that helped to fuel a major and rapid demographic change.

In the 1960s, we were repeatedly told by social scientists that it was unlikely that birthrates would fall to replacement level in the United States until after the year 2000, even if the government encouraged smaller families. The government, of course, did nothing of the sort, but family size dropped to below replacement in a few years in the early 1970s. Clearly, when circumstances are ripe, dramatic changes, even in things thought to be very personal and difficult to alter (like reproductive behavior), can happen very fast.

Similarly, we know that the economic system can be transformed very rapidly, given the proper stimulus. In about a year in 1942 the U.S. economy went onto a wartime footing. Factories were converted from making automobiles to making tanks, women were recruited into the work force in large numbers, rationing and price controls were instituted, and so on. In 1945–46, the entire process was reversed. Then it took only a little more than a decade to rebuild the war-shattered economies of Europe and Japan. All that was required was for the vast majority of people to agree that the necessary changes had to be made and the required price paid. Economies are more complex now, and resources scarcer, but an economic transformation in the absence of wartime destruction clearly could be made in a decade or so, given the will.

There is no substitute for an informed citizenry, if rapid progress is to be made in solving the population problem and other elements of the human predicament. The mass media have made politicians all too aware that they are operating in a goldfish bowl. What is needed today is voters well versed on population and environmental matters carefully peering into the bowl and making sure that the goldfish are doing the things required to limit population size and solve the other parts of the human predicament.

Perhaps the very best way to approach American politicians is with an analogy. In recent years people have become very worried by the state of the aircraft flown by U.S. air carriers. The average age of the jet fleet is now thirteen years, roughly twice that of airlines of other industrialized countries, and there have been disturbing accidents that appear to be traceable to the deteriorating condition of the fleet. Whatever the actual danger, people are worried that the safety margin in flying is being reduced. The Federal Aviation Administration has mandated steps to strengthen older airliners in an attempt to preserve the margin of safety originally designed into them. When new aircraft are constructed, of course, they are made as "fail-safe" as possible within the limitations of weight and economics. That is, they are designed so that if one structural component or system fails, there is a backup system that will prevent the first failure from causing a crash.

Curiously enough, though, when it comes to the size of the human population and its impact on the deteriorating structure and systems of spaceship Earth, there is no general consensus in our government (or in those of most other nations) that a fail-safe design be maintained—that a margin of error be provided against catastrophic failure of human life-support systems. In fact, much of the public discourse is just the other way around. For a long time, efforts to abate acid rain were opposed because there was no "proof" that it could be damaging to lakes and forests. Steps to slow climate change induced by the greenhouse warming have been opposed because it is not certain what direction those changes will take. And, above all, population growth has been encouraged as if an experiment were being run to see just exactly how many people could be jammed onto Earth before the population crashed.

It is difficult to see the point of such an experiment. Those who believe in the intrinsic good of having large numbers of people (for instance, as future souls to be processed into a better world) clearly should wish for a population size stabilized at well below the carrying capacity at any given time. Having, say, one billion people alive all the time for four million more years obviously would create a greater cumulative total than topping out at 10 billion in the next century and then dying out or collapsing to a population of a few hundred thousand people eking out a livelihood on an impoverished planet for the next four million years. Is it somewhere written that a major goal of humanity should be to maximize the number of human beings living *all at once?*

We hope that you already are the sort of citizen who will carry such messages to your political representatives, or that you will become one. We urge you to "tithe to society" —to put at least one tenth of your time into learning about the human predicament and working to make a better world for yourself and your descendants. Only a mass movement can solve the population/resource/environment crisis before it overwhelms us.

► **TAKE-HOME MESSAGES** ◄

We hope that you have gained some insights about the seriousness and importance of population trends from reading this book. To summarize the most significant aspects of the subject, we have devised the following list of "take-home" messages, to keep in mind when you see, read, and hear discussions about the human dilemma in the future.

THE 1990 POPULATION OF EARTH IS OVER 5.3 BILLION PEOPLE, AND SOME 95 MILLION ARE BEING ADDED YEARLY.

UNPRECEDENTED OVERPOPULATION AND CONTINUING POPULATION GROWTH ARE MAKING SUBSTANTIAL CONTRIBUTIONS TO THE DESTRUCTION OF EARTH'S LIFE-SUPPORT SYSTEMS.

OVERPOPULATION IS A MAJOR FACTOR IN PROBLEMS AS DIVERSE AS AFRICAN FAMINES, GLOBAL WARMING, ACID RAIN, THE THREAT OF NUCLEAR WAR, THE GARBAGE CRISIS, AND THE DANGER OF EPIDEMICS.

OVERPOPULATION IN RICH COUNTRIES IS, FROM THE STANDPOINT OF EARTH'S HABITABILITY, MORE SERIOUS THAN RAPID POPULATION GROWTH IN POOR COUNTRIES.

RAPID POPULATION GROWTH IN POOR NATIONS IS AN IMPORTANT REASON THEY STAY POOR, AND OVERPOPULATION IN THOSE NATIONS WILL GREATLY INCREASE THEIR DESTRUCTIVE IMPACT ON THE ENVIRONMENT AS THEY STRUGGLE TO DEVELOP.

THERE IS NO QUESTION THAT THE POPULATION EXPLOSION WILL END SOON. WHAT REMAINS IN DOUBT IS WHETHER THE END WILL COME HUMANELY BECAUSE BIRTHRATES HAVE BEEN LOWERED, OR TRAGICALLY THROUGH RISES IN DEATH RATES.

ANYONE WHO OPPOSES CONTROLLING THE NUMBER OF BIRTHS IS UNKNOWINGLY PROMOTING MORE PREMATURE DEATHS.

EARTH CANNOT LONG SUSTAIN EVEN 5.3 BILLION PEOPLE WITH FORESEEABLE TECHNOLOGIES AND PATTERNS OF HUMAN BEHAVIOR. IF CIVILIZATION IS TO SURVIVE, POPULATION *SHRINKAGE* BELOW TODAY'S SIZE EVENTUALLY WILL BE NECESSARY.

POPULATION CONTROL IS THE MOST PRESSING OF HUMAN PROBLEMS BECAUSE OF THE ENORMOUS LAG TIME BETWEEN BEGINNING AN EFFECTIVE PROGRAM AND STARTING POPULATION SHRINKAGE.

A MAXIMUM NUMBER OF PEOPLE WILL LIVE EVENTUALLY IF THE POPULATION IS REDUCED TO A SUSTAINABLE SIZE AND MAINTAINED FOR MILLIONS OF YEARS. TRYING TO SEE HOW MANY CAN LIVE *ALL AT ONCE* IS A RECIPE FOR A POPULATION CRASH THAT WILL LOWER EARTH'S CARRYING CAPACITY AND REDUCE THE NUMBER OF PEOPLE THAT CAN EVER EXIST.

THE POPULATION/RESOURCE/ENVIRONMENT PREDICAMENT WAS CRE-
ATED BY HUMAN ACTIONS, AND IT CAN BE SOLVED BY HUMAN ACTIONS.
ALL THAT IS REQUIRED IS THE POLITICAL AND SOCIETAL WILL. THE
GOOD NEWS IS THAT, WHEN THE TIME IS RIPE, SOCIETY CAN CHANGE
ITS ATTITUDES AND BEHAVIOR RAPIDLY.

WE MUST ALL TITHE TO SOCIETY IN ORDER TO RIPEN THE TIME.

► **SAMPLES OF LETTERS SENT TO** ◄
INFLUENTIAL PEOPLE

LETTER FROM A CITIZEN TO A CONGRESSMAN

June 12, 1989

Congressman Tom Campbell
1730 Longworth Building
Washington, DC 20515

Dear Congressman Campbell:

It seems as though the problems of overcrowding in the
San Francisco Bay Area get worse every day. The air quality
is often terrible, there is near-gridlock on the highways at all
hours of the day and night, and green hillsides are giving way
to suburbs and other urban development. It's past time for you
and other Bay Area Congressmen to hold back growth and plan
for the future before we end up with another Los Angeles right
here.

Unfortunately, what's happening here is just a manifesta-
tion of a global problem. I am concerned about the kind
of world that we will be leaving to our children and grandchildren. Issues such as the greenhouse warming, acid deposition, and ozone depletion need immediate attention, but
these problems will never be solved without addressing the
underlying problem, the human population. These problems
are not just for the rest of the world to worry about, but
for the United States as well. I'm afraid that the trend
started in the Reagan administration of working against

population control (not to mention lack of leadership in tackling other global issues) is continuing. The administration's recent proposal on air quality is somewhat encouraging, but my perception is that it ignores both population and global contexts.

I urge you and your colleagues to start immediately on legislation to bring U.S. population growth to a halt, indeed to start a slow decline, and to provide appropriate aid to other nations wishing to do the same thing. I realize that you will be opposed in your efforts, but if you provide leadership on this issue, I can promise that you will create dedicated new supporters who will work hard to see that you are returned to Washington in the next election to carry on the fight for our futures.

Sincerely,
PAMELA MATSON

LETTER FROM A CITIZEN TO THE PRESIDENT

May 10, 1989

President George Bush
White House
Washington, D.C.

Dear President Bush:

During the 1988 campaign, I was pleased when you announced that you would become the "environmental president." It disturbs me, however, to see that you apparently don't realize that one cannot be the environmental president without also being the *population* president. There is, of course, a great deal that can and should be done directly to protect our environment by becoming cleverer in our use of technology and by reducing America's wasteful consumption of natural resources. But in the long run, it will all be to no avail, unless the numbers of Americans, and people around the world can be brought under control.

I understand that the issue of population limitation is a

political hot potato—but leaders are supposed to be able to deal with hot potatoes. It is high time that you called for a national population policy, made it clear that "patriotic Americans stop at two," and started the United States on the road back to the international forefront on this issue—instead of behaving like a banana republic in the 1950's.

Anyone who flew a torpedo bomber off an aircraft carrier in the Second World War has got to have had courage. Show us you still have it, and make a singular place for yourself in world history by taking the lead now while there is still chance to keep our civilization intact.

Sincerely,
GRETCHEN DAILY

LETTER FROM A CATHOLIC SCIENTIST TO THE POPE

Department of Biological Sciences
Stanford University
Stanford, California 94305

June 3, 1989

His Holiness Pope John Paul II
Vatican City
Rome, Italy

Your Holiness:

In 1968 I wrote to Pope Paul VI that "a change in the teaching of the Church with regard to birth control would be reasonable and consistent with the concept of development of doctrine that has so long been part of Christian tradition." I was seriously concerned about the possibility of famines related to overpopulation, and indeed those famines have occurred. On the order of 200 million people have died needlessly as a result of hunger and hunger-related diseases since I tried to alert Pope Paul to the deteriorating population situation. And now your advisors are continuing the inhumane policies that, all over the world, force Catholics to choose between what their intelligence and moral sense tell them and a doctrine which is dangerously outmoded.

As a Catholic botanist I was extremely disturbed by the statement of your bishops (made at the time of the Reaffirmation of Humanae Vitae) that the world could theoretically feed 40 billion people. I do not have a single scientific colleague who believes that that "theory" has anything to do with the realities humanity now faces. Indeed, the best scientists are convinced that it will be nearly impossible to give even the 5.2 billion people on earth today all a diet such as you and I enjoy, and that trends in agriculture are leading us toward a massive population–food imbalance in the next decade or so.

Obviously everything possible should be done to maximize food production, short of doing long-term damage to the food producing system itself. But that kind of long-term damage is exactly what is being inflicted right now—through deforestation causing climate change and the extinction of the relatives of crops, through massive erosion, through the "mining" of aquifers, and so on. Each year farmers must feed 90 million more people using 25 billion tons less topsoil.

I am sad to tell you that reaffirming Humanae Vitae was a great mistake. Anyone working to prevent bringing human birth rates down today is simply working to increase death rates. I know that is not your intention, but intentions have no influence on natural systems. For the good of humanity and the future of our Church, I urge you to reconsider your position on this issue, and get the Church back on the side of humanity instead of dogma.

Sincerely yours,
JOHN H. THOMAS
Professor

LETTER FROM A CITIZEN TO A STATE GOVERNOR

May 15, 1989

Governor George Deukmejian
State Capitol Building
Sacramento, CA 95814

Dear Governor Deukmejian:

As a native Californian, I have become increasingly de-
pressed by the decline in the quality of life in our state. The
air is foul, the freeways are jammed, the flower-filled fields
where I used to like to hike have become occupied by subdi-
visions, water shortages are increasing, crime rates are rising,
hideous new resorts are defiling the coastline, suburban sprawl
is marching up our hillsides, and off-road vehicles are tearing
up our once-beautiful deserts.

Much of the decline of our state can be traced to an insane
policy of growth for growth's sake—a policy that has made
California more populous than the entire nation of Canada.
And yet, you have, incredibly, chosen to attack state support
for family planning programs.

I beg you to reverse your position. We have more than
enough people, and more than enough children bearing children. Indeed, in the absence of any action at the federal level,
I plead with you to become the first governor of California to
take the lead in pushing for population control at both the
national and state level. Unless something is done about the
burgeoning numbers of Californians, I see nothing but trouble
ahead for our once-beautiful state. There will be increasing
demands for northern Californians to ship water to the south,
an area where *air* is in short supply.

There will also be increasing conflicts between residential,
industrial, and agricultural uses of that water. Gridlock on our
freeways will make life a nightmare for our commuters, and
our scientific and industrial base will be eroded as highly talented people who are attracted to California's life style move
to the southeast, northwest, and elsewhere to escape California's deteriorating environment.

California should be at the front line of providing demographic information, sex education, and contraceptive services in public schools (making condoms available to high school students and teaching them to use them will not only help curb teenage pregnancies, but also will cut down on the transmission of AIDS). This state should encourage the enactment of zoning ordinances everywhere to severely restrict or stop further water and sewer hook-ups and generally discourage both people and industry from coming into our state.

Obviously, California cannot solve the nation's or the world's population problem as a whole, but it *can* start setting an example. Remember, as Edward Abbey put it, "Perpetual growth is the creed of the cancer cell." By reversing your course you could go down in history as a great leader.

Sincerely,
DENNIS D. MURPHY

LETTER TO A PROTESTANT CLERGYMAN

The Reverend Mr. Wm. Norman

Dear Bill:

In recent decades there has been a cheering increase in the religious community of concern for people in the here and now. Ministers, priests, and rabbis have been at the forefront of the civil rights movement, campaigns for disarmament, and the fight for economic equity—to bring health to our growing population of poor and homeless people.

I am writing to urge you to put much more of your effort into assuring that we will retain a world in which those battles can be fought and, hopefully, won. The explosion of human numbers and affluence (among the already rich) and the faulty technologies with which we try to meet increasing demands for goods, are threatening to destroy the habitability of our planet.

It is especially important in view of the lack of political leadership in Washington and Sacramento that the clergy fill the void and help to solve a problem that contributes to almost all of the ills that afflict humanity. If we stop human population growth, that will not automatically remove the threat of nuclear war, it will not restore our environment, it will not end racism, sexism, religious prejudice, and gross economic inequity. But unless the size of the human population is controlled, we won't even get the chance to try and solve those problems.

I have personally worked long and hard to see that all people have access to family planning services. I am now afraid that the assault on Roe v. Wade will be successful and that both the personal rights of women and the future of my children and grandchildren will be threatened. Any leadership you can provide on this issue will be deeply appreciated.

Sincerely yours,
MARGO HEATH

ENCOURAGING LETTER TO A SENATOR

July 1, 1989

Senator Timothy Wirth
380 Russell Senate Office Building
Washington, D.C. 20510

Dear Senator Wirth:

I just wanted to write and thank you for the effort you have put in over the last few years in trying to keep our planet habitable. Your pioneering work on global warming legislation was especially appreciated. The fact that you recognized the population component to the global warming problem makes you a stand-out among legislators.

As residents of Colorado, we are especially proud to have you representing our state. In the next election, we will be working to see to it that you continue to be a force for good in Washington. Keep up the good work.

Sincerely,
ALANSON HEGEMAN
MARCIA HEGEMAN

►   **ORGANIZATIONS WORKING TO SOLVE**   ◄
               POPULATION PROBLEMS

Activist Population Organizations

The following are the most prominent groups that not only carry out public educational programs on population matters, but also lobby Congress or (in the case of CAPS) state legislatures.

Californians for Population Stabilization (CAPS)
1025 Ninth Street, No. 217
Sacramento, CA 95814

National Abortion Rights Action League (NARAL)
1101 Fourteenth Street NW, 5th floor
Washington, D.C. 20005

Planned Parenthood Federation of America, Inc.
810 Seventh Avenue
New York, NY 10019
Planned Parenthood operates the largest private network of family-planning services in the United States, as well as actively lobbying for population concerns, both domestic policies and the U.S. population-assistance programs. It is the U.S. member of the International Planned Parenthood Federation (headquartered in London), which, through its national affiliates, provides family-planning services to people around the world.

Zero Population Growth (ZPG)
1400 Sixteenth Street NW, Suite 320
Washington, D.C. 20036
ZPG is a lobbying and public education organization.focusing primarily on U.S. policies.

Activist Environmental Groups

Many environmental organizations have population programs or policies; the following are some of the better-known ones.

Friends of the Earth/Environmental Policy Institute
218 D Street SE
Washington, D.C. 20003

National Audubon Society, Inc.
950 Third Avenue
New York, NY 10022

The Sierra Club, Inc.
730 Polk Street
San Francisco, CA 94109

Population Organizations

The following are leading sources of information and public education focusing primarily on population issues. The list is by no means exhaustive. Several universities (for instance, Johns Hopkins, Princeton, and the Universities of North Carolina and Michigan) have excellent population-studies programs.

Alan Guttmacher Institute (AGI)
111 Fifth Avenue
New York, NY 10003
As the educational affiliate of Planned Parenthood, AGI publishes, among other things, *Family Planning Perspectives* and *International Family Planning Perspectives*.

Population Council
One Dag Hammerskjold Plaza
New York, NY 10017
An organization long involved with family-planning programs in developing nations, the Population Council produces numerous publications on the subject, including *Population and Development Review*.

Population Crisis Committee
1120 Nineteenth Street NW, Suite 550
Washington, D.C. 20036-3605

Population Institute
110 Maryland Avenue NE
Washington, D.C. 20002

Population Reference Bureau, Inc.
777 Fourteenth Street NW, Suite 800
Washington, D.C. 20005

The PRB is the source of the annual *World Population Data Sheet*, *Population Bulletin*, and a plethora of other useful publications, including materials for school programs.

Organizations Involved in Public Education on Population/Resource/Environment Issues Combined

Center for Conservation Biology, *and*
Morrison Institute of Population and Resource Studies
Department of Biological Sciences
Stanford University
Stanford, CA 94305
These two research and educational organizations are separate but share many concerns; some projects are co-sponsored by both groups.

Global Tomorrow Coalition
1325 G Street NW, Suite 915
Washington, D.C. 20005
The coalition serves as a liaison organization among numerous population and environmental organizations, and sponsors "Globescope" conferences.

Population/Environment Balance
1325 G Street NW, Suite 1003
Washington, D.C. 20005

World Resources Institute
1735 New York Avenue NW
Washington, D.C. 20006
WRI produces the detailed biennial report *World Resources* and numerous useful reports on different subjects in the population/resource/environment field.

Worldwatch Institute
1776 Massachusetts Avenue NW
Washington, D.C. 20036
Worldwatch Institute produces the annual *State of the World* volume, a series of *Worldwatch Reports*, and the new magazine *World Watch*, all full of useful information on the human predicament.

World Wildlife Fund
1250 Twenty-fourth Street NW
Washington, D.C. 20037
The international organization, now calling itself World-Wide
Fund for Nature to reflect its broader interests, has begun to
incorporate population growth into its concerns.

Some Other Social Groups Concerned with Population Issues

Federation for Action on Immigration Reform (FAIR)
1424 Sixteenth Street NW, Room 701
Washington, D.C. 20036

National Organization for Women (NOW)
15 West 18th Street
New York, NY 10011
NOW has been active in promoting women's rights, including
rights to abortion and access to birth control.

Other Sources of Population Information

United Nations Fund for Population Activities (UNFPA)
220 East 42nd Street
New York, NY 10017

U.S. Department of Health and Human Services
National Center for Health Statistics
3700 East–West Highway
Hyattsville, MD 20782

The World Bank
1818 H Street NW
Washington, D.C. 20433

▶   BOOKS FOR FURTHER READING   ◀

Although potential sources of additional information can be
located in the Notes and obtained from organizations noted
above, we list here a few books which supply concentrated
doses of supplementary material. Some periodic sources,

rather than standard books, are key resources. Worldwatch Institute's superb annual volume *State of the World* and the Population Reference Bureau's information-packed annual *World Population Data Sheet* are both essential if you wish to stay well informed about the population crisis and related issues.

Brundtland, G. H., Chairman, World Commission on Environment and Development. *Our Common Future*. Oxford University Press, Oxford, 1987. The importance of this work is not that it contains any new analysis, but that it was issued by a quasi-governmental entity and conveys some sense of urgency, despite its impeccably conservative source.

Daly, H. E. *Steady State Economics*. W. H. Freeman, San Francisco, 1977. Probably the most important book on economics of this century.

Ehrlich, A. H., and P. R. Ehrlich. *Earth*. Franklin Watts, New York, 1987. A broad, nonquantitative overview of the population/resource/environment-conflict situation, with color illustrations.

Ehrlich, P. R. *The Machinery of Nature*. Simon and Schuster, New York, 1986. Describes the ecological and evolutionary scientific background of the human predicament.

———, L. Bilderback, and A. H. Ehrlich. *The Golden Door: International Migration, Mexico, and the United States*. Wideview Books, New York, 1981. An overview of the migration component of population problems, focused on the U.S. and Mexico.

———, and A. H. Ehrlich. *Extinction: The Causes and Consequences of the Disappearance of Species*. Random House, New York, 1981. An overview of the loss of one of the most precious parts of the human legacy, the other life forms that ultimately support humanity.

———, and S. Feldman. *The Race Bomb: Skin Color, Prejudice and Intelligence*. New York Times/Quadrangle, New York, 1977. Explodes the myth that there are genetically superior groups of people who should be encouraged to breed and genetically defective ones who should be discouraged.

Harte, John. *Consider a Spherical Cow: A Course in Environmental Problem Solving.* William Kaufmann, Los Altos, Calif., 1985. An excellent primer if you want to learn how to do your own "back of the envelope" calculations.

Myers, Norman. *Gaia: An Atlas of Planet Management.* Doubleday/Anchor, New York, 1984. A gold mine of information on population/resource/environment issues.

Ornstein, R., and P. Ehrlich. *New World/New Mind: Moving Toward Conscious Evolution.* Doubleday, New York, 1989. A discussion of why people have so much difficulty perceiving and acting on the gradual environmental trends (such as population growth) that threaten our future, and of what can be done to end that difficulty.

Schneider, S. H. *Global Warming.* Sierra Club Books, San Francisco, 1989. An in-depth analysis of what is probably the most serious population-related problem, by an outstanding scientist.

APPENDIX

▲

Aspects of How
Earth Works

▼

A lack of basic background on the history and functioning of our planet is a major barrier to many people's understanding the seriousness of the population/resource/environment crisis. It's a pity, for the history and functioning of our planet and our population are fascinating subjects, as well as being crucial knowledge if we are to increase our individual and collective chances of survival. Here we expand on some background topics that are important to understanding the influence of human population growth in shaping our future.

Earth, the only known life-bearing planet, is a marvelously intricate self-sustaining system. During the four billion or so years that life has existed here, it has evolved into millions of distinctly different kinds of organisms. Over the ages, these evolving life forms have reshaped the planet itself in a variety of ways to make it more hospitable. For instance, the very composition of the atmosphere—the oxygen-rich air that animals breathe—is a result of the activities of organisms, primarily green plants, over eons of Earth's history. Nonhuman organisms are still active in maintaining a favorable balance of atmospheric gases.

▶   **THE FIRST GREEN REVOLUTION**   ◀

The sun provides virtually all the energy that powers the Earth system—both living and nonliving components.[1] Green plants and some microorganisms (which from here on we will often simply call "green plants"),[2] both in the oceans and on land, are able to capture the energy in sunlight in a complicated process known as photosynthesis and convert it into chemical energy. In this process, they extract carbon dioxide from the atmosphere and combine it with water to produce carbohydrates (sugars, starches, and cellulose). Some of the sun's energy is captured in the bonds that hold these large chemical molecules together. The "waste" product of photosynthesis is oxygen; if it were not for green plants, Earth's atmosphere would have no oxygen.

The green plants use some of the energy "fixed" in this fashion in the chemical bonds of carbohydrates for their own life processes—maintenance, growth, and reproduction. The energy stored in green plants is the foundation of life for all other organisms. All animals and decomposer organisms gain their energy by feeding on green plants, directly or indirectly. And they use the plants' waste oxygen to extract energy efficiently from their food and drive their own life processes.[3]

Green plants, in addition to providing the energy to support the rest of the living world, also make proteins and other relatively complex organic chemicals (such as vitamins), using not only carbon dioxide and water but a variety of other minerals obtained from soil or (by aquatic plants) water. These elements, needed by most forms of life and made available by plants, are known as nutrients.

Some nutrients are quite common in the Earth system (carbon, nitrogen); others exist in smaller amounts (sulfur, iron, calcium) or in tiny trace amounts (copper, selenium). All are required by most life forms, including ourselves. Because they are essential for life, the global community of organisms cycles these materials in complex paths through the living and nonliving parts of the system. The green plants—producers—first provide energy and nutrients to animals that feed on these plants, and these animals in turn pass them on to animals that eat the plant-eaters, and so on. All of these are consumers, and this series of steps from producers to plant-eaters and those that devour them is known as a food chain. At each step in a food chain, decomposer organisms feed on wastes and dead bodies of both plants and animals, digesting them and returning the elemental nutrients in them to the soil or the body of water, where they will again be available to green plants.[4]

BIOTIC COMMUNITIES

This picture highlights the interdependence that indeed exists among life forms. Groups of plants, consumers, and decomposers in any one place are known as communities. Often, the plants, animals, and microorganisms that coexist in a community have evolved together over a long period of time.

Natural communities are relatively rarely plagued by "pests." Most ecosystems are composed of thousands of different species of plants, animals, and microorganisms; and the existence of several potential predators and parasites for each organism, whether herbivore (plant-eater) or carnivore (animal-eater), usually prevents the buildup of any population to pest levels. Despite the rarity of pest outbreaks in ecosystems, producers run the risk of being consumed completely, which, of course, would be the end of the community.

Green plants can't run away, but they are by no means defenseless. A plant species can hide among other plants by having a widely scattered population, which defeats animals and plant diseases that specialize on it. This creates some problems for the plants' reproduction, but various devices, such as relying on the wind, water, or animals (birds, insects, mammals, etc.) to transfer pollen and disperse seeds, have been developed to overcome this disadvantage. Camouflage and mechanical defenses, such as thorns and tough skin, also discourage consumers. And many plants, having coevolved with their consumers for ages, have developed a great variety of chemical defenses—poisons and noxious odors and flavors —to protect themselves.[5]

Animals too have evolved numerous ways of defending themselves against predators, some of which resemble the plants' strategies. They hide, rely on camouflage, use poisons and noxious substances (sometimes obtained directly from plants), wear armor (clams, beetles, turtles, and armadillos), live in large groups (herds of antelope, schools of fishes), fight, and escape by flying, swimming, or running away.

At the same time, predators have evolved ways to overcome the defenses of their prey. Herbivores have ways of finding their preferred foods and of circumventing physical and chemical defenses. Plant-eating insects, with their short generation times, are especially adept at rapidly evolving resistance to the poisons employed by plants. Predators on animals too have evolved ways to overcome the defenses of their prey: by detecting hidden quarry, pursuing it, or cutting vulnerable individuals out of the herd. Plants and herbivores, like predators and prey, are often involved in "coevolutionary races," in which the winner gains access to rich resources and the loser faces extinction.

Coevolution has produced any number of intimate relationships among organisms besides that of predator and prey. Many species compete for the same or similar resources, such as food, water, or living space. But competition for food may be reduced by specializing on slightly different prey organisms, or by feeding at different times or in different places.

Another kind of coevolved relationship is mutualism—in which two very different organisms may coexist in mutually beneficial ways. Examples include the algae and fungi that coexist as complex structures called lichens; the algae obtain energy through photosynthesis, and the fungi supply protective covering and storage capacity and extract nutrients from rock, soil, or air. Somewhat less intimately, a honeybee obtains nectar in exchange for transferring a plant's pollen. Another very important case is certain kinds of bacteria that live in nodules on the roots of legumes (members of the pea family), capturing atmospheric nitrogen and converting it to a form usable by plants in exchange for sugar provided by the legume. This particular mutualistic relationship thus plays an important part in one of the most critical nutrient cycles operated by ecosystems.

Many coevolutionary interactions occur in the most complex ecosystems on Earth, humid tropical forests, which contain by far the greatest diversity of organisms. Perhaps 40 percent or more of Earth's complement of species are found in those regions, although they occupy only a small fraction—less than 7 percent—of the world's land surface.[6]

ECOSYSTEMS

The organisms that comprise a community and the physical environment with which they interact—including soil, water, atmosphere, terrain, etc.—are collectively known as an "ecosystem."

While both nutrients and energy move through the food webs (interwoven food chains) of an ecosystem, they follow paths that differ in one important respect. Nutrients are continually cycled through an ecosystem and are mostly retained within it (although major parts of the cycles may occur in the nonliving portions of the system). They make up the great "biogeochemical cycles" of carbon, nitrogen, sulfur, potassium, and so on.[7] When an animal dies, for example, the materials of its body are broken down by decomposers and the nutrients are released to soil, water, or air, from which they again become available to plants. Energy, by contrast, moves only one way through food chains. Usually, most of the energy is lost at every step, because each organism uses some of it to operate its own life processes, and when energy is used, some of it is always degraded to less available forms.[8] As a rule of thumb, only about one tenth of the energy present at each level in a food chain is available to the consumer at the next step upward.

This loss of usable energy has crucial implications for the way ecosystems are organized. A diagram of energy availability is shaped like a pyramid, with the greatest amount flowing into the green plants, much less being available for the plant-eaters (herbivores), and rapidly diminishing quantities going into each level of meat-eaters (carnivores). Likewise, the weight of living material at each level in an ecosystem is usually pyramidal.[9] The green plants at the base have the greatest mass, and succeeding levels of consumers are proportionately smaller, with the predators at the tops of food chains generally having the least living weight (biomass). There is a greater weight of grass than of antelopes, a greater weight of antelopes than of lions, and a greater weight of lions than of ticks that live on the lions.

The small amount of energy available at the upper ends of food chains limits the population sizes of animals in those positions. Human beings get an important part of the protein for their diets by feeding high on food chains. One likely consequence of the explosive growth of the human population is that *Homo sapiens*, on average, will be forced to find more of its food lower down—that is, become more vegetarian.

A TAMED PLANET

The taming of Earth, a planet originally very hostile to life, was a long and arduous process. For most of the nearly four billion years Earth has existed, life was confined to the oceans. In those oceans, the first photosynthesizing organisms were bacteria. Very gradually, over billions of years, the photosynthetic activities of oceanic organisms built up the concentration of free oxygen—that waste product of photosynthesis—in the oceans and the atmosphere.

The slow buildup of oxygen in the atmosphere made it possible for life to survive on land in two ways. One important change was the availability of oxygen in the air for respiration —the main process by which energy in carbohydrates is released and used—by both plants and animals. Respiration is the slow "burning" process by which oxygen is used to release the energy stored in chemical bonds; it is, in essence, the opposite of photosynthesis, resulting in an uptake of oxygen and a release of carbon dioxide.

The other way was less obvious, but was essential for life to flourish on land. Some of the oxygen reacted under the influence of ultraviolet radiation to produce an unusual form, ozone, which has three oxygen atoms joined together instead of the two found in a normal oxygen molecule. Ozone formed a diffuse layer high in the upper atmosphere, the stratosphere, where it absorbs the sun's radiation in the near-ultraviolet part of the spectrum.[10] Ultraviolet radiation of those wavelengths is broadly damaging to most life forms, and until it was screened out by the ozone shield in the atmosphere, organisms could survive only under water, which also filters out ultraviolet.

In the photosynthetic process, carbon was taken (as carbon dioxide) from the oceans and the atmosphere and incorporated into the tissues of organisms.[11] Much later, some of this carbon was isolated from the natural carbon cycles for eons as undecomposed dead plants and microbes were buried and preserved by geological processes. This had two important consequences: the accumulation of oxygen in the atmosphere was accelerated, and the preserved carbon-rich organic material was slowly transformed into fossil fuels.

Once established on land, plants, animals, and microorganisms evolved into a diversity of new forms and in turn substantially modified their new environments. The process was anything but smooth, however. Continents move around the planet's surface on gigantic "plates" in a process called plate tectonics.[12] The drifting continents crept from one climatic region to another—from the tropics to the poles—subjecting their living passengers, over time, to enormous changes in climatic regimes as well as to physical changes in Earth's surface and varying sea levels.[13] The result of all these slow environmental changes was a further diversification of organisms as they evolved in response to changed conditions. The distribution of mineral deposits beneath Earth's surface today also is the result of billions of years of this tectonic movement and associated geological phenomena, such as volcanic activity and mountain-building.

ANCIENT EXTINCTIONS

In addition to the gradual environmental changes induced by the extremely slow geological phenomena such as shifts of the continents, relatively rapid and severe environmental changes apparently occurred on several occasions, with catastrophic consequences for the life forms existing at those times. The best-known and most recent such event took place some 65 million years ago, when the dinosaurs disappeared from Earth along with a wide array of other kinds of organisms.[14] It is not clear from the fossil record whether this massive extinction event took place over a few hundred thousand years in response to a widespread change in climate or other environmental factors, or whether it occurred much more suddenly as a result of some externally caused cataclysm.

Possible causes for such a catastrophe include Earth's being sideswiped by a comet with a very erratic orbit or struck by an unusually large meteorite, either of which could have hurled billions of tons of dust into the atmosphere, blocking out most of the sunlight for several months. The darkness and lower temperatures would have killed or severely damaged most green plants and decimated the animals dependent on them both on land and in the sea. The fireball resulting from the impact would have produced enough nitrogen oxides to destroy the ozone layer completely, subjecting Earth's surface to a deadly flux of ultraviolet-B radiation.[15] A large fraction of the life forms existing then, even major groups of plants and animals, could have perished from such conditions.

The consequent gross impoverishment of flora and fauna would have led to profound changes in communities and ecosystems, and the recovery of life to its former luxuriance took a very long time. Climates apparently changed substantially around that time, favoring new directions for evolution. The absence of many kinds of organisms also opened new opportunities for those that had survived. Thus the disappearance of the previously dominant dinosaurs is thought to have opened the way for diversification of the previously obscure mammals, a diversification that eventually produced humanity.

Whether these wrenching changes in Earth's flora and fauna occurred abruptly or over many thousands of years, their long-term result is our own existence and the assemblage of species that now share the planet with us. Indeed, this episode in the evolution of our planet not only led to the appearance of human beings but put the finishing touches on our hospitable environment. Many of the kinds of organisms and communities most familiar to us, and on which we have based our civilization, also appeared during the past several million years. Thus gradually, over its long history, Earth has been dramatically changed by the evolution of life itself, making it increasingly habitable (from the human point of view).

VEGETATION AND CLIMATE

But, unbeknownst to most people, the process continues. Natural ecosystems are still actively engaged in maintaining the planet's habitability—making it possible for over 5 billion people to survive and a billion or two to thrive. Other organisms are functioning parts of those natural ecosystems; to the degree that we exterminate them, we imperil the capacity of Earth to support us and our descendants.

The community of life on Earth generated and still maintains the composition of the atmosphere. Green plants capture and make available the energy that sustains all other life forms. And organisms of all kinds participate in the great biogeochemical cycles. These movements of materials through the living and nonliving parts of the biosphere constantly renew supplies of essential nutrients, replenish soils, and dispose of wastes. But several other life-supporting functions are also carried out continuously by members of living communities.

The climate of any given place on Earth is governed principally by the amount of sunlight received at the surface, which in turn is determined by latitude and season, and the circulation patterns of the atmosphere and the oceans, which are affected by the locations and shapes of landmasses. But climate, particularly over land, is also heavily influenced and moderated by the kind of vegetation present. This determines its surface reflectivity and thus its surface temperature. The cycling of water from land surfaces to the atmosphere and back to the surface in precipitation is regulated to a large extent by forests and other plant communities.

Similarly, the fate of water that reaches the land surface is very largely determined by the presence and type of plant community there. Forests are most efficient at capturing, retaining, and recycling water. Tropical rain forests, such as cover the Amazon basin of South America, capture and recycle prodigious quantities of water. Less than half of the rainfall runs off into the rivers—and the mammoth size of the Amazon and its tributaries can give a small idea of how much water does fall there. Most of the moisture is reevaporated from the trees, forming the almost constant cloud cover characteristic of the region.

Forests and dense grasslands can keep even heavy rainfalls from running off rapidly; instead the water sinks deep into the soil, and some of it recharges underground stores of fresh water (aquifers). Soils in such areas typically remain moist for long periods between rains, and water is released slowly in springs and steadily flowing streams. Sparse vegetation, by contrast, such as one sees in semiarid regions, is much less efficient at retaining moisture, which tends to run off in floods, often carrying soil with it (especially from steep slopes). Between rains, such areas are frequently subject to drought. These conditions are most extreme in areas where land is bare, such as the driest deserts or as a result of human intervention, as in clear-cut forest areas, overgrazed ranges, or fallow cropland.

Of course, we have just touched on a few aspects of the functioning of the global ecosystem here. More detailed information can be found in references cited in the Notes.

Notes

▼

PREFACE

1. P. Ehrlich, *The Population Bomb* (Ballantine, New York, 1968).
2. Ibid., p. xi. The mortality estimate is based primarily on information from UNICEF, WHO, and other sources on infant/child mortality and may be conservative. For example, it is now estimated that 40,000 children die daily (14.6 million a year) from hunger-related diseases, according to *International Health News*, September 1987. The number "at least 200 million" is based on an average of 10 million deaths annually for 21 years. See also a discussion in World Resources Institute/International Institute for Environment and Development, *World Resources 1987* (Basic Books, New York, 1987), pp. 18–19. The exact number, of course, can never be known with precision (see note 15, Chapter 4).
3. That is, 28 people will be born and 10 will die. The growth rate is now 3 people per second.
4. L. R. Brown, *The Changing World Food Prospect: The Nineties and Beyond*, Worldwatch Paper 85 (Worldwatch Institute, Washington, D.C., October 1988).
5. P. Ehrlich, *The Population Bomb*, p. 61.
6. The situation has been analyzed and reanalyzed in the technical and popular literature. Two key technical papers are P. R. Ehrlich and J. P. Holdren, "The Impact of Population Growth," *Science*, vol. 171 (1971), pp. 1212–17, and J. P. Holdren and P. R. Ehrlich, "Human Population and the Global Environment," *American Scientist*, vol. 62 (1974), pp. 282–92. Much important information can be found in works by Lester Brown and his colleagues in the excellent *State of the World* series issued by Worldwatch Institute and published by W. W. Norton, New York, and in the *World Resources* series issued by the World Resources Institute (WRI) and the International Institute for Environ-

ment and Development (IIED), in collaboration with the United Nations Environment Program (UNEP), (published by Basic Books, New York). Two other landmark works are the *Global 2000 Report to the President*, issued in 1980 by the Council on Environmental Quality and the Department of State, and the World Commission on Environment and Development's 1987 report *Our Common Future* (the "Brundtland Report," named for the commission's chairwoman, the Prime Minister of Norway), published by Oxford Univ. Press, Oxford. A detailed exposition of the connection of population growth to the rest of the human predicament can be found in P. R. Ehrlich, A. H. Ehrlich, and J. P. Holdren, *Ecoscience: Population, Resources, Environment* (W. H. Freeman, San Francisco, 1977). The most recent extensive popular treatment is A. H. Ehrlich and P. R. Ehrlich, *Earth* (Franklin Watts, New York, 1987).

CHAPTER 1: WHY ISN'T EVERYONE AS SCARED AS WE ARE?

1. The world population in 1990 is about 5.3 billion. Most demographic information in this book, unless otherwise noted, is from *1989 World Population Data Sheet*, issued by the Population Reference Bureau (PRB), 777 Fourteenth St. NW, Suite 800, Washington, D.C. 20005. In some cases, as above, we have made simple extrapolations for the 1990 figures. Besides the fine annual data sheet, PRB produces several very useful publications on population issues.

2. Note that the U.S. population was growing much faster before then, spurred by substantial numbers of immigrants. It *quadrupled* in the 6 decades before 1928, turning a post–Civil War society largely restricted to the eastern half of the nation into a cosmopolitan world power spanning the continent.

3. This evolutionary blind spot is discussed at length in R. Ornstein and P. Ehrlich, *New World/New Mind* (Doubleday, New York, 1988).

4. D. Johanson and M. Edey, *Lucy: The Beginnings of Mankind* (Simon and Schuster, New York, 1981). While there is still controversy over details of human history, there is no dispute that an erect, small-brained hominid something like Lucy was one of our ancestors. This exciting book beautifully presents the view of human origins of one outstanding group of scientists. For more on the controversies and on other discoveries, see R. Lewin's excellent *Bones of Contention* (Simon and Schuster, New York, 1987).

5. Note that we are considering *Homo sapiens* as the latest human species and are applying the term "human" to all hominids since the australopithecines (just as the term "ape" is applied to several species). Some people would restrict the term "human" to *Homo sapiens*.

6. When annual growth rates are under 5 percent, a working estimate of the number of years required to double the population at that rate can be obtained by simply dividing the percentage rate into 70. Thus, with Kenya's growth rate of 4.1 percent, the estimate of doubling time is $70/4.1 = 17.1$ years. A recent decline in Kenya's birthrate was reported in J. Perlez, "Birth Control Making Inroads in Populous Kenya," *New York Times*, Sept. 10, 1989, but the population still has a doubling rate of less than 20 years.

7. Exponential growth occurs when the increase in population size in a given period is a *constant* percentage of the size at the beginning of the period. Thus a population growing at 2 percent annually or a bank account growing at 6 percent annually will be growing exponentially. Exponential growth does not have to be fast; it can go on at very low rates or, if the rate is negative, can be exponential shrinkage.

Saying a population is "growing exponentially" has almost come to mean "growing very fast," but that interpretation is erroneous. True exponential growth is rarely seen in human populations today, since the percentage rate of growth has been changing. In most cases, the growth rate has been gradually declining since the late 1960s. Nevertheless, it is useful to be aware of the exponential model, since it is implied every time we project a population size into the future with qualifying statements such as "if that rate continues."

8. For mathematical details on exponential growth, see P. R. Ehrlich, A. H. Ehrlich, and J. P. Holdren, *Ecoscience: Population, Resources, Environment* (Freeman, San Francisco, 1977), pp. 100–104. The term "exponential" comes from the presence in the equation for growth of a constant, e, the base of natural logarithms, raised to a power (exponent) that is a variable (the growth rate multiplied by the time that rate will be in effect).

9. The potential for surprise in repeated doublings can be underlined with another example. Suppose you set up an aquarium with appropriate life-support systems to maintain 1,000 guppies, but no more. If that number is exceeded, crowding will make the fishes susceptible to "ich," a parasitic disease that will kill most of the guppies. You then begin the population with a pair of sex-crazed guppies. Suppose that the fishes reproduce fast enough to double their population size every month. For eight months everything is fine, as the population grows $2 \rightarrow 4 \rightarrow 8 \rightarrow 16 \rightarrow 32 \rightarrow 64 \rightarrow 128 \rightarrow 256 \rightarrow 512$. Then within the ninth month the guppy population surges through the fatal 1,000 barrier, the aquarium becomes overcrowded, and most of the fishes perish. In fact, the last 100 guppies appear in less than five days—about 2 percent of the population's history.

10. Note that "doubling times" represent what would happen if the growth rates of the moment continued unchanged into the future. Demographic projections include changes in growth rates, usually caused by reductions in birthrates and/or *declines* in death rates (demographers classically don't consider rises in death rates in their global projections). Projections therefore often show the population taking more, and occasionally less, time to double than was indicated by the "doubling time" of a recent year.

11. For a fine discussion of climate models, see S. H. Schneider, *Global Warming* (Sierra Club Books, San Francisco, 1989).

12. "Eco-Refugees Warning," *New Scientist*, June 10, 1989.

13. Synergisms occur when the joint impact of two (or more) factors is greater than the sum of their separate impacts.

14. See S. H. Schneider, *Global Warming*, and the extensive references therein.

15. Statement released Sept. 3, 1988, at the Pugwash Conference on Global Problems and Common Security, at Dagomys, near Sochi, USSR. The

signatories were Jared Diamond, UCLA; Paul Ehrlich, Stanford; Thomas Eisner, Cornell; G. Evelyn Hutchinson, Yale; Gene E. Likens, Institute of Ecosystem Studies; Ernst Mayr, Harvard; Charles D. Michener, University of Kansas; Harold A. Mooney, Stanford; Ruth Patrick, Academy of Natural Sciences, Philadelphia; Peter H. Raven, Missouri Botanical Garden; and Edward O. Wilson, Harvard.

The National Academy of Sciences and the American Academy of Arts and Sciences are the top honorary organizations for American scientists and scholars, respectively. Hutchinson, Patrick, and Wilson also are laureates of the Tyler Prize, the most distinguished international award in ecology.

16. May 4, 1989, by Philip Shabecoff, a fine environmental reporter. In general, the *Times* coverage of the environment is excellent. But even this best of American newspapers reflects the public's lack of understanding of the urgency of the population situation.

17. *Washington Post*, Nov. 19, 1988, p. C-15.

18. Italy is a not freak case. Catholic France has an average completed family size of 1.8 children, the same as Britain and Norway; Catholic Spain, with less than half the per-capita GNP of Protestant Denmark, has the same completed family size of 1.8 children. We are equating "completed family size" here with the *total fertility rate*, the average number of children a woman would bear in her lifetime, assuming that current age-specific birth and death rates remained unchanged during her childbearing years—roughly 15–49. In the United States, a Catholic woman is more likely to seek abortion than a non-Catholic woman (probably because she is likelier to use less-effective contraception). By 1980, Catholic and non-Catholic women in the U.S. (except Hispanic women, for whom cultural factors are strong) had virtually identical family sizes. (W.D. Mosher, "Fertility and Family Planning in the United States: Insights from the National Survey of Family Growth," *Family Planning Perspectives*, vol. 20, no. 5, pp. 202–17, Sept./Oct. 1988.) On the role of the Vatican, see, for instance, Stephen D. Mumford, "The Vatican and Population Growth Control: Why an American Confrontation?," *The Humanist*, September/October 1983, and Penny Lernoux, "The Papal Spiderweb," *The Nation*, April 10 and 17, 1989.

19. J. Simon, *The Ultimate Resource* (Princeton Univ. Press, Princeton, N.J., 1981).

20. B. Wattenberg, *The Birth Dearth* (Pharos Books, New York, 1987).

21. R. W. Kates, R. S. Chen, T. E. Downing, J. X. Kasperson, E. Messer, S. R. Millman, *The Hunger Report: 1988* (The Alan Shawn Feinstein World Hunger Program, Brown University, Providence, R.I., 1988). The data on distribution in this paragraph are from this source.

22. The name of a series of reports on KRON-TV's news programs, San Francisco, the week of May 8, 1989.

23. For an amusing analysis of the "outer-space" fairy tale, see Garrett Hardin's classic essay "Interstellar Migration and the Population Problem," *Journal of Heredity*, vol. 50, pp. 68–70 (1959), reprinted in G. Hardin, ed., *Stalking the Wild Taboo*, 2nd ed. (William Kaufmann, Los Altos, Calif., 1978). Note that some things have changed; to keep the population of Earth from growing today, we would have to export to space 95 million people annually!

24. This story received broad coverage in both electronic and print media; for instance, *New York Times*, May 8, 1989.

25. For a discussion of natural selection and evolution written for nonspecialists, see P. R. Ehrlich, *The Machinery of Nature* (Simon and Schuster, New York, 1986).

26. As discussed in Chapter 10, "population control" does not require coercion, only attention to the needs of society.

CHAPTER 2: THE ONE-TIME BONANZA

1. Including synthetic substances such as plastics derived directly from the fossil fuels themselves.

2. L. Brown et al., *State of the World 1989* (Norton, New York, 1989). See also Council on Environmental Quality and the Department of State, *The Global 2000 Report to the President* (Government Printing Office, Washington, D.C., 1980).

3. All the organisms—plants, animals, and microbes—that live in an area are the *community* (more technically, "biological community") of that area. The community and the physical environment with which it interacts are an *ecosystem*. It is usually important to specify the ecosystem one is discussing. The plants, fishes, snails, and microorganisms in an aquarium along with the water and the gravel are an ecosystem; so is the entire "shell" near the surface of Earth that contains all living organisms. For more on ecosystems (and communities), see P. Ehrlich, *The Machinery of Nature* (Simon and Schuster, New York, 1986). For a more technical treatment, see P. Ehrlich and J. Roughgarden, *The Science of Ecology* (Macmillan, New York, 1987).

4. For a brief overview of soil ecosystems, see P. Ehrlich, *The Machinery of Nature*. More detail is provided in P. Ehrlich, A. Ehrlich, and J. Holdren, *Ecoscience: Population, Resources, Environment* (Freeman, San Francisco, 1977).

5. Brown et al., *State of the World 1989*.

6. L. R. Brown, *Building a Sustainable Society* (Norton, New York, 1981), p. 13.

7. An excellent discussion of America's profligate use of the limited water of its semidesert West can be found in Marc Reisner, *Cadillac Desert: The American West and Its Disappearing Water* (Viking, New York, 1986). This book reads like a novel—a true horror story of how part of humanity's one-time bonanza is being consumed. Numbers on overdrafts come from this source. See also M. Glantz and J. Ausubel, "The Ogallala Aquifer and Carbon Dioxide: Comparison and Convergence," *Environmental Conservation*, vol. 11, pp. 123–31 (1984). Curiously, the latter doesn't mention population control as part of the solution to either the overdraft of the aquifer or the rise in greenhouse gases.

8. Quoted in Reisner, *Cadillac Desert*, p. 11.

9. Reisner, op. cit., p. 10.

10. G. M. Oza, "Water Crisis for the Indian Subcontinent," *Environmental Awareness (Baroda)*, vol. 12, pp. 1–2 (1989).

11. Data from *China Environmental Review*, reported in K. Forestier, "The Degreening of China," *New Scientist*, July 1, 1989, p. 52.

12. Unlike oil burned as a source of energy, water can be reused if it is

cleaned up. In practice, however, in some uses such as agriculture, much of the water cannot be recovered. In general, we are converting a basically renewable resource into a nonrenewable one by draining aquifers too rapidly and by polluting surface waters beyond our capability of economically purifying them.

13. A. Ehrlich and J. Birks, eds., *Hidden Dangers*, in press (Sierra Club Books, San Francisco, 1990). See also A. Makhijani, "The Hidden Nuclear Legacy," *Technology Review*, August/September 1988; and Radioactive Waste Campaign, *Deadly Defense* (625 Broadway, New York, NY 10012, 1988).

14. For overviews of the biodiversity crisis, see N. Myers, *The Sinking Ark* (Pergamon Press, New York, 1979); P. Ehrlich and A. Ehrlich, *Extinction: The Causes and Consequences of the Disappearance of Species* (Random House, New York, 1981); and E. O. Wilson, ed., *Biodiversity* (National Academy Press, Washington, D.C., 1988).

15. For more details, see Ehrlich and Ehrlich, *Extinction*.

16. If you are unfamiliar with the concept of an ecosystem, see pages 256–57.

17. See appendix. More can be found in P. Ehrlich, *The Machinery of Nature*. A more technical treatment can be found in Ehrlich and Roughgarden, *The Science of Ecology*.

18. Aldo Leopold, *Round River* (Oxford Univ. Press, New York, 1953). Available in paperback in *A Sand County Almanac, with Essays from Round River* (Ballantine Books, New York, 1966), p. 197.

19. For more on coevolution, see the Appendix.

20. Here we refer to all the organisms found in tropical forests. Sometimes ecologists will discuss a community restricted to a particular taxonomic group such as the "bird community of the Amazon basin" or the "fish community of the Great Barrier Reefs."

21. For more on the potential of developing new crops, and on the problems caused by the decay of biodiversity in general, see Ehrlich and Ehrlich, *Extinction*; and N. Myers, *A Wealth of Wild Species: Storehouse for Human Welfare* (Westview, Boulder, Colo., 1983).

22. Overpopulation often forces people to live in areas where they are more vulnerable to disasters, and the situation isn't limited to poor nations. Lack of space in the San Francisco Bay Area has resulted in tens of thousands of people residing on unstable bay fill and along slide-prone cliff faces. This guarantees longer casualty lists after the next giant earthquake. The phenomenon of differential impacts on large populations resulting from climatic and other factors seemingly not related to population size was first pointed out by H. Andrewartha and L. C. Birch, in their classic text *The Distribution and Abundance of Animals* (Univ. of Chicago Press, Chicago, 1953).

23. A. Wijkman and L. Timberlake, *Natural Disasters: Acts of God or Acts of Man?* (Earthscan, Washington, D.C., 1984), p. 69. Since this section was written, a new work has appeared analyzing the Himalayan situation and showing it to be extremely complex. See J. D. Ives and B. Messeric, *The Himalayan Dilemma: Reconciling Development and Conservation* (Routledge, London, 1989).

24. See any recent edition of United Nations Food and Agriculture Organization (FAO), *Production Yearbook* (FAO, Rome, Italy).

25. For details, see the Appendix, pages 259–60.

26. P. M. Vitousek, P. R. Ehrlich, A. H. Ehrlich, and P. A. Matson, "Human Appropriation of the Products of Photosynthesis," *BioScience*, vol. 36 (1986), pp. 368–73.

27. Ibid.

28. Study of Critical Environmental Problems, *Man's Impact on the Global Environment* (MIT Press, Cambridge, Mass., 1970).

29. See, for example, J. G. Speth, "A Luddite Recants," *The Amicus Journal*, Spring 1989. People realize, of course, that if the population doubles with just a doubling of economic activity, gigantic levels of poverty will be perpetuated. They therefore hope that development can greatly increase the size of the economic pie and pull many more people out of poverty. It is basically a humane idea, made insane by the constraints nature places on human activities (constraints that, by the way, Speth partially recognizes in his article, which is a plea for a "greening" of technology).

30. It means the wise or knowing man. Carl von Linné did the actual naming more than two centuries ago, but people have adopted the epithet with abandon.

31. M. Forbes, "Fact and Comment II," *Forbes*, March 20, 1989. This short article is an unwitting plea for more education on population/resource/environment issues in America's boardrooms.

32. Population Reference Bureau, *1989 World Population Data Sheet*.

33. Paul Harrison, *The Greening of Africa* (Penguin, New York, 1987).

34. Part of the notion that overpopulation is a matter of density traces to experiments with rats (J. B. Calhoun, "Population Density and Social Pathology," *Scientific American*, February 1962). If rats are crowded far beyond the densities that are usually found in nature, they start turning homosexual and become irresponsible parents—even eventually eating their young! That condition of overpopulation is self-correcting. But even in cities like New York and Tokyo, which have enormous human population densities, the number of people is not controlled either by a decline of heterosexuality or by cannibalism. Large cities usually have more social problems than small cities, but so many other factors are at work, and cities differ in so many characteristics besides size, that it's not possible to say much about what constitutes overpopulation in terms of density. The results of experimental research on human crowding are interesting, but shed little light on the issues discussed here. (For the little that is known, see P. R. Ehrlich and J. L. Freedman, "Population, Crowding, and Human Behavior," *New Scientist*, April 1, 1971.)

35. Defining the area occupied by a human population can be a very complex matter. Parts of New Mexico and Arizona are clearly part of the Los Angeles "area," since electricity for the city is generated there. Much of the city's water comes from the Rockies in Wyoming and Colorado; some comes from northern California. And food for Los Angeles comes from all over the world. The entire U.S. in this sense "occupies" much more area than is found within its borders and contributes to the degradation of the long-term carrying capacity of a great deal of that outside territory. The same, of course, applies to the discussion of the "Netherlands Fallacy" below.

36. See P. Ehrlich and A. Ehrlich, *Population, Resources, Environment: Issues in Human Ecology* (Freeman, San Francisco, 1972), p. 257; Ehrlich, Ehrlich, and Holdren, *Ecoscience*.

37. 1984–86 data from World Resources Institute (WRI) and International Institute for Environment and Development (IIED), *World Resources 1988–89* (Basic Books, New York, 1989).

38. In 1986, the Netherlands consumed some 3×10^{18} joules of commercial energy, and its 1984 proven recoverable reserves of natural gas were 1.5×10^{12} cubic meters. Each cubic meter contains 3.9×10^{7} joules, so that amounts to roughly 6×10^{19} joules, or a 20-year supply (data from *World Resources 1988–89*; conversions are in John Harte's *Consider a Spherical Cow* [Wm. Kaufmann, Los Altos, Calif., 1985]). Of course, this calculation assumes no substantial changes either in consumption or in the extent of the reserves.

39. It is, in essence, the definition used in technical ecological work. When a population starts depleting its resources, it is said to be above the carrying capacity of the environment, and a subsequent decline is assumed. Natural populations ordinarily are constrained by the availability of renewable resources and rarely "pollute" their environments. Note that, while a rough definition of human carrying capacity is easily given, calculating that carrying capacity for a given area is usually extremely difficult.

40. World Bank figures cited in WRI and IIED, *World Resources 1988–89*. The World Health Organization in its annual *Report on World Health* in 1989 noted that one billion people are suffering from malnourishment or disease (reported in *New York Times*, Sept. 26, 1989).

41. If China were included, that rate in 1989 would have been 2.1 percent, with a doubling time of 32 years. China, with 1.1 billion people, had a rate of natural increase of 1.4 percent in 1989, but the birthrate was going up ("China Population Hits 1.1 Billion—Births Called 'Out of Control,' " *San Francisco Chronicle*, April 15, 1989).

42. *Times of India*, Feb. 20, 1989.

43. Numerous reports and articles have appeared recently documenting the economic redistribution of wealth in the U.S. since 1980; for example: P. Passell, "Forces in Society, and Reaganism, Helped Dig Deeper Hole for Poor," *New York Times*, July 16, 1989; E. F. Hollings, "Decaying America: The Underside of Reagan Legacy," *Washington Post Weekly Edition*, May 8–14, 1989; P. Peterson, "The Morning After," *Atlantic Monthly*, October 1987; S. H. Preston, "Children and the Elderly in the U.S.," *Scientific American*, December 1984.

44. The exact relationship of urban problems such as crime to population size and growth is not well understood, and many other factors are clearly involved. The issue is discussed further in Chapter 7.

45. The present status of the rich nations is best described as "overdevelopment" (see Ehrlich, Ehrlich, and Holdren, *Ecoscience*, pp. 926–30).

46. R. Ornstein and P. Ehrlich, *New World/New Mind: Moving Toward Conscious Evolution* (Doubleday, New York, 1989).

CHAPTER 3: CRITICAL MASSES

1. Some would not count our ancestors as having been truly human until the "cultural revolution" of some 35,000 years ago, when a highly and rapidly innovative modern *Homo sapiens* emerged. For a fine exposition of that point of view, see J. Diamond, "The Great Leap Forward," *Discover*, May 1989. We prefer to define humanity as beginning with the first fully upright, small-brained australopithecine hominids some 4 million years ago. It is, of course, just a question of definition; there is little dispute on the facts.

2. Births and immigrations are the "input" side of the demographic equation, while deaths and emigration are the "output" side. Here we are ignoring immigration, and we will ignore emigration in the discussion of output as well. On a global scale, of course, migration can be ignored. In the demography of some individual nations, such as the U.S., migration can be important and must be included in calculations of growth rates. In such situations, "rate of natural increase" is the difference between birth and death rates, while "growth rate" takes migration (a net gain or loss) into account.

   More details on the mathematics of population growth can be found in P. Ehrlich, A. Ehrlich, and J. Holdren, *Ecoscience: Population, Resources, Environment* (Freeman, San Francisco, 1977). If you find dealing with the mathematical aspects of population and related issues daunting, we strongly recommend John Harte's *Consider a Spherical Cow: A Course in Environmental Problem Solving* (Wm. Kaufmann, Los Altos, Calif., 1985).

3. Once again, all 1989 population data are from the *World Population Data Sheet 1989*, produced by the Population Reference Bureau (PRB). Anyone interested in population issues should join this excellent organization and receive the wealth of information it supplies to members. In some cases, the PRB numbers have been rounded for simplicity, so our examples may not always match the data sheet exactly. Normally, the estimated midyear population is used as the divisor. Census statistics, especially in developing countries, are somewhat unreliable (those in the U.S. also contain significant errors, especially when compared with those from nations like Sweden). That is the reason for all the "weasel" words (e.g., "roughly," "about") accompanying population numbers. Note, however, that it makes no difference to the message of this book whether the midyear population in 1989 was 5.1 or 5.4 billion, or whether the birthrate was 26 or 29 per 1,000. Such uncertainties make little difference in the long run.

4. 146/5200 = .028. Remember, a billion is 1,000 million.

5. 51/5200 = .010.

6. Again, we're ignoring migration.

7. Technically, demographers say that when birth and death rates are equal, there is no "natural increase" and the population is "stationary." Zero population growth, however, has become much more widely used in the popular literature; it is also the name of the premier organization pushing to get population growth in the United States under control.

8. There is evidence, still being debated, that some groups of people had

settled in the Western Hemisphere much earlier, but they may have
been less effective hunters than the invaders that arrived around 12,000
years ago.

9. See P. S. Martin and R. G. Klein, eds., *Quaternary Extinctions: A
Prehistoric Revolution* (Arizona Univ. Press, Tucson, 1984). The last
word is not in, however, on the debate about Pleistocene extinctions.

10. For more details and references, see Ehrlich, Ehrlich, and Holdren,
Ecoscience, chap. 5.

11. T. Jacobsen and R. M. Adams, "Salt and Silt in Ancient Mesopotamian
Agriculture," *Science*, vol. 128, pp. 1251–58 (1958). The degree to
which problems with the irrigation system contributed to the downfall
of the civilization is controversial.

12. For a fine brief overview of the environmental impact of the Greeks and
Romans, see J. D. Hughes, *The Ecology of Ancient Civilizations* (Univ.
of New Mexico Press, Albuquerque, 1975). There are those, however,
who doubt that ecological factors had much to do with the decline of
either Greece or Rome; see, e.g., T. H. van Andel and C. Runnels,
Beyond the Acropolis (Stanford Univ. Press, Stanford, Calif., 1987).
Even those authors, however, concede that human activity has brought
the Mediterranean basin to its present degraded state.

13. See, for instance, J. A. Sabloff, "The Collapse of the Classic Maya
Civilization," in J. Harte and R. Socolow, *Patient Earth* (Holt, Rinehart
and Winston, New York, 1971), pp. 16–27; T. P. Culbert, ed. *The
Classic Maya Collapse* (Univ. of New Mexico Press, Albuquerque,
1973), especially chap. 15 (W. T. Sanders, "The Cultural Ecology of
the Lowland Maya: A Reevaluation"); E. S. Deevey, D. S. Rice,
H. H. Vaughan, M. Breener, and M .S. Flannery, "Mayan Urbanism:
Impact on a Tropical Karst Environment," *Science*, vol. 206, pp. 298–
306 (1979). Other scholars have cast doubt on this idea, citing evidence
of a well-developed, sustainable soil-preserving agricultural system.

14. A more detailed discussion of the history of human population growth
can be found in Ehrlich, Ehrlich, and Holdren, *Ecoscience*, chap. 5.

15. Since there are few reliable census statistics available for most of the
world before this century, dates for when the total human population
reached various levels tend to be informed guesses. We have long
accepted 1850 as the approximate time that the population reached a
billion (based on various sources); the PRB now uses 1800. They know
more than we do, so we have switched to their estimate.

16. Or at least less of an asset than they were on the farm.

17. Some social scientists believe that a demographic transition is an automatic part of the demographic history of societies. They complacently
assume that sooner or later today's less-developed countries will
undergo such a transition and birthrates will fall to industrial levels,
regardless of population policies. That assumption is supported by the
recent gradual decline of birthrates in many nations. But this simple
view is a dubious proposition, as we outline in Chapter 9. An example
of an otherwise excellent analysis that tacitly accepts this assumption
is John R. Weeks, "The Demography of Islamic Nations," *Population
Bulletin*, vol. 43, no. 4 (December 1988).

18. Details in Ehrlich, Ehrlich, and Holdren, *Ecoscience*, chap. 5.

19. J. P. Holdren and P. R. Ehrlich, "Human Population and the Global Environment," *American Scientist*, vol. 62 (1974), pp. 282–92. This basic formulation was first published in P. R. Ehrlich and J. P. Holdren, "Impact of Population Growth," *Science*, vol. 171, pp. 1212–17 (1974). For a detailed discussion, see Ehrlich, Ehrlich, and Holdren, *Ecoscience*, chap. 12. Note that the formula is simplified, since the multiplicative factors are not entirely independent. "Consumption" is in some ways a more accurate term than "affluence," but PAT is a much handier acronym than PCT.

20. Excluding the People's Republic of China. If China is included, the figure is 37 percent.

21. Demographers usually consider only females when calculating reproductive rates. At any moment, one can picture these rates as being calculated by taking a hypothetical group of 1,000 newborn female babies and, using a computer, running the group through the current death and birth rates for each age group in the population. At first there are no births, but a few deaths occur; as the age of puberty arrives, the hypothetical survivors (still the vast majority) start producing babies. When the childbearing years are over, the computer adds up the number of female babies ever born to the original group of females, and divides it by 1,000. The resulting number is called the net reproductive rate (NRR). If 2,000 female babies had been produced, the population would be growing like a skyrocket, doubling every generation, and the NRR would be $2,000/1,000 = 2$. If the original 1,000 female babies produced exactly 1,000 female babies, there would be replacement reproduction, or a net reproductive rate of one $(1,000/1,000 = 1)$.

    The number usually quoted, however, is the current total fertility rate (TFR), which is simply the average number of babies of both sexes that would be born per woman in her lifetime if current age-specific fertility rates remained constant; or the average completed family size, as it is sometimes expressed.

22. Technically, the timing depends on the precise trajectories of age-specific birth and death rates, but those details need not concern us here. From a policy point of view, a year or two's difference in reaching replacement reproduction is of little consequence—although a decade's difference can be *very* significant.

23. News release, "1990s a Crucial Decade for World Population Stabilization," Population Reference Bureau, Washington, D.C., May 24, 1989.

24. For an overview of human migration, with special attention to the relationship between Mexico and the U.S., see P. Ehrlich, L. Bilderback, and A. Ehrlich, *The Golden Door: International Migration, Mexico, and the United States* (Wideview Books, New York, 1981). The numerous difficult ethical questions that surround the immigration dilemma are explored in that book.

25. J. Jacobsen, *Environmental Refugees: A Yardstick of Habitability*, Worldwatch Paper 86 (Worldwatch Institute, Washington, D.C., 1988). This fine paper describes a horrifying worldwide problem.

26. This is assuming a net natural increase of 1.75 million (about 4 million births minus 2.25 million deaths) and (conservatively) a net immigration

of 0.6 million, giving a total annual increase of 2.35 million people. The contribution of migration is then $0.6/2.35 = .255$, or 25.5 percent. Immigration at this rate is sufficient to raise the 1989 U.S. population growth rate from 0.7 to 0.95 percent. For an interesting discussion of recent Census Bureau projections of the future U.S. population, see Leon Bouvier, "The Census Bureau's 1989 Projections of Future U.S. Population: Which Scenario Is Reasonable?" *CIS Backgrounder* (Center for Immigration Studies, 1424 Sixteenth St. NW, Washington, D.C., March 27, 1989).

27. We are not counting the USSR as a *very* rich nation, and the Soviet border with China is heavily militarized.

28. That study is Ehrlich, Bilderback, and Ehrlich, *The Golden Door*. Much of the material in this paragraph and the discussion that follows comes from this source.

29. Today, population growth in the U.S. has a component of natural increase (because of demographic momentum) and one of net immigration (surplus of immigrants over emigrants). If family sizes do not increase, the first component will gradually shrink to zero and then become negative. What will happen to net immigration (and whether it will increase and thereby keep the U.S. population growing, even in an era of natural decrease) we cannot predict.

30. Unfortunately, the U.S. has long interfered in the affairs of Mexico, doing so in a way that has helped to worsen our southern neighbor's problems. Our meddling goes back to the days of U.S. Minister Joel Poinsett in 1822, but was most blatant during the Mexican War (which the Mexicans call "the War of American Intervention") of 1846–47 and the dictatorship of Porfirio Díaz (1876–1911). It continues to this day in the form of trade and investment policies. Few Americans realize that our nation took more than half of Mexico's territory by force in the Mexican War and even considered making the entire nation part of the U.S., which certainly would have solved any "migration" problems.

31. We ignore here Woodrow Wilson's Mexican adventure just before World War I. The U.S., Mexico, and Canada have all been at peace with each other since the Mexican War.

32. A step in that direction occurred in October 1989 when the Canadian government announced that it was joining the Organization of American States (OAS) (reported on CNN *World Report*, Oct. 29).

Chapter 4: Food: The Ultimate Resource

1. An intelligent exposition of this view can be found in F. M. Lappé and J. Collins, *Food First* (Houghton Mifflin, Boston, 1977). Their book does not seriously consider the potential for absolute shortage, but offers much information on how more people could be fed by changing diets, changing socioeconomic arrangements (who controls and participates in food production), and better distribution. Unfortunately, it ignores an array of environmental and economic issues that are dealt with later in this chapter.

2. R. W. Kates, R. S. Chen, T. E. Downing, J. X. Kasperson, E. Messer, and S. R. Millman, *The Hunger Report: 1988* (The Alan Shawn Feinstein World Hunger Program, Brown University, Providence, R.I., 1988).

3. WRI and IIED, *World Resources 1988–89* (Basic Books, New York, 1989). The numbers come from the World Bank, which has tracked the increase in their numbers for a few decades and defines them as "absolute poor"—meaning too poor to buy enough food.

4. For an overview of the current food situation, see L. R. Brown, *The Changing World Food Prospect: The Nineties and Beyond,* Worldwatch Paper 85 (Worldwatch Institute, Washington, D.C., October 1988); and L. R. Brown et al., *State of the World 1989* (Norton, New York, 1989).

5. Sadly, food "gluts" and hunger often exist simultaneously because the poor don't have the money to buy sufficient food even when it's available.

6. It is instructive that Lappé and Collins (note 1) focus on China (as they should) as an example of a nation with "food first" policies. Nevertheless, only a dozen years after they wrote, China again faces the prospect of serious nutritional trouble.

7. K. Forestier, "The Degreening of China," *New Scientist,* July 1, 1989. Other Chinese agricultural problems include a large decline in irrigated farmland, a shift of population off the farm that has not been accompanied by increased efficiency on the farm, and a sharp drop in investment in agriculture.

8. A study by the Society for Promotion of Wastelands Development in India, cited in L. R. Brown et al., *State of the World 1988.*

9. B. B. Vohra, *A Policy for Land and Water,* Sardar Patel Memorial Lecture, New Delhi, 1980.

10. P. Spitz, "The Green Revolution Re-examined in India," in B. Glaeser, ed., *The Green Revolution Revisited* (Allen and Unwin, London, 1987), pp. 56–75.

11. E. Goldsmith and N. Hildyard, *The Earth Report: The Essential Guide to Global Ecological Issues* (Price Stern Sloan, New York, 1988), p. 159.

12. UN Food and Agriculture Organization (FAO), *Tropical Forest Resources,* Forestry Paper 30 (Rome, 1982); Centre for Science and Environment, *The State of India's Environment 1984–85* (New Delhi, 1985); Associated Press, Oct. 27, 1987. Exact rates of deforestation and degradation of woodlands are not available, hence the vague projection. Some reports say the forests will be largely gone around the year 2000.

13. Associated Press, Oct. 27, 1987.

14. See K. S. Valdiya, "Vulnerable Lands of the Indian Subcontinent," paper presented at conference on Global Warming and Climate Change: Perspectives from Developing Countries, sponsored by the Tata Energy Research Institute, New Delhi, India, Feb. 21–23, 1989 (proceedings in press).

15. L. R. Brown, "World Population Growth, Soil Erosion, and Food Security," *Science,* vol. 214, pp. 995–1002 (1981). Note that it is impossible to estimate accurately the number of people who starve to death annually. Governments don't publish statistics on how many of their people have died from lack of food—indeed, officials try to cover up that sign of their own incompetence. Nature aids them in that cover-

up, since malnourished people don't ordinarily die of starvation, but from the attack of some disease-causing pathogen—such as diarrhea, measles, or pneumonia—that easily overwhelms immune systems compromised by malnutrition. Thus officials can credit the deaths to "disease" when lack of food was the basic cause.

16. "Trees: Appropriate Tools for Water and Soil Management," in B. Glaeser, ed., *The Green Revolution Revisited*, p. 116.

17. World Bank, *Poverty and Hunger: Issues and Options for Food Security in Developing Countries* (World Bank, Washington, D.C., 1986).

18. L. R. Brown, *The Changing World Food Prospect*.

19. S. H. Wittwer, "Food Problems in the Next Decades," in D. B. Botkin, M. F. Caswell, J. E. Estes, and A. A. Orio, *Changing the Global Environment: Perspectives on Human Involvement* (Academic Press, Boston, 1989), p. 119.

20. L. R. Brown, "Reexamining the World Food Prospect," in *State of the World 1989*, p. 43.

21. B. E. Goldstein, "Indonesia Reconsiders Resettlement," *World Watch*, March/April 1988.

22. The forest–agriculture situation in the Philippines is detailed in G. Porter and D. Ganapin, Jr., *Resources, Population, and the Philippines' Future: A Case Study*, World Resources Institute Paper no. 4, October 1989.

23. Goldsmith and Hildyard, *The Earth Report*, p. 158.

24. B. Glaeser, "Agriculture Between the Green Revolution and Ecodevelopment: Which Way to Go?," in Glaeser, ed., *The Green Revolution Revisited*, p. 5.

25. Much of the material on Brazil in the following paragraphs is from A. R. Romeiro, "Alternative Developments in Brazil," in Glaeser, ed., *The Green Revolution Revisited*, pp. 79–110.

26. That is, the workers may be hungry, but they don't have money to buy more food. The money, not the need, creates "demand" in the economic sense used here.

27. More information on tropical deforestation can be found in N. Myers, *The Primary Source: Tropical Forests and Our Future* (Norton, New York, 1984), and Independent Commission on International Humanitarian Issues, *The Vanishing Forest: The Human Consequences of Deforestation* (Zed Books, London, 1986).

28. Brown et al., *State of the World 1989*.

29. Despite the migration northward of several hundred thousand each year. For more on Mexican migration, see P. R. Ehrlich, L. Bilderback, and A. H. Ehrlich, *The Golden Door: International Migration, Mexico, and the United States* (Wideview Books, New York, 1981).

30. A. H. Ehrlich, "Development and Agriculture," in P. R. Ehrlich and J. P. Holdren, eds., *The Cassandra Conference: Resources and the Human Environment* (Texas A & M Press, College Station, 1988), pp. 75–100.

31. Independent Commission on International Humanitarian Issues, *Famine: A Man-Made Disaster?* (Vintage Books, New York, 1985).

32. Ibid., p. 54.

33. L. R. Brown and E. C. Wolf, "Getting Back on Track," in *State of the World 1985* (Norton, New York, 1985), p. 230.

34. WRI and IIED, *World Resources 1988–89.*

35. L. R. Brown et al., *State of the World 1987* (Norton, New York, 1987).

36. A. H. Ehrlich, "Development and Agriculture."

37. U.S. Dept. of Agriculture, *World Agriculture: Situation and Outlook Report,* March 1989.

38. Brown et al., *State of the World 1989.*

39. Much of our information on South Africa was gleaned from various sources, including family-planning workers, professional biologists, wildlife specialists, and environmentalists, during an extended trip there in 1988. South Africa must end apartheid as soon as possible and launch a cooperative effort to achieve a sustainable society, or it will soon find itself overwhelmed by its environmental problems—on top of the social ones.

40. Brown et al., *State of the World 1989.*

41. The "tons" here and throughout this chapter are metric tons, equal to 1,000 kilograms or 1.102 short (or English) tons. For the purposes of this book, the 10 percent difference between short and long tons is unimportant and often would be lost in errors of estimation anyway.

42. P. Ehrlich, A. Ehrlich, and J. Holdren, *Ecoscience: Population, Resources, Environment* (Freeman, San Francisco, 1977); data on fisheries yields from UN *1983/84 Statistical Yearbook* (United Nations, New York); and WRI and IIED, *World Resources 1988–89.*

43. L. R. Brown, "Maintaining World Fisheries," in *State of the World 1985* (Norton, New York, 1985); WRI and IIED, *World Resources 1988–89.*

44. That was in May 1989; whether or not she was correct should be evident in the next few years. Our informant wished to remain anonymous for fear of offending local people. There is strong support for all extractive industries in Alaska, a state that has sold its soul for oil. Fortunately, there appears to be a growing realization in that beautiful state that its present economy is not long sustainable.

45. You can keep casual track of the fisheries situation by noticing how many of your local restaurants offer "blackened" fish dishes. The trend to harvesting less and less desirable fish stocks as the more desirable ones are overfished seems bound to continue ("desirable" means tasty; people will pay more for desirable fishes). One way restaurants have of dealing with fishes that don't taste good is to coat them in so many spices and sauces that you can't taste the fish.

46. More information on the altercation and the North Atlantic fisheries situation can be found in Ehrlich, Ehrlich, and Holdren, *Ecoscience.*

47. WRI and IIED, *World Resources 1988–89.*

48. Yang Wenhe, deputy director of the National Bureau of Oceanography, quoted in K. Forestier, "The Degreening of China," p. 53.

49. Quoted in Forestier, op. cit.

CHAPTER 5: THE ECOLOGY OF AGRICULTURE

1. The sun's energy arrives at an average rate of about 145 watts for each square yard of land surface. Only about half of that energy lies in the part of the solar spectrum that the plants can use, and they actually manage to use only about one percent of that on average. Suppose crops could bind solar energy at a rate of 2 watts per square yard over and above what they need to run their own life processes and that they could do it all year round (an extremely optimistic assumption). By comparison, about 120 watts of energy are needed to run the life processes of an average person. If a person could extract 5 percent of the energy available in the crop plants to support his or her life processes, then each square yard of crop field would yield about 0.1 watts (.05 × 2). One acre of cropland would thereby support 4 people, 2.5 acres would support roughly 10 individuals, and a square mile could feed 2600.

2. By far the best overall treatment of how the climate works and what it means, addressed to a lay audience, is S. H. Schneider and R. Londer, *The Coevolution of Climate and Life* (Sierra Club Books, San Francisco, 1984).

3. The degree of accuracy to which climate/weather ever will be predictable is still a matter of debate, depending in part on the role chaos may play in the system.

4. See S. Pimm, *The Balance of Nature?* (Univ. of Chicago Press, Chicago, 1990).

5. L. R. Brown et al., *State of the World 1987* (Norton, New York, 1987).

6. L. R. Brown, "Reducing Hunger," in *State of the World 1985* (Norton, New York, 1985), p. 32. See also E. C. Wolf, "Raising Agricultural Productivity," in L. R. Brown et al., *State of the World 1987*.

7. A. H. Ehrlich, "Development and Agriculture," in P. Ehrlich and J. Holdren, eds., *The Cassandra Conference: Resources and the Human Environment* (Texas A & M Press, College Station, 1988).

8. L. R. Brown et al., *State of the World 1986* (Norton, New York, 1986).

9. "Economics and Financial Aspects of the Plan of Action to Combat Desertification," paper presented at UN Conference on Desertification, Nairobi, Kenya, Aug. 29–Sept. 7, 1977.

10. Council of Environmental Quality and Department of State, *Global 2000 Report to the President* (1980), vol. 2, p. 279.

11. Quoted in "Points of View," *Surviving Together*, Fall/Winter 1988. See also "Soviet Union Planned Paddy Fields for Aral Sea," *New Scientist*, May 20, 1989.

12. See P. Ehrlich and A. Ehrlich, *Extinction: The Causes and Consequences of the Disappearance of Species* (Random House, New York, 1981).

13. Vitousek et al., "Human Appropriation of the Products of Photosynthesis," *BioScience*, vol. 36, pp. 368–73 (1986).

14. M. S. Swaminathan, "Global Agriculture at the Crossroads," *Earth '88: Changing Geographic Perspectives* (National Geographic Society, Washington, D.C., 1988), pp. 316–29.

15. L. R. Brown et al., *State of the World 1989* (Norton, New York, 1989).

16. Goldsmith and Hildyard, *The Earth Report: The Essential Guide to Global Ecological Issues* (Price Stern Sloan, New York, 1989), p. 142, based on U.S. Dept. of Agriculture statistics.

17. J. Sokoloff, *The Politics of Food* (Sierra Club Books, San Francisco, 1988).

18. S. Postel, Worldwatch Institute, personal communication.

19. Sokoloff, *The Politics of Food*, p. 36.

20. PRE observed the incompetence firsthand when he, along with several colleagues in entomology and biology, was called in to consult on the problem.

21. S. Postel, personal communication.

22. N. A. Berg, "Making the Most of the New Soil Conservation Initiatives," *Journal of Soil and Water Conservation*, January/February 1987.

23. Technically, the economic system is too much based on a high discount rate to allow such long-range factors to be considered. From the viewpoint of standard economics, the family farmer has "noneconomic" reasons for conserving soil. For example, he may wish to pass on to his children a farm fully as productive as (or more so than) the farm he inherited.

24. Sokoloff, *The Politics of Food*. See also F. M. Lappé and J. Collins, *Food First* (Houghton Mifflin, Boston, 1977).

25. International Institute for Applied Systems Analysis (IIASA), "Hunger amid Abundance," *Options*, no. 1–2 (1987).

26. UN Food and Agriculture Organization (FAO), the UN Fund for Population Activities (UNFPA), and IIASA in Austria, *Potential Population Supporting Capacities of Lands in the Developing World*, Technical Report of Project on Land Resources for the Future, FPA/INT/513, Rome, Italy, 1982. Using the year 1975 as a baseline, the researchers attempted to integrate detailed information on soils and potential yields of crops with population projections for the developing countries, and determine whether or not they could, at least potentially, be self-sufficient in food after 2000.

27. See, e.g., R. Repetto and M. Gillis, eds., *Public Policies and the Misuse of Forest Resources* (Cambridge Univ. Press, Cambridge, 1988).

28. See N. Myers, *The Primary Source: Tropical Forests and Our Future* (Norton, New York, 1984); and C. Caulfield, *In the Rainforest* (Alfred A. Knopf, New York, 1985).

29. A. H. Ehrlich, "Development and Agriculture," and references therein.

30. Ehrlich and Ehrlich, *Extinction*; and N. Myers, *A Wealth of Wild Species: Storehouse for Human Welfare* (Westview, Boulder, Colo., 1983).

31. Some successful efforts to establish sustainable agricultural-assistance programs are described in W. V. C. Reid, J. N. Barnes, and B. Blackwelder, *Bankrolling Successes: A Portfolio of Sustainable Development Projects* (Environmental Policy Institute and National Wildlife Federation, Washington, D.C., 1988).

32. J. S. Douglas and R. A. de J. Hart, *Forest Farming* (Intermediate Technology Publications, London, 1984).

33. S. R. Gleissman, E. Garcia, and A. M. Amador, "The Ecological Basis for the Application of Traditional Agricultural Technology in the Management of Tropical Agro-ecosystems," *Agro-ecosystems*, vol. 7, pp. 173–85 (1980).

34. They were veterans demanding that Congress help them in their time of need by accelerating payment of a bonus due in 1945.

35. M. Lofchie, "The Decline of African Agriculture," in M. Glantz, *Drought and Hunger in Africa: Denying Famine a Future* (Cambridge Univ. Press, Cambridge, 1987), pp. 85–109. Here again the Marxist focus on factory workers rather than peasants often has played a role.

36. K. Hart, "The State of Agricultural Development," in *The Political*

Economy of West African Agriculture (Cambridge Univ. Press, Cambridge, 1982), p. 10.

37. Independent Commission on International Humanitarian Issues, *Famine: A Man-Made Disaster?* (Vintage Books, New York, 1985).

38. Techniques of biotechnology are very diverse and include such things as cell culture (especially with cloning, which makes the culture genetically uniform), tissue culture, cell fusion, fermentation, artificial insemination, embryo transfer, artificial selection, genetic engineering, and so on.

39. For an excellent brief discussion of this issue and of genetic engineering of crops, see P. H. Raven, R. F. Evert, and S. E. Eichorn, *Biology of Plants*, 4th ed. (Worth, New York, 1986). This book is a gold mine of information on plants in general.

40. The ability to produce uniformly high-quality corn plants depends on making each generation in the field the product of crosses between two different inbred strains. In order for this to be done, seed must be produced without self-pollination of the corn plants. Originally, this was done by hand removal of the tassels (pollen-producing structures); now it is accomplished by using genetically determined male sterility. Self-pollination is eliminated, but the genetic composition of the strains is manipulated so that the sperm produced by the pollen of one can fertilize the ovules of the other, producing viable hybrid seed. Unfortunately, one side effect of this process is that the crops are genetically uniform and therefore may be very susceptible to pathogens and pests.

41. A. H. Jamal, "The Socioeconomic Impact of New Biotechnologies in the Third World," *Development Dialogue*, 1988, no. 1–2, pp. 5–8.

42. Independent Commission, *Famine: A Man-Made Disaster?*, p. 87.

43. Address to the Forum on Global Change of the National Academy of Sciences/Smithsonian Institution in Washington, D.C., May 3, 1989. See also "Reexamining the World Food Prospect," in *State of the World 1989*, p. 49.

44. Personal communication. The basis of the estimate will be published in the forthcoming *State of the World, 1990* (Norton, New York, 1990).

CHAPTER 6: GLOBAL ECOSYSTEM HEALTH

1. For more discussion of ecosystem services, see P. Ehrlich and A. Ehrlich, *Extinction: The Causes and Consequences of the Disappearance of Species* (Random House, New York, 1981).

2. For a detailed and authoritative treatment of this topic, see S. H. Schneider's *Global Warming* (Sierra Club Books, San Francisco, 1989). Also excellent, but more technical, is D. E. Abrahamson, ed., *The Challenge of Global Warming* (Island Press, Washington, D.C., 1989).

3. *Calypso Log*, June 1989, p. 7.

4. *Nature*, April 20, 1989.

5. T. Maugh II, "Ocean Data Shows Global Warming May Have Begun," *Los Angeles Times*, April 20, 1989.

6. For a detailed discussion of the evolutionary reasons why we have so much trouble paying attention to long-term trends, and what should be done about it, see R. Ornstein and P. Ehrlich, *New World/New Mind* (Doubleday, New York, 1989).

7. Conservation is by far the environmentally most benign and readily available alternative. With appropriate incentives we believe the transition could be made in about 15 years.

8. He Bochuan, a professor of philosophy at Zhongshan Univ., Guangdon, claims that to evade the one-child policy, many families do not register their children, so that the standard 1.1 billion figure is an undercount. Reported in K. Forestier, "The Degreening of China," *New Scientist*, July 1, 1989, p. 53.

9. China in 1987 burned some 650 millions tons of coal, accounting for about three quarters of its total energy consumption (about 850 million tons of coal-equivalent). The official government plan is for an annual consumption of between 1.4 and 1.5 billion tons of coal-equivalent by 2000, with coal accounting for an even higher proportion of energy use than it does today. In 1985, U.S. fossil-fuel consumption injected some 1.2 billion tons of carbon into the atmosphere (CO_2 emissions are usually measured in tons of carbon); China's injected slightly over 500 million. Under the scenario presented here, China would very nearly have caught up with the U.S. by the turn of the century, provided U.S. emissions did not increase. The basic source for this information is Stephen Meyer, ed., *Proceedings of the Chinese-American Symposium on Energy Markets and the Future of Energy Demand, Nanjing, China, June 22–24, 1988*, published by Lawrence Berkeley Laboratory (available from NTIS, Springfield, VA 22161). Interestingly, in the same symposium the 3.2 million cars in China in 1985 were projected to increase to 13 million by 2000. Professor Lu Yingzhong of the Institute of Nuclear Energy and Technology, Beijing, looks further ahead in his apparently unpublished 1989 paper, "Some Comments on CO_2 Issues in PRC." He gives a "low-nuclear-power" projection of coal use in 2025 as 2.6 billion tons; a "high-nuclear-power" projection of 1.75 billion tons. It is therefore pretty clear that China plans to emit more CO_2 than the U.S. could offset by 2025 at the latest. China, by the way, had coal reserves in 1985 of 780 billion tons, about a third of the world total. Global warming will clearly restrain China's coal use long before supply becomes a significant constraint.

10. Material on population, coal, and CO_2 is from P. R. Ehrlich and A. H. Ehrlich, "How the Rich Can Save the Poor and Themselves: Lessons from the Global Warming," in press in proceedings of conference on Global Warming and Climate Change: Perspectives from Developing Countries, held in New Delhi, India, Feb. 21–23, 1989, sponsored by the Tata Energy Research Institute, New Delhi.

11. The projection, of course, also optimistically presumes that India will somehow avoid massive rises in its death rates from starvation, disease, or social breakdown—something that seems highly unlikely to us.

12. Roughly 1–3 billion tons of carbon are added annually by deforestation as compared to about 5.5 billion tons from burning of fossil fuels. There is considerable controversy surrounding the estimates of the contributions of deforestation.

13. S. Postel, "A Green Fix to the Global Warm-up," *World Watch*, September/October 1988, pp. 29–36.

14. Norman Myers, *The Primary Source: Tropical Forests and Our Future* (Norton, New York, 1984); J. O. Browder, "Public Policy and Defores-

tation in the Brazilian Amazon," in R. Repetto and M. Gillis, eds., *Public Policies and the Misuse of Forest Resources* (Cambridge Univ. Press, Cambridge, 1988), pp. 247–97.

15. Because of poor and erosion-prone soils, crop pests, malaria and other tropical diseases, insufficient farm credit, and lack of sound agricultural advice and support.

16. Associated Press, Oct. 27, 1987.

17. R. Hutchinson, "A Tree-Hugger Stirs Villagers in India to Save Their Forests," *Smithsonian*, February 1988.

18. Li Jinchang, Kong Fanwen, He Naihui, and L. Ross, "Price and Policy: The Keys to Revamping China's Forestry Resources," in R. Repetto and M. Gillis, eds., *Public Policies and the Misuse of Forest Resources*, p. 211.

19. Reported in Forestier, "The Degreening of China." The information that follows on fires is attributed to him and other forestry experts.

20. Quoted in Forestier, "The Degreening of China."

21. S. Postel, "Global View of a Tropical Disaster," *American Forests*, November/December 1988. According to FAO estimates, in 1980 almost 1.2 billion people in poor countries were cutting fuelwood faster than it grew; by 2000 half the people in developing countries will lack a sustainable supply of fuelwood. In many areas women and children spend a large portion of their time traveling in search of wood, which keeps them from other productive activities. It also affects diets, since quick-cooking cereals and tubers are substituted for more nutritious, slower-cooking foods such as beans.

22. *Calypso Log*, June 1989, p. 8.

23. See N. Myers, *The Primary Source: Tropical Forests and Our Future* (Norton, New York, 1984), chap. 7; also N. Myers, ed., *Gaia: An Atlas of Planet Management* (Doubleday, New York, 1984).

24. This holds true only as long as more forests exist to move to as each previous tract gives out. A new study indicates that even this destruction procedure is less remunerative than sustainable use even in the relatively short term (W. Booth, "Study Offers Hope for Rain Forests," *Washington Post*, June 29, 1989; C. Peters, A. Gentry, and R. Mendelsohn, "Valuation of an Amazonian Rainforest," *Nature*, vol. 339, pp. 655–56, June 29, 1989), although some of the estimates in the study were probably too optimistic.

25. N. Myers, *Primary Source*, pp. 104–5.

26. The state has long been run by a reactionary rural minority given control by gerrymandered electoral districts.

27. The industry claims the forests will regenerate, apparently not realizing that many of the plants require the microclimatic conditions of the forests to grow, and that the animals can't go into suspended animation to wait for the forests to return.

28. The economic reasons for "taking the capital" rather than harvesting on a sustainable-yield basis are discussed on pp. 164–65. In at least one case, the corporation is under pressure to pay off the junk bonds used in the takeover of the lumber company.

29. For an informative overview of forest policies globally, see R. Repetto and M. Gillis, eds., *Public Policies and the Misuse of Forest Resources* (Cambridge Univ. Press, Cambridge, 1988).

30. Natural bogs and marshes and termite flatus are also major sources.

31. It has been estimated that cow farts contribute annually almost 100 million tons of methane to the atmosphere (F. Pearce, "Methane: The Hidden Greenhouse Gas," *New Scientist*, May 6, 1989). A cow produces over 700 times as much methane as a human being, so the most obvious direct connection to human population growth is not critical. (See P. J. Crutzen, I. Anselmann, and W. Seiler, "Methane Production by Domestic Animals and Humans," *Tellus*, vol. 388, pp. 271–80, 1986.)

32. For a recent review of the role of methane in global warming see Pearce, "Methane: The Hidden Greenhouse Gas."

33. There are so many uncertainties in the levels of greenhouse gas emissions and the speed of the climatic system's response to it, that average warming by 2050 could be anything from as much as 9° F. to as little as 0.65° F., with about a 10 percent chance of the change being outside of those boundaries. The chances are around 50-50 that the pace of change will be some 10 to 60 times faster than long-term average natural rates of change. See S. H. Schneider, *Global Warming*.

34. S. H. Schneider, "The Greenhouse Effect: Scientific Basis and Policy Implications," testimony before Subcommittee on Water and Power Resources, Committee on Interior and Insular Affairs, U.S. House of Representatives, Sept. 27, 1988.

35. S. H. Schneider, *Global Warming*, and personal communication.

36. S. Postel, "Stabilizing Chemical Cycles," in L. Brown et al., *State of the World 1987* (Norton, New York, 1987).

37. About all that can be said of the studies done so far (many of them nicely summarized in Schneider, *Global Warming*) is that they indicate the situation will be very complex.

38. See, for example, D. Lincoln, D. Couvet, and N. Sionet, "Response of an Insect Herbivore to Host Plants Grown in Carbon Dioxide Enriched Atmospheres," *Oecologia (Berlin)*, vol. 69, pp. 556–60 (1986); D. Lincoln and D. Couvet, "The Effect of Carbon Supply on Allocation to Allelochemicals and Caterpillar Consumption of Peppermint," ibid., vol. 78, pp. 112–14 (1989); E. Fajer, M. Bowers, and F. Bazzaz, "The Effects of Enriched Carbon Dioxide Atmospheres on Plant–Insect Herbivore Interactions, *Science*, vol. 243, pp. 1198–1200 (1989).

39. We do not count the (tiny and overdue) raising of the automobile fuel-efficiency standards in 1989 as "significant"—although it was at least a move in the right direction.

40. New wetlands will doubtless eventually replace the old ones in some areas, but the rate of their formation is likely to lag far behind the rate of inundation. Furthermore, many new shoreline areas will be already occupied by cities, highways, farms, and so on, and will not be readily available for conversion to coastal marshes.

41. Schneider testimony, "The Greenhouse Effect." See also Schneider's *Global Warming*, chap. 6.

42. See P. Ehrlich, G. Daily, A. Ehrlich, P. Matson, and P. Vitousek, *Global Change and Carrying Capacity: Implications for Life on Earth*, Paper 0022, Morrison Institute for Population and Resource Studies, Stanford University, 1989; in press, proceedings of National Academy of Sciences/Smithsonian Institution Forum on Global Change, Washington, D.C., May 3, 1989. The details of the model will be given in G.

Daily and P. Ehrlich, "An Exploratory Model of the Impact of Rapid Climate Change on the World Food Situation," in preparation.

43. A food model developed at the International Institute for Applied Systems Analysis (*Options*, 1987, no. 1–2) concludes that lower food prices do not eliminate hunger, but "high-price scenarios yield increased numbers of starving, despite the consequent higher long-term food production in developing countries."

44. At the moment, we also have the theoretical option of consuming less livestock (especially those that are grain-fed) and using land now devoted to growing feed to producing food for human beings. But this "fail-safe" mechanism is certainly not "designed" for that role, and it is highly unlikely to function (we suspect the rich would continue to eat meat while the poor died in large numbers).

45. Technically, "acid deposition," since acid reaches the ground through rain, fog, snow, and dry deposition.

46. For an excellent overview, see J. Harte, "Acid Rain," in P. Ehrlich and J. Holdren, eds., *The Cassandra Conference* (Texas A & M Press, College Station, 1988), pp. 125–46.

47. The production of significant acid precipitation is a complex response to the injection of sulfur and nitrogen oxides into the atmosphere. For instance, when local pollution problems resulted in the building of much taller power-plant stacks, local air-pollution problems were rapidly converted to regional acid-precipitation problems. There also may be significant nonlinearities in the atmospheric chemistry.

48. For an extreme example, see J. Harte, "An Investigation of Acid Precipitation in Qinghai Province, China." *Atmospheric Environment*, vol. 17, pp. 403–8 (1983). In northern China, airborne dust tends to neutralize acid rain, but in southern China rainfall with an average pH less than 4.5 falls in 13 cities (reported in J. Silvertown, "A Silent Spring in China," *New Scientist*, July 1, 1989, p. 57). In Guandong, Guangxi, and Hubei provinces (all southern) the pH of the rain is between 4 and 4.2 (Forestier, "The Degreening of China"). Rainfall with a pH of about 4.5 caused great biological difficulties in Adirondack lakes. Its impacts on Chinese natural aquatic communities and aquaculture facilities will depend on the buffering capacity of the soil.

49. M. Simons, "High Ozone and Acid-Rain Levels Found Over African Rain Forests, *New York Times*, June 19, 1989.

50. The severity of damage to biological systems from acid deposition, and the speed with which that damage appears, are very largely a function of the buffering capacity of the soil. Ecosystems with very alkaline soils may show very little damage over very long time periods.

51. Quoted in Simons, "High Ozone and Acid Rain."

52. How the climate system works was described early in chapter 5; more information is in the Appendix. See also S. H. Schneider and R. Londer, *The Coevolution of Climate and Life* (Sierra Club Books, San Francisco, 1984).

53. CFCs, if uncontrolled, could account for as much as a quarter of the warming in the next century (Schneider, *Global Warming*).

54. *Development Forum*, May–June 1989.

55. H. E. Dregne, *Desertification of Arid Lands* (Harwood, New York,

1983), and "Combating Desertification: Evaluation of Progress," *Environmental Conservation*, vol. 11, pp. 115–21 (1984).

56. D. Ferguson and N. Ferguson, *Sacred Cows at the Public Trough* (Maverick Publications, Bend, Ore., 1983).

57. M. A. F. Kassas, "Ecology and Management of Desertification," in H. J. De Blij, ed., *Earth '88: Changing Geographic Perspectives* (National Geographic Society, Washington, D.C., 1988), p. 198; UNEP, *General Assessment of Progress in the Implementation of the Plan of Action to Combat Desertification*, Report of the Executive Director, 1984, Nairobi, UNEP/GC.12/9.

58. Dregne, op. cit.

59. Independent Commission on International Humanitarian Issues, *The Encroaching Desert: The Consequences of Human Failure* (Zed Books, London, 1986).

60. R. Nelson, quoted in B. Forse, "The Myth of the Marching Desert," *New Scientist*, Feb. 4, 1989, p. 32.

61. Ibid.

62. N. Myers, *Gaia: An Atlas of Planet Management*; P. R. Ehrlich, A. H. Ehrlich, and J. P. Holdren, *Ecoscience: Population, Resources, Environment* (Freeman, San Francisco, 1977), p. 628.

63. P. R. Ehrlich, *The Machinery of Nature* (Simon and Schuster, New York, 1986); David Hopcraft, personal communication.

64. R. Baker, "Famine: The Cost of Development," *Ecologist*, vol. 4, pp. 170–75 (June 1974).

65. Ferguson and Ferguson, *Sacred Cows at the Public Trough*. Overstocking in the U.S. West has no significant human-population component, since the relatively tiny amount of beef produced does not go to hungry people or even allow pressures to be reduced on tropical forests being cleared for pasture. It is mostly a story of greed, stupidity, and the ignorance and incompetence of people ranging from senators to bureaucrats, as this fine book shows.

66. Southern African Development Coordination Conference, *SADCC Agriculture: Toward 2000* (FAO, Rome, Italy, 1984).

67. L. R. Brown, and C. Flavin, "The Earth's Vital Signs," in Brown et al., *State of the World 1988* (Norton, New York, 1988), p. 9.

68. Forestier, "The Degreening of China."

69. The Everglades have been under threat for a long time; see J. Harte and R. Socolow, "The Everglades: Wilderness Versus Rampant Land Development in South Florida," in J. Harte and R. Socolow, eds., *Patient Earth* (Holt, Rinehart and Winston, New York, 1971), pp. 181–202.

70. A distinctive, pure white south-Florida population of the common great blue heron.

71. G. V. N. Powell, A. H. Powell, and N. K. Paul, "Brother, Can You Spare a Fish?," *Natural History*, February 1988, pp. 34–38.

72. John Harte, personal communication. Fresh water, of course, floats on salt water, so the saltwater intrusion amounts to making the underground reservoir shallower.

73. Harte and Socolow, "The Everglades."

74. U.S. Bureau of the Census, *Statistical Abstract of the United States:*

1982–83 (103d ed.; Washington, D.C., 1982). The Chinese number is said to have increased to 3.2 million by 1985.

75. These estimates are based on 1986 statistics from WRI and IIED, *World Resources, 1988–89* (Basic Books, New York, 1988). Note that the assumptions in the statement include that energy-use differentials will remain the same as the babies grow up, and that technological changes will be parallel in all nations. Statistics are also very rough estimates, especially in the poorer nations, and a disproportionately larger fraction of damage from energy use is likely to come from *noncommercial* energy use (such as agricultural burning and the gathering of fuelwood by individual families). None of this changes the validity of the basic point.

76. P. 130.

CHAPTER 7: POPULATION AND PUBLIC HEALTH

1. For more detail, see P. Ehrlich, A. Ehrlich, and J. Holdren, *Ecoscience: Population, Resources, Environment* (Freeman, San Francisco, 1977).

2. Garbage from New York City is now hauled to the Middle West; Seattle is negotiating to send its refuse to eastern Oregon.

3. We are using the term loosely, since in this case no single factor of production is "fixed" in the classical sense.

4. The point where diminishing returns are encountered will vary with the specific situation, but in most cases humanity is now well beyond that point.

5. M. Renner, "Car Sick," *World Watch*, November/December 1988.

6. S. Postel, "Global View of a Tropical Disaster," *American Forests*, November/December 1988.

7. Renner, "Car Sick." Much of the following material is also from this source.

8. I = 0.67, P = 1.25, AT = .54; if P had remained at 1, then I = .54. Note that with the per-capita number of cars increased as well as the mileage driven (A), the T factor has been impressively reduced by more efficient engines with superior pollution-control equipment. A has probably almost doubled, meaning that, on average, emissions per mile driven (T) have been reduced some 75 percent (so that AT is roughly .5).

The reductions, of course, vary with the substance. Lead has been reduced 96 percent, for example; carbon monoxide, only 39 percent. This detail is lost when lumped estimates are given (M. Weisskopf, "A Qualified Failure: The Clean Air Act Hasn't Done the Job," *Washington Post Weekly*, June 19–25, 1989).

9. "Group Gives Gloomy Prognosis," *Denver Post*, July 18, 1989.

10. The biggest problems with industrialized agriculture are that it is generally unsustainable and does serious damage to ecosystem health. Cancer statistics do not indicate the upsurge many of us feared two decades ago when pesticide contamination of food was first widely recognized; however, on first principles we still would recommend stiff laws to control residues and a general policy of minimizing the use of many synthetic chemicals of questionable safety.

11. W. McNeill, *Plagues and People* (Doubleday, New York, 1976).

12. A. Crosby, *The Columbian Exchange: Biological and Cultural Consequences of 1492* (Greenwood Publishing, Westport, Conn., 1972), p. 52.
13. A. Crosby, op. cit. and *Ecological Imperialism: The Biological Expansion of Europe, 900–1900* (Cambridge Univ. Press, Cambridge, 1986).
14. F. Black, "Measles Endemicity in Insular Populations: Critical Community Size and Its Evolutionary Implications," *Journal of Theoretical Biology*, vol. 11, pp. 207–11 (1966).
15. The existence of nonspecific inherited resistance is somewhat controversial and its mechanism uncertain. Nonetheless, on evolutionary grounds it seems very likely to be a major explanation for the high susceptibility of populations to new infections and their high morbidity-mortality rates in comparison to populations long associated with pathogens that are capable of inflicting high mortality. See also T. A. Cockburn, "Infectious Diseases in Ancient Populations," *Current Anthropology*, vol. 12, pp. 45–54 (1971), and the discussion following.
16. Black, "Measles Endemicity"; T. A. Cockburn, "Infectious Diseases in Ancient Populations."
17. Syphilis is caused by the spirochete *Treponema pallidum*; yaws, by its very close relative, *T. pertenue*. Yaws is now largely restricted to hot, humid areas. In earlier times when people huddled together for warmth naked or semiclothed in the winter, it was common in Europe.
18. M. Burnet, and D. O. White, *The Natural History of Infectious Disease*, 4th ed. (Cambridge Univ. Press, Cambridge, 1972), p. 122.
19. H. Temin, "Is HIV Unique or Merely Different?" *Journal of Acquired Immune Deficiency Syndromes*, vol. 2, pp. 1–9 (1989).
20. A monoculture in agriculture is a substantial area in which a single crop is grown. As we have seen, humanity is getting close.
21. L. Altman, "Fearful of Outbreaks, Doctors Pay New Heed to Emerging Viruses," *New York Times*, May 9, 1989. Similar concerns were expressed in 1968 in *The Population Bomb*, pp. 70–71.
22. Altman, "Fearful of Outbreaks . . ."
23. The disease was transmitted by mosquitoes and perhaps bedbugs. It produced severe joint pains, headache, fever, swollen glands, and an itching rash; but after about a week they subsided, and recovery was ordinarily complete. The relationship of the virus to that of another disease, Chikungunya (Chik), that occurred in Tanganyika and the Congo around the same time is not clear. For details, see R. Fiennes, *Zoonoses of Primates: The Epidemiology and Ecology of Simian Diseases in Relation to Man* (Weidenfeld and Nicolson, London, 1967), from which we've drawn much of our information on O'nyong-nyong fever.
24. Ibid., pp. 7–8.
25. Such a mortality rate creates a very strong selective pressure on the pathogen to become less lethal, which is exactly what happened to the myxomatosis virus (see F. Fenner, B. McAuslan, C. Mims, J. Sambrook, and D. White, *The Biology of Viruses* [Academic Press, New York, 1974]). Of course, that isn't much comfort for the victims who create the selective pressure.
26. In addition to those mentioned below, there is also monkey-B virus and several new hemorrhagic-fever viruses.

27. Ehrlich, Ehrlich, and Holdren, *Ecoscience*, chap. 10.

28. "New Outbreak of Marburg Disease," *New Scientist*, Oct. 28, 1976, p. 199.

29. R. Chandra, "Nutrition, Immunity, and Infection: Present Knowledge and Future Directions," *Lancet*, March 26, 1983, pp. 688–91.

30. Called simian immunodeficiency viruses.

31. AIDS Monitor, "French Probe New Virus from Wild Chimp as Other Monkey Viruses Shed Light on Origin of HIV," *New Scientist*, June 9, 1988, p. 40.

32. A discussion of the possible African origin of AIDS with extensive documentation can be found in P. Epstein and R. Packard, "The Social Context of AIDS in Africa," *Science for the People*, January/February 1987, pp. 10–17, 32. It is not at all clear that the speculations in this article are correct, but it provides a sense of the complexity of the issue. See also M. A. Gonda, "The Natural History of AIDS," *Natural History*, 1986, no. 5, pp. 78–81.

33. For an interesting discussion of many of the issues surrounding "blame" for the AIDS epidemic, see Renée Sabatier, *Blaming Others: Prejudice, Race and Worldwide AIDS* (Panos Institute, London, 1988).

34. W. Langer, "The Black Death," *Scientific American*, February 1964.

35. Like all other RNA viruses.

36. B. Larder, G. Darby, and D. Richman, "HIV with Reduced Sensitivity to Zidovudine (AZT) Isolated During Prolonged Therapy," *Science*, vol. 243, pp. 1731–34 (1989).

37. Temin, "Is HIV Unique or Merely Different?" Our discussion of changed transmissibility leans heavily on this source, but see the more pessimistic view of Lederberg, cited below (quoted in R. Weiss, "Waiting for the Real-life Andromeda Strain," *Washington Post Weekly*, Oct. 16–22, 1989).

38. F. Fenner, B. McAuslan, C. Mims, J. Sambrook, and D. White, *The Biology of Viruses*, 2nd ed. (Academic Press, New York, 1974).

39. This may be explained by factors other than differences in viral strains, such as a high incidence of sexually transmitted diseases whose lesions aid the passage of HIV, less male circumcision, and more female circumcision.

40. See N. Kreiger, "The Epidemiology of AIDS in Africa," *Science for the People*, January/February 1987, pp. 18–20; S. Kingman, "Ten Times More AIDS Cases in Africa," *New Scientist*, Sept. 22, 1988, p. 20. For a discussion of the social downside of examining the origins of AIDS, see R. Sabatier et al., *Blaming Others*.

41. M. John, "A Model of HIV-1 Transmission in Developing Countries" (1988). Manuscript.

42. J. H. Callicott, "Amoebic Meningioencephalitis Due to Free-living Amoebas of the *Hartmanella* (Acanthomoeba) *naegleria* Group," *American Journal of Clinical Pathology*, vol. 49 (1968), p. 84.

43. T. Daniels and R. Falco, "The Lyme Disease Invasion," *Natural History*, July 1989.

44. K. Warren, "Precarious Odyssey of an Unconquered Parasite," *Natural History*, May 1974.

45. Quoted by Peter Raven in *Calypso Log*, June 1989. This is also the source of the figure on scientists and technologists.

46. B. Commoner, "How Poverty Breeds Overpopulation and Not the Other Way Around," *Ramparts*, August/September 1975.

47. See discussion in Ehrlich, Ehrlich, and Holdren, *Ecoscience*, especially pp. 778–79.

48. What is often not equal is the quality of sanitation and the availability of medical care. Japan is quite crowded and the population density in Tokyo is extraordinary, yet public-health measures keep mortality from disease very low.

49. McNeill, *Plagues and People*, p. 275.

50. UN Centre for Human Settlements, *Global Report on Human Settlements 1986* (Oxford Univ. Press, New York, 1986); WRI and IIED, *World Resources 1988–89* (Basic Books, New York, 1988).

51. Recently, city planners have scaled back previous forecasts of 25 million for São Paulo—see E. Robinson, "Straddling the First and Third Worlds," *Washington Post Weekly*, July 10–16, 1989.

52. WRI and IIED, *World Resources 1987* (Basic Books, New York, 1987).

53. E. Goldsmith and N. Hildyard, *The Earth Report: The Essential Guide to Global Ecological Issues* (Price Stern Sloan, New York, 1988).

54. R. Weintraub, "Bombay—Hell in a Very Small Place," *Washington Post Weekly*, Dec. 19–25, 1988.

55. WRI and IIED, *World Resources 1988–89*; PRE and AHE personal observations in 1987; Robinson, "Straddling the First and Third Worlds."

56. E. Hollings, "Decaying America: The Underside of the Reagan Legacy," *Washington Post Weekly*, May 8–14, 1989.

57. Administered by the organization Zero Population Growth in 1988.

58. The criteria (in italics) were assessed as follows: For *population change*, cities growing rapidly or shrinking were reckoned to be less desirable places to live in than those with relatively stable populations. *Crowding* was measured by the percentage of housing units classed as crowded by the Census Bureau, and *education* by per-pupil expenditures and proportion of the adult population having finished high school. *Violent crime* was evaluated both by the rate of such crimes per 100,000 population and by changes in that rate. *Community economics* was measured by unemployment rates and Moody's rating of the city's municipal bonds; and *individual economics* by the percentage of families and individuals below the poverty line and changes in per-capita income between 1979 and 1985. *Births* to women under the age of 20 was another criterion, as were four general measures of environmental quality: *air quality* (compliance with EPA standards), *hazardous wastes* (number of hazardous or potentially hazardous sites), ground and surface *water quality* (U.S. Geological Survey ratings), and *sewage* treatment (EPA reports on quality and capacity).

59. No doubt there are complex interactions among these factors that may never be sorted out fully. A careful study of the degree to which population *change*, poverty, and lack of education may be causative variables would be desirable. Teenage pregnancy, of course, *is* a factor in population growth and thus in making cities larger.

60. United States Commission on Population Growth and the American Future, *Population and the American Future*, 6 vols. (U.S. Government Printing Office, Washington, D.C., 1972).

61. P. Ehrlich and J. Freedman, "Population, Crowding, and Human Behavior," *New Scientist*, April 1, 1971.
62. J. Forrester, "Counterintuitive Behavior of Social Systems," *Technology Review*, vol. 73, pp. 52–68 (1971).

CHAPTER 8: POPULATION, GROWTHISM, AND NATIONAL SECURITY

1. H. George, 1902, *Progress and Poverty*, 4th ed. (Doubleday, Page, New York, 1902), p. 141. The book was originally published two decades earlier; George was responding to a Malthusian statement by John Stuart Mill.
2. Quoted in P. Ehrlich, A. Ehrlich, and J. Holdren, *Ecoscience: Population, Resources, Environment* (Freeman, San Francisco, 1977), p. 807.
3. Quoted by L. Grant, "Too Many Old People or Too Many Americans? Thoughts About the Pension Panic," *NPG Forum*, July 1988. Boulding is himself an extremely distinguished economist, whose classic article "The Economics of the Coming Spaceship Earth," in H. Jarrett, ed., *Environmental Quality in a Growing Economy* (Johns Hopkins Press, Baltimore, 1966), should be read by every economics student right after completing a course in ecology.
4. A recent source for this and many of the other specious arguments for population growth found in this chapter is B. Wattenberg, *The Birth Dearth* (Pharos Books, New York, 1987). See also J. Rauch, "Kids as Capital," *Atlantic Monthly*, August 1989.
5. Demographers speak of the "dependency ratio"—the proportion of people in the productive age classes, defined as 15–64 years of age. In the U.S., that ratio has fluctuated between 61 and 66 percent between 1940 and 1985, with no perceptible impact on the economy. If fertility doesn't change much in the future, it will climb to about 69 percent by 2010 and then decline to 63 percent by 2025. The source of these figures is L. Grant, "Too Many Old People or Too Many Americans?"
6. L. Grant, op. cit.
7. Early followers of Adam Smith, economists David Ricardo and John Stuart Mill developed the theory of comparative advantage and showed the benefits of free trade under the assumption that (as Ricardo put it) people's disinclination to leave the country of their birth and subject themselves to the laws of strangers would "check the emigration of capital." These pioneers never envisioned that capital would become mobile. They could not imagine that an American television manufacturer might set up shop in Taiwan to take advantage of lower labor costs, or that a Taiwanese manufacturer might move his capital and technological expertise to Bangladesh for the same reason. They did not know a world of multinational corporations in which transfers internal to the firm could be international. Modern economists so love the old logical argument for comparative advantage that they have ignored that its foundation, capital immobility, has crumbled, and that, as a result, absolute advantage will increasingly rule.

This issue is discussed in depth in H. Daly and J. Cobb, Jr., *For the Common Good: Redirecting the Economy Toward Community, the*

Environment, and a Sustainable Future (Beacon Press, Boston, 1990). This book is a must for all those interested in the state of Earth's economic system—it doesn't oppose international trade, but presses for balanced trade between national communities as opposed to free trade among individuals across national boundaries.

8. "Steady-State Versus Growth Economics: Issues for the Next Century," paper given at Hoover Institution Conference on Population, Resources and Environment, Stanford University, Feb. 1–3, 1989.

9. Although this discussion is focused on the U.S., we must point out that there is much more wastage of minds in poor countries, where millions of children are retarded by malnutrition and have little or no opportunity for education.

10. As Edward Abbey used to say. He is sadly missed; his last book, *The Fool's Progress* (Henry Holt, New York, 1988), is a novel that touches cogently on many of the issues discussed in this book.

11. Daly's work has been built on foundations laid by John Stuart Mill, Kenneth Boulding, and Nicholas Georgescu-Roegen. See, for example, H. Daly, *Steady State Economics: The Economics of Biophysical Equilibrium and Moral Growth* (Freeman, San Francisco, 1977); and Daly and Cobb, Jr., *For the Common Good*. Daly's brilliant writings are the best introduction to ecological economics.

12. We have been cheered by the writings of John Gowdy at Rensselaer Polytechnic and Joseph Vogel at the University of Southern Mississippi. Sadly, the economics departments at the most prestigious universities tend to be both the most isolated from reality and the most dogmatic. Resource economists, who understand many of the issues discussed here, have had little impact on the profession as a whole.

13. R. Repetto, W. Magrath, M. Wells, C. Beer, and F. Rossini, *Wasting Assets: Natural Resources in the National Income Accounts* (World Resources Institute, Washington, D.C., 1989).

14. More technically, the central economic question ought to be: How can the costs to society of the impacts of the different economic agents on the functioning of ecosystems be internalized in such a way that those agents will respond to those "true" costs, which are now externalities? If that could be properly done, the scale of the economic system would presumably adjust itself so as to leave ecosystem services largely unimpaired.

15. W. Beckerman, "Economists, Scientists, and Environmental Catastrophe," Inaugural lecture, University College, London (unpublished).

16. J. Parsons, *Population Fallacies* (Elek/Pemberton, London, 1977). This excellent book contains much material pertinent to this chapter.

17. This, of course, refers to economic growth *per capita*.

18. For a more detailed discussion see Ehrlich, Ehrlich, and Holdren, *Ecoscience*. Over the last couple of millennia there in fact has been a pattern of alternating economic growth and shrinkage—*not* constant growth. For example, the purchasing power of builders' wages in the south of England was higher in 1500 than it was in 1850.

19. A nation's GNP is its total annual output of goods and services. It is a convenient economic indicator, but per-capita GNP unfortunately is often confused with an index of the quality of life (QOL). To claim that

per-capita GNP does measure quality of life (as some would) involves making some extremely culturebound value judgments and concluding that the average American has a life twice as high in quality as an average New Zealander and 10 times as high as an average Costa Rican. It requires one to believe that a Los Angeleno is perhaps 100 times better off than one of America's Founding Fathers or a Bushman or an Eskimo before contact with European culture. Only someone who equates quality of life primarily with quantity of gadgets could hold such a view.

20. It is also based on the "common-pool" problem of economics, discussed later under the rubric "the tragedy of the commons."

21. Technically, this belief allows economists to think we can live in a world of high discount rates forever.

22. H. Barnett and C. Morse, *Scarcity and Growth: The Economics of National Resource Availability* (Johns Hopkins Univ. Press, Baltimore/London, 1963), p. 11.

23. The ultimate homogeneity would even destroy the distinctions between the atoms.

24. The largely unmeasured ultimate social and environmental costs of such "successful" substitutions may one day give us an entirely different perspective—and greatly dampen expectations of reducing the environmental damage done by growing populations by working on the T factor in the $I = PAT$ equation. Is paper actually saved by computers? You certainly couldn't prove it from the flow from high-speed printers in our vicinity! And what are the costs in loss of privacy when everyone's financial transactions are in computers? Computers may make the storing of library materials more convenient, but what do they do to the cost and convenience of using them? How do we evaluate the military uses of computers, especially if they begin to take control of military decision-making (as they would if the U.S. or the Soviet Union went into a "launch-on-warning" strategic posture)? We are heavy users of computers ourselves, but it is nonetheless not certain that their benefits outweigh their costs; the issue is complex.

25. P. Ehrlich and H. Mooney, "Extinction, Substitution, and Ecosystem Services," *BioScience*, vol. 33, pp. 248–54 (1983).

26. P. Ehrlich, "The Limits to Substitution: Meta-Resource Depletion and a New Economic-Ecological Paradigm," *Ecological Economics*, vol. 1, pp. 9–16 (1989).

27. WRI and IIED, *World Resources 1988–89* (Basic Books, New York, 1988).

28. An exception here is South Africa, where the disenfranchised majority is badly in need of economic growth.

29. That, of course, doesn't mean that no further research is required; more information is badly needed so that recommendations can be fine-tuned and our progress (or lack of it) monitored. It is already clear, for instance, that the flux of greenhouse gases into the atmosphere should be reduced as rapidly as possible, but additional knowledge will be required to enable us to make sound predictions of the pace and direction of regional climate change, and to make judgments on the most effective measures to take to mitigate them.

30. First issue published January 1989 by Elsevier Science Publishers, P.O. Box 330, 1000 AH Amsterdam, The Netherlands.

31. Many graduate students in economics, realizing that advancement in the field requires emphasis on such questionable exercises, conclude "that graduate economics education is succeeding in narrowing students' interests." But a survey by two economists (D. Colander and A. Klamer, "The Making of an Economist," *Journal of Economic Perspectives*, vol. 1, pp. 95–111 [1987]), from which the quote is taken, of the students' opinions of the importance of reading in other fields to their development as economists did not even list ecology or any other biological science among the fields to be scored by the students. Moreover, the lowest score given was to physics. Only 2 percent of the students considered it very important, 6 percent important, and 27 percent moderately important, whereas 64 percent rated it unimportant. Small wonder the equivalents of perpetual-motion machines remain embedded in economic thought!

32. A major barrier to this, as well as to other interdisciplinary work, is the conservatism and highly bureaucratic structure of universities.

33. Suggestions on how to do this can be found in R. Ornstein and P. Ehrlich, *New World/New Mind* (Doubleday, New York, 1989). We do not suggest special courses at these levels, since most school systems are already failing to turn out students adequately prepared in English, mathematics, geography, history, science, or even the basics of how our government works. There is little point in teaching about the loss of biodiversity in the Amazon basin if the students don't know where (or what) the Amazon is.

34. B. Wattenberg, *The Birth Dearth*.

35. Germany forced Russia to sue for peace even though the Germans were also fighting the French, the British, the Italians, and the Americans (combined populations about 220 million, not counting colonies) on the western front.

36. The Japanese conquered much of China, destroyed British and Dutch power in the Pacific, and (briefly) gave the United States and Australia a run for their money, in spite of the enormous population differentials in favor of the Allies. We didn't add in the British, Dutch, and Australian populations, since many of their resources had already been expended against Germany and Italy. For a thorough examination of the basic elements of national strength, see P. Kennedy, *The Rise and Fall of the Great Powers* (Random House, New York, 1987). For a fine brief look at how Japan managed to be so successful for the first 6 months after Pearl Harbor, and at how Isoruku Yamamoto and others realized that the comparative strengths of the industrial plants of the U.S. and Japan preordained Japan's defeat, see J. Keegan, *The Price of Admiralty* (Viking, New York, 1988).

37. Numbers also don't count much today in the great East–West confrontation. The Soviet Union outnumbers the U.S. (1990 Soviet population, 292 million; U.S., 251 million). Nonetheless, the Soviet side is weaker by most military standards. NATO nations have greater technological capability than those of the Warsaw Pact. That difference in capability applies to the Soviet forces themselves. Their weapons are less sophisticated, and major units of the Soviet ground forces are composed of minority troops that do not speak Russian. In many Soviet infantry and armored units, the average soldier isn't even trained to read a map. (For an interesting, if controversial, look at the Soviet Army from the inside, see V. Suvorov, *Inside the Soviet Army* [Macmillan, New York, 1982]. Other important books on this subject are A. Cockburn, *The Threat: Inside the Soviet Military Machine* [Random House, New York, 1983], and T. Gervasi, *The Myth of Soviet Military Supremacy* [Harper and Row, New York, 1986]).

Above all, the Russians can't be certain which side their various satellite armies would fight for. Military strength often can be more a question of the quality of allies than of brute numbers. Our Joint Chiefs of Staff have repeatedly testified that they wouldn't trade our forces for the Soviet forces. Indeed, since it would take only a couple of dozen nuclear weapons to destroy the Soviet Union as a functioning entity (and about the same number for the U.S.), the Israelis alone probably have enough military power to deter any sane Soviet leader from attacking them. (Midair-refueled, nuclear-capable Israeli aircraft could bomb cities in southern Russia, and Israel has reputedly acquired intermediate-range ballistic missiles. There is no reason to think that the Soviets would be willing to trade, say, Odessa and Rostov for the destruction of Israel.)

38. A. Westing, ed., *Global Resources and International Conflict* (Oxford Univ. Press, New York, 1986).
39. G. Hardin, "The Tragedy of the Commons," *Science*, vol. 162, pp. 1243–48 (1968).
40. The original commons referred to by Hardin was undivided pastureland, used communally. It was to everyone's individual advantage to maximize the number of sheep herded on the commons; in aggregate, this led to overgrazing and disaster for all herdsmen.
41. J. Cooley, "The War over Water," *Foreign Policy*, no. 54, pp. 3–26 (1984).
42. S. Postel, personal communication.
43. N. Myers. "The Environmental Dimensions of Security Issues." Mimeo. Myers has written extensively on these subjects. See also his "Population, Environment, and Conflict," *Environmental Conservation*, vol. 14, no. 1, pp. 15–22 (1987).
44. P. Ehrlich, D. Bilderback, and A. Ehrlich, *The Golden Door: International Migration, Mexico, and the United States* (Ballantine, New York, 1979).
45. S. Hamburg and C. Cogbill, "Historical Decline of Red Spruce Populations and Climatic Warming," *Nature*, vol. 331, pp. 428–30 (1988).

CHAPTER 9: THE BANG, THE WHIMPER, AND THE ALTERNATIVE

1. For early descriptions of the possible atmospheric effects of nuclear war, see T. Stonier, *Nuclear Disaster* (World Publishing, Cleveland, 1964); P. R. Ehrlich, "Population Control or Hobson's Choice," in L. R. Taylor, ed., *The Optimum Population for Britain* (Academic Press, London, 1969); and P. Ehrlich and A. Ehrlich, *Population, Resources, Environment; Issues in Human Ecology* (Freeman, San Fran-

cisco, 1970), pp. 191–93. The central papers of the more recent analysis by the scientific community are R. Turco, O. Toon, T. Ackerman, J. Pollack, and C. Sagan, "Nuclear Winter: Global Consequences of Multiple Nuclear Weapons Explosions" (known as the "TTAPS" study), *Science*, vol. 222, pp. 1283–92 (Dec. 23, 1983); and P. Ehrlich, J. Harte, M. Harwell, P. Raven, C. Sagan, G. Woodwell, J. Berry, E. Ayensu, A. Ehrlich, T. Eisner, S. Gould, H. Grover, R. Herrera, R. May, E. Mayr, C. McKay, H. Mooney, N. Myers, D. Pimentel, and J. Teal, "Long Term Biological Consequences of Nuclear War," ibid., pp. 1293–1300.

More recent overviews are P. Ehrlich, "The Ecology of Nuclear War," in P. Ehrlich and J. Holdren, eds., *The Cassandra Conference: Resources and the Human Predicament* (Texas A & M Press, College Station, 1988); and A. Ehrlich, "Nuclear Winter: Is Rehabilitation Possible?," in J. Cairns, Jr., ed., *Rehabilitating Damaged Ecosystems*, vol. II (CRC Press, Boca Raton, Fla, 1988). A treatment of these issues including fine coverage of the social and economic effects on a society of a nuclear attack can be found in the report of the Greater London Area War Risk Study Commission, *London Under Attack* (Basil Blackwell, Oxford, 1986). Some of the physical studies subsequent to the TTAPS study indicated that climatic effects might not be as severe as originally expected, and this brought great joy to some fans of nuclear war. But more recent work is pushing the pendulum in the other direction (e.g., J. Nelson, "Fractility of Sooty Smoke: Implications for the Severity of Nuclear Winter," *Nature*, vol. 339, pp. 611–13 [June 22, 1989]). It really makes little difference, since, although there remains considerable uncertainty about the precise atmospheric effects of a large-scale nuclear war, one anywhere within the range of possibilities would translate into an ecological and social disaster of unprecedented magnitude.

2. P. 61.
3. S. H. Schneider, *Global Warming* (Sierra Club Books, San Francisco, 1989).
4. S. Camp, ed., *Population Pressures—Threat to Democracy* (Population Crisis Committee, 1120 19th St. NW, Suite 550, Washington, D.C. 20036, 1989). Indicators employed for demographic pressures were rates of population increase, urbanization, and labor-force growth; age composition, and heterogeneity (the existence of major ethnic, religious, or language divisions). Indicators of political stability were number of changes of government between 1962 and 1989, political freedoms (participation in the political process), civil liberties (right of free expression and assembly, freedom of religion, etc.), communal violence (violent conflicts between groups), and frustrated expectations (a proxy indicator of the gap between employment expectations and opportunities). Since most of the unstable nations in this study are poor ones, the argument may be made that it only illustrates that poverty causes instability. Arguing about this is probably a waste of time, returning to the question of whether poverty causes population growth or vice versa. We think both rising standards of living *and* gradual population shrinkage would be conducive to political stability.
5. In *The Population Bomb* we tried to deal with uncertainties about the

course of events by using scenarios—little stories about the future as an aid to thinking about it. That was a mistake, because people took the scenarios as predictions, and some concluded that because they had not "come true" the basic message of the book was wrong. But, of course, the entire purpose of the book and the scenarios was to stimulate the kind of action that would *prevent* events such as those described in the scenarios from occurring. (Unfortunately, as we have seen, much of the action that *was* stimulated by the food problems of the late 1960s turned out to be a short-term cure which has made the long-term situation worse.) At any rate, we're avoiding scenarios in this book. We would not be surprised, however, if some reviewer dismissed *The Population Explosion* because the scenarios in *The Population Bomb* did not actually materialize. Live and learn.

6. Witness the great popularity of ethnic restaurants and the interest in other cultures manifested in entertainment, magazines, travel/learning programs, museums, and so on. Of course, only a minority of the population manifests most of the appreciation, but nonetheless it's a start.

7. This trend is present not only in places like Canada, Northern Ireland, Kenya, India, and Lebanon, but recently in the Soviet Union and, upon the partial collapse of the civil-rights consensus with encouragement from the Reagan administration, in the U.S. Interconnected social units with varied structures and values might come to replace the mass culture that now predominates. Such a trend in the U.S. can be seen, for example, in the diversification of cable-television systems at the expense of a few nationwide networks. Ethnic refragmentation in the world is occurring at a time of a shrinking resource pie, environmental deterioration, and massive and growing economic inequity. While ethnic identification can be a source of strength, it obviously also can lead to conflict unless carefully guided by wise leaders. Unless the problems that divide groups can be alleviated, the end of the road may well be a breakdown of civilization into numerous small warring fragments.

8. For example, Prince Philip's "Living Off the Land," BBC "Dimbleby" lecture, March 7, 1989, and also the collection of his speeches and writings, *Down to Earth* (Collins, London, 1988).

9. Literally thousands have written or told us in person that reading *The Population Bomb* led them to have smaller families. Needless to say, this is not a scientific sample, but it does convince us that the book had an impact.

10. Economists may object that building mass transit is extremely expensive and thus not often feasible because it won't "pay for itself." This is just another example of the need to change the way economists think of costs. The comparison should be made to the high costs to the environment (and the human stress) caused by the use of automobiles and the costs of maintaining the infrastructure to support their use. One recent estimate for the repair and replacement of the U.S. interstate freeway system alone for the next few decades is $600 billion. Similarly stratospheric estimates have been made for repairing New York City's poorly maintained bridges. Finally, the economists' calculations are based on an assumption that gasoline will always be cheap. If all those costs are taken into account, mass-transit systems become very economical indeed.

CHAPTER 10: CONNECTIONS AND SOLUTIONS: I

1. This issue is dealt with in detail in R. Ornstein and P. Ehrlich, *New World/New Mind* (Doubleday, New York, 1989).

2. Killing of individuals deemed dangerous was standard practice in Eskimo groups until very recently; it is still deemed a social remedy in nations as disparate as the U.S. and the People's Republic of China.

3. R. Ornstein and P. Ehrlich, *New World/New Mind*, gives a long series of suggestions on how to achieve conscious evolution.

4. A technique for promoting small families that is already widely in use in China and India.

5. W. Wisbaum, "Costa Rica Battles High Fertility Rate," *Popline*, May–June 1989.

6. *New York Times*, Oct. 20, 1985.

7. Oxford Univ. Press, Oxford. The excerpt that follows is from p. 95.

8. Remember, the essence of natural selection is differential reproduction; the winners leave more offspring than the losers.

9. Maximizing reproduction ordinarily means having the maximum possible offspring survive to be reproductive adults in the next generation. This is not necessarily achieved by a woman starting childbearing as early as possible and having a maximum number of births as close together as possible. Such behavior is known to increase risks to the mother's health and life and can reduce the total production of offspring over her lifetime. Having too many children too early and too close together jeopardizes the survival of the children to reproductive age; infant and child deaths in such families are consistently much higher than among children in well-spaced families—even among the rich and well fed.

10. A further reduction in Austria, Luxembourg, West Germany, and Italy, which have TFRs of 1.4 or less, should not be necessary.

11. PRE discussed the issue with him personally a couple of decades ago when Bush headed the special Republican Task Force on Population and Earth Resources.

12. The quote is from the foreword Bush wrote to Phyllis Piotrow's *World Population Crisis: The United States Response* (Praeger, New York, 1973). The entire document shows Bush's sensitivity to the issues, and in particular to the taboos against discussion of population issues.

13. Italy's population has not yet started to shrink; its birthrate is 10 per 1,000 and its death rate 9. But it will soon join West Germany and Hungary in "negative population growth" if its average completed family size stays this low.

14. It seems unlikely to us that in the foreseeable future abortion (legal or illegal) will totally disappear as a backup to contraception in rich nations. Much of the present need, however, might be met primarily by an abortifacient pill such as RU 486. The problem of abortion in poor nations is much more complex, especially where women resort to it clandestinely as a means of avoiding children their husbands desire. Greatly reducing abortion in poor nations while achieving population control may be much more difficult than in rich nations.

15. If you've had some biology, you'll remember that sperm and eggs are the haplophase of the human life cycle, where each cell contains just

one set of chromosomes. From zygote to adult, we are in the diplophase, and most cells contain two sets of chromosomes, one received from the sperm and one from the egg. We're very impressed by the diplophase, since that is the phase that all antiabortionists, biologists, attorneys, and politicians are in. If people were like mosses, however, it would be the start of the haplophase that we would consider the "beginning of life." The dominant part of a moss's life cycle, the phase of the familiar moss plant, is the haplophase. Debates over the sanctity of human life often become just plain silly because the debaters know so little of elementary biology.

16. Personally, we agree with the old saying "Life begins when the kids leave home and the dog dies."

17. The section that follows leans heavily on the work of our Stanford Law School colleague John Kaplan, one of the most thoughtful legal analysts of social problems. See, in particular, his excellent "What If the Supreme Court Changed Its Mind?," *Stanford Lawyer*, Fall 1988.

18. A first step in that direction may have been taken in the Court's July 3, 1989, decision upholding a Missouri law which forbade the use of public funds or facilities for abortions and placed restrictions on doctors' ability to do late abortions. The main effect of this decision will simply be to make getting abortions much more difficult for poor women, while not affecting women who come from the classes represented by the justices who were in the majority.

As Richard Cohen put it in *The Washington Post Weekly*, July 10–16, 1989, "It is not surprising that the indifference Ronald Reagan showed the poor during his presidency would become a fixture of his Supreme Court. Every molehill of an obstruction—every form to fill out, every permission slip needed, every bus that has to be taken to another state—is a mountain to the poor." Further changes in abortion laws may be made by the Court before this book appears.

19. S. Henshaw and J. Silverman, "The Characteristics and Prior Contraceptive Use of U.S. Abortion Patients," *Family Planning Perspectives*, vol. 20, p. 4 (July–August 1988).

20. After this section was written, a brilliant and comprehensive overview of the situation in the U.S. regarding the development and deployment of new contraceptives appeared: C. Djerassi, "The Bitter Pill," *Science*, vol. 245, pp. 356–61 (July 28, 1989).

CHAPTER 11: CONNECTIONS AND SOLUTIONS: II

1. An excellent description of the attitudes of peasants in India is given in Mahmood Mamdani, *The Myth of Population Control: Family, Caste, and Class in an Indian Village* (Monthly Review Press, New York, 1972). This book, although lacking a broad grasp of population problems, gives much insight into the failures of India's family-planning programs.

2. For an in-depth discussion of the myth that some groups of people are intrinsically better than others, see P. Ehrlich and S. Feldman, *The Race Bomb: Skin Color, Prejudice, and Intelligence* (New York Times/ Quadrangle, New York, 1977).

3. "China on the Population Question," *China Reconstructs*, vol. 23, no. 11 (1974). This journal is published for foreign readers in English and several other languages by the China Welfare Institute to present official views of the PRC.

4. The degree of voluntarism is a matter of some debate, and there is no doubt some sterilizations were coerced. It is difficult to evaluate, since the society had determined that sterilization should take place after a second child (or after the first, if one had signed up for the one-child program). When the rules were broken, forced sterilization was the punishment.

5. In calculating per-capita production, economists had been using too small a divisor.

6. Qu Geping, "Over the Limit," *Earthwatch* (supplement to *New Scientist*), no. 34, p. 2 (1989). Dr. Qu is vice-chairman of China's Environmental Protection Commission and administrator of the National Environmental Protection Agency. We suspect that his estimate of China's long-term carrying capacity is high, but since the nation appears doomed to grow to *at least* twice that number, the point will be moot for a very long time.

7. Some of the mathematical implications of the one-child family in China are explored in J. Harte, *Consider a Spherical Cow: A Course in Environmental Problem Solving* (Wm. Kaufmann, Los Altos, Calif., 1985), pp. 216–23. A great deal of information on China's demographic situation can be found in *People* (International Planned Parenthood Federation, London), vol. 16, no. 1 (1989).

8. The trend clearly is in the wrong direction, since in 1989 it is moving toward coercing pregnant poor women to bear their children whether they want to or not. George Bush's veto in October 1989 of a bill to provide abortion services to poor women who are victims of rape and incest underlined the Supreme Court's retrograde action in this area.

9. Even using official figures. One Chinese scholar, Prof. He Bochuan of Zhongshan University, Guangdong, thinks that there is serious underreporting of births because of the one-child policy, and that China's population in 1989 may have been 1.2 billion (reported in K. Forestier, "The Degreening of China," *New Scientist*, July 1, 1989, p. 53).

10. United Nations, *Demographic Yearbook: Historical Supplement* (UN, New York, 1979). This is the basic source of the pre-1977 demographic statistics used here and below.

11. For a summary of information on family-planning goals, see P. R. and A. H. Ehrlich, *Population, Resources, Environment: Issues in Human Ecology*, 2nd ed. (Freeman, San Francisco, 1972), Table 10–4.

12. B. Crossette, "Why India Is Still Failing to Stop Its Population Surge," *New York Times*, July 9, 1989.

13. United Nations, *Statistical Yearbook, 1985/86* (UN, New York).

14. *Population Bomb*, p. 18.

15. WRI and IIED, *World Resources 1988–1989* (Basic Books, New York, 1988). The following statistics in this paragraph are from the same source.

16. Based on numbers cited in "Kenya Faces Burgeoning Workforce," *Popline*, May–June 1989.

17. J. Perlez, "Birth Control Making Inroads in Populous Kenya," *New York Times*, Sept. 10, 1989.

18. These are Population Reference Bureau figures based on official statistics. But such statistics are very uncertain in most of the Third World, and in Africa in particular. For example, Dr. Muriel Wilson wrote to us about census-taking in Nigeria (letter of March 17, 1989): ". . . attempts to count the numbers are only rough estimates, varying between 100 million, and at least 130 or 140 million, depending on who is doing the estimating. Census takers told me that in the 1970's they had tried to do local counts, and the Heads had said there were about 30 people in their area. When they discovered that the census was not for taxation purposes, but were advised that areas with more than 35,000 population were eligible for a new hospital, they changed their tune, and agreed that yes, there were at least 35,000 people around . . . "

19. J. Weeks, "The Demography of Islamic Nations," *Population Bulletin*, vol. 43, no. 4 (December 1988).

20. Weeks, p. 7.

21. See, for example, Penny Lernoux's "The Papal Spiderweb," *The Nation*, April 10 and 17, 1989. While the hierarchy has been a retrograde force, many individual priests have been supportive of both individual rights and the limitation of families.

22. E. van de Walle and J. Knodel, "Europe's Fertility Transition: New Evidence and Lessons for Today's Developing World," *Population Bulletin*, vol. 34, no. 6 (February 1980).

23. It is a proposition based on confusing correlation with causation. Fertility today tends to be lower in nations that are more developed—or, more technically, fertility and development are "negatively correlated." But that does not mean that development causes birthrates to fall, any more than falling birthrates in China over the last decade have been caused by you personally growing older or by the rise in CO_2 levels in the atmosphere—even though Chinese fertility is negatively correlated with both your age and atmospheric CO_2 concentration.

    Similar points could be made about the observed negative correlation between level of development and rates of malnutrition and illiteracy. Many hunter-gatherer societies, such as Australian aborigines (about as "underdeveloped" as one could get), suffered less malnutrition than one finds in the U.S. today. China's illiteracy rate is about as high as Brazil's, even though by conventional measures Brazil is roughly six times more developed. Clearly, observed correlations of such social factors with levels of development as defined by economists tell us little about underlying mechanisms.

24. N. Birdsall, "Population Growth and Poverty in the Developing World," *Population Bulletin*, vol. 35, no. 5 (December 1980).

25. Ehrlich, Ehrlich, and Holdren, *Ecoscience: Population, Resources, Environment* (Freeman, San Francisco. 1977), p. 781; see also J. E. Kocher, *Rural Development, Income Distribution, and Fertility Decline*, Population Council Occasional Papers, 1973; J. P. Grant, "Development: The End of Trickle Down?," *Foreign Policy*, no. 12 (Fall 1973), pp. 43–65; A. Sweezy, *Recent Light on the Relation Between Socioeconomic Development and Fertility Decline*, Caltech Population Program Occasional Papers, series 1, no. 1 (1973).

26. P. Mauldin and B. Berelson, "Conditions of Fertility Decline in Developing Countries, 1965–1975," *Studies in Family Planning*, vol. 9, no. 5 (1978), p. 104; "Status of Women Key to Future," *Development Forum*, May–June 1989 (reporting on the UN Fund for Population's *State of the World Population Report 1989*).

27. Recent research has demonstrated that this effect holds in developed nations too. In the U.S., a study reported in 1989 that husbands of educated women in the U.S. are likely to live longer and have fewer heart attacks than men with less educated wives.

28. Something like this was originally envisioned as the next step after global distribution and assimilation of the *Global 2000 Report* (Council on Environmental Quality and U.S. State Department [Government Printing Office, Washington, D.C., 1980]), produced at the request of President Jimmy Carter. Ronald Reagan tried to suppress the report; as of this writing (July 1989), George Bush has shown no sign of understanding the need for such planning.

29. These OECD statistics (from the *Christian Science Monitor*, July 3, 1989) will come as a surprise to many Americans long taken in by tales of our generosity—which always focus on the record *absolute* amount we donate (almost $10 billion annually). Information on Japan from C. Foy, "Whither the Japanese Surplus?," *OECD Observer*, no. 158 (June–July 1989), pp. 23–27.

30. "Aid to Population Programs," *Population Today* (published by Population Reference Bureau), vol. 17, no. 3 (March 1989), p. 5.

31. Quoted in *World Development Forum*, vol. 6, no. 20 (Nov. 15, 1988).

32. Sometimes these might require sacrifices of "performance." For example, with the banning of CFCs for use in plastic foams and cooling systems, more efficient and durable refrigerators might not only be more expensive but have smaller capacities relative to their outside dimensions. Paying that price may be necessary to keep society going.

33. See, for example, D. Hayes, *Repairs, Reuse, Recycling: First Steps Towards a Sustainable Society*, Worldwatch Paper 23 (1978).

34. Much of the material in this section is based on P. R. Ehrlich and A. H. Ehrlich, "The Environmental Dimensions of National Security," delivered at the Pugwash Conference, Dagomys, USSR, September 1988.

Chapter 12: What You Can Do

1. *ZPG Reporter*, April 1989. The figure is only for basic maintenance—it doesn't include such things as orthodontia, summer camp, or piano lessons.

2. Of course, this doesn't apply to people who end up trying to raise children alone not by choice but because of divorce or the death of their partners; they deserve sympathy and help.

3. See, for example, H. Breland, "Family Configuration and Intellectual Development," *Journal of Individual Psychology*, vol. 31, pp. 86–96 (1977); R. B. Zajonc, "The Decline and Rise of Scholastic Aptitude Scores," *American Psychologist*, vol. 41, no. 8, pp. 862–67 (1986); Judith Blake, *Family Size and Achievement* (Univ. of California Press, Berkeley, 1989).

4. The level of illegal immigration into the U.S. is only a guesstimate now, and of course is even more uncertain in the future. We suspect that the Census Bureau's projections of immigration are optimistically low. If we saw more action addressing the underlying causes of immigration (see P. Ehrlich, L. Bilderback, and A. Ehrlich, *The Golden Door*, updated ed. [Wideview Books, New York, 1981]), we'd be more inclined to be optimistic, too.

5. "Census Predicts Population Drop in Next Century," *New York Times*, Feb. 1, 1989.

6. You guessed it, we're in the process of writing that book.

7. There remain in our society a great many people who believe that IQ tests are the ultimate index of human quality and who fear that if intelligent people restrain their reproduction, society will quickly be composed of fools. For a recent example of this recurring fallacy, see "A Confederacy of Dunces," *Newsweek*, May 22, 1989.

8. P. Ehrlich and S. Feldman, 1977, *The Race Bomb: Skin Color, Prejudice, and Intelligence* (New York Times/Quadrangle, New York, 1977).

9. One of our greatest resources is a network of friends who have different areas of expertise. If we have a question on energy policy, we know that John Holdren at Berkeley will give us a sound, unbiased answer. If we have to check a critical point on climate change, we call Steve Schneider at the National Center for Atmospheric Research—who is a leading figure in the area of climate change and its impact on society. If we need to check a population statistic, Carl Haub at the Population Reference Bureau is most helpful. Historian Loy Bilderback of Fresno State University is always happy to give us brutal criticisms on things we write, as are psychologist Bob Ornstein, economists Herman Daly and Tim and Lisa Daniel, our fellow biologists at Stanford, and many other friends and colleagues.

   Such professional assistance and criticism is essential when your life is dedicated to trying to keep detailed track of various aspects of the human predicament, weave them together into an integrated whole, and publish the analyses. Of course, this would be overkill for a concerned citizen with another life to lead, but spare-time activism is possible at various levels and can be highly effective.

10. Grossman attacked *Time* magazine's "conversion" issue, in which it "discovered" the environment and even the population problem in poor (but not rich) nations. He was especially upset with *Time*'s failure to point out the central role that many big corporations play in wrecking the environment, and by its refusal to point the finger and name names. We agreed with some of it, and disagreed with some. But it was a good read that would be especially informative for executives both in governments and in firms like Exxon. It was published as "Of Time and Tide" in *Earth Island Journal*, Spring 1989.

11. The key Supreme Court decisions on school desegregation were made in 1954 and 1955, and the first civil-rights law since Reconstruction, protecting voting rights, was passed in 1957. Sit-ins to desegregate restaurants started in the mid-1950s (we were involved in them in Lawrence, Kan.) and became national news when they began in the Deep South in 1960–61. In 1964 an omnibus civil-rights law banned discrim-

ination in public accommodations, jobs, etc., dramatically changing the status of blacks and beginning another decade of progress which, though marred by the assassination of Martin Luther King, Jr., and other setbacks, completely changed race relations in the United States. We've come a long way fast, but of course (as the Reagan rollback of civil rights in the 1980s demonstrated) we still have a long way to go.

APPENDIX: ASPECTS OF HOW EARTH WORKS

1. The major exception is the energy of radioactive decay which drives tectonic movements.
2. Other photosynthetic organisms include several kinds of bacteria, algae, and some algae-containing mutualistic associations such as lichens and corals.
3. Plants also oxidize carbohydrates to extract the energy from their chemical bonds and use it to grow, repair themselves, and reproduce. One can think of the oxidations that go on in the cells of organisms as the equivalent of slow chemical "fires"—since fires transform energy by rapid oxidation.
4. Much of the material on ecology in this appendix is expanded upon at a nontechnical level in P. R. Ehrlich, *The Machinery of Nature* (Simon and Schuster, New York, 1986). A more technical treatment can be found in P. R. Ehrlich and J. Roughgarden, *The Science of Ecology* (Macmillan, New York, 1987).
5. Coevolution is simply the reciprocal evolutionary interaction of two kinds of organisms that are ecologically intimate, such as herbivores influencing the evolution of plants and vice versa (see Ehrlich, *Machinery of Nature*, chap. 4). For more technical information see P. R. Ehrlich and P. H. Raven, "Butterflies and Plants: A Study in Coevolution," *Evolution*, vol. 8, pp. 506–8 (1964), and P. R. Ehrlich, "Coevolution and the Biology of Communities," in K. L. Chambers, ed., *Proc. 29th Ann. Biol. Colloq. 1968* (Oregon State Univ. Press, Corvallis, 1970). More recent reviews are: D. J. Futuyma and M. Slatkin, *Coevolution* (Sinauer, Sunderland, Mass., 1983), and K. C. Spencer, ed., *Chemical Mediation of Coevolution* (Academic Press, New York, 1988).
6. The reasons there are so many more species in the tropics than in other regions are poorly understood. For a discussion of current conjectures, see P. R. Ehrlich and J. Roughgarden, *The Science of Ecology*, pp. 400–402.
7. For details on biogeochemical cycles see P. Ehrlich, A. Ehrlich, and J. Holdren, *Ecoscience: Population, Resources, Environment* (Freeman, San Francisco, 1977).
8. This loss of useful energy is described by the second law of thermodynamics. For more details see Ehrlich, Ehrlich, and Holdren, *Ecoscience*.
9. We say "usually" because if the producers in a food chain are small organisms such as oceanic phytoplankton, they can live and die so fast that they will have a smaller biomass at any given time than longer-lived organisms higher on the food chain. High turnover, in this case,

substitutes for high biomass; and the pyramid of biomass is turned upside down. More energy is still flowing into the lower level, however, and the energy pyramid is right side up.

10. Ozone high in the atmosphere serves as a critical shield for life; near the surface (where it is produced by human activities) it is also a pollutant that is damaging to plants.

11. Carbon, of course, was incorporated into organisms by other processes before photosynthesis evolved.

12. At least once, probably several times, the continents were melded into one huge supercontinent, then slowly broken up into the six major landmasses existing today.

13. For a summary of plate tectonics, see Ehrlich and Roughgarden, *The Science of Ecology*.

14. For more on extinctions and the dinosaurs, see Ehrlich and Roughgarden, op. cit.

15. As shown by a recent computer simulation by Starley Thompson and Paul Crutzen (S. H. Schneider, personal communication, July 1989).

▲

Acknowledgments

▼

We thank the following people who were kind enough to review part or all of the manuscript for us: D. Loy Bilderback (Department of History, Fresno State University), Lester Brown and Sandra Postel (Worldwatch Institute), Gretchen Daily, Marcus Feldman, Patricia Jones, Sharon Long, Harold A. Mooney, Peter Vitousek (Department of Biological Sciences, Stanford University), Herman E. Daly (World Bank), Lisa Daniel and Timothy Daniel (Bureau of Economics, Federal Trade Commission), Carl Haub (Population Reference Bureau), John Harte (Energy and Resources Group, University of California, Berkeley), Mary Ellen Harte (Rocky Mountain Biological Laboratory), John P. Holdren (Energy and Resources Group, University of California, Berkeley), Sally Mallam and Robert Ornstein (Institute for the Study of Human Knowledge), Pamela Matson (NASA, Ames), Irwin Remson (Department of Applied Earth Sciences, Stanford University), Stephen H. Schneider (National Center for Atmospheric Research), and Howard M. Temin (McArdle Laboratory for Cancer Research, University of Wisconsin). Their efforts are very much appreciated, but of course the final responsibility for all opinions and errors lies with us.

Gene Coan (Sierra Club), Sam Hurst (NBC News), Thomas

Merrick (Population Reference Bureau), Norman Myers (Oxford, England), Peter Myers (Audubon Society), Peter Raven (Missouri Botanic Garden), Susan Weber (Zero Population Growth), Muriel Wilson (Victoria, British Columbia), and Scott Wissinger (Biology Department, Allegheny College) were most helpful in providing information or other assistance. As usual, the staff of Stanford's Falconer Biology Library assisted us repeatedly in digging up obscure references; the assistance of Claire Shoens, Gill Senn, and Joe Wible was especially appreciated. Claire is retiring this year, and we want particularly to thank her for innumerable kindnesses over the past twenty-three years. Steve Masley and Pat Browne once again did yeoman service at the copying machine. Peggy Vas Dias helped immeasurably in dealing with a wide array of problems with the manuscript. Our agent, Ginger Barber (Virginia Barber Agency), gave important critical comments on the manuscript, and Bob Bender, our editor, did the same and patiently oversaw the book's production. We also are grateful for the help given by our copy editor, Vera Schneider, who sadly did not live to see the book in print. We would also like to thank our numerous colleagues in ecology, evolutionary biology, and behavior who have helped us in so many ways and have provided important moral support, over the twenty-two years since *The Population Bomb* was written. We must also acknowledge that since ther the job of keeping track of the population/resource/environment situation has been greatly facilitated by the expanded programs of the Population Reference Bureau and by the fine work of the Worldwatch Institute.

Finally, we would like to thank all those who have generously supported our work over the years, especially Peter and Helen Bing, John and Susan Boething, Haydi Danielson, John Gifford, Stanley and Marion Herzstein, the late Joseph Koret and Susan Koret, the late Dean Morrison and Virginia Morrison, and Alan Weeden, and of course our deepest appreciation and love go once again to LuEsther, without whom none of this would have been possible.

Index

Abbey, Edward, 244
abortions, 19, 22, 195–200
absolute poverty, 41
acid rain, 11, 17, 123–24, 132–33, 173, 176–77, 188–89, 220, 228, 236, 238–39
acquired immune deficiency syndrome (AIDS), 11, 17, 34, 143–50, 156, 177, 200
Africa, 82, 122, 188, 217
  acid rain in, 123–24
  agricultural policy in, 105
  AIDS in, 146–49
  arable land in, 96
  declines in death rates in, 56
  demographic momentum in, 61
  desertification in, 83, 127–28
  droughts in, 62, 83
  epidemics in, 144–47
  famines in, 80–81, 83, 126, 128
  food production in, 10, 68, 80–84, 211
  impact of early *Homo sapiens* on, 49
  neglect of indigenous crops in, 103
  overpopulation of, 39–40
  population density of, 38
  population growth in, 14–15, 82–83, 210–12

rise of human species in, 46
starvation in, 21
agriculture, 36, 50–55, 132, 211
  and assault on biotic diversity, 31
  climatic disruption and, 171–72
  climatic sensitivity of, 89–90, 95, 120–23
  and demographic changes, 51–52
  in depletion of natural resources, 26–30
  disruption of, 175–76
  ecology of, 88–109
  fossil fuels used in, 57
  genetic variability in, 33
  government policies on, 97–99, 104–6, 108
  industrial, 76
  inputs and outputs, 91–95
  invention of, 14, 26
  land required by, 88–89
  modernization of, 77
  organic, 137, 184
  ozone layer depletion and, 125
  tropical, *see* tropical agriculture
  weather sensitivity of, 89–91, 95
  see also food production
Agriculture Department, U.S., 98
aircraft safety, 236
air pollution, 43, 53, 136, 138, 154, 173, 181, 220

Alan Guttmacher Institute (AGI),
247
Alaskan National Wildlife Refuge,
133
Alaskan oil spill, 15
American Academy of Arts and
Sciences, 18
Andes, deforestation of, 79
animals, 25–26
extinction of, 30–37, 57
herding of, 51
impact of hunting on, 49–50
predator defenses of, 255
aquifers:
in irrigation, 93, 95
overdrafting of, 28–30, 70–71,
93, 95, 133
poisoning of, 30, 131, 178
Aquino, Corazón, 75
Aral Sea, 94
Arctic National Wildlife Refuge,
220
Argentina, 41, 79, 84, 214
arms races, 45, 175
artificial selection, 106
Asia, 53
arable land in, 96
declines of death rates in, 56
demographic momentum in, 61
desertification in, 127
early human species in, 46
food production in, 43, 69–75,
84, 86
Asia Minor, origins of agriculture
in, 50
Asociación Demográfica
Costarricense, 190
atmospheric gases, 31–32, 37
Audubon Society, 130, 247
Australia, 56, 144
deforestation in, 117
desertification in, 127
economic growth in, 167
food production in, 84
australopithecines, 14
Aztecs, 140–41

Bangladesh, 34, 72–73, 129, 188
Barnett, Harold, 165–66
Barnett, Patricia, 178

Beckerman, Wilfred, 163
Bering Sea, 85
Bihar, 42, 71
biochemicals, 33
biodiversity, 30–37, 95–96
loss of, 34, 42, 228
overpopulation and, 34
biogeochemical cycles, 256
biotechnology, impact of, 106–9
biotic communities, 254–56
birth control, 17, 61
abortion as, 19, 196–200
Catholic Church policy on, 18–
20, 241–42
see also population control and
family planning
birthrates, 23, 152
declines in, 16, 55–56
definition of, 47
demographic momentum and,
59–61
in early hunter-gatherer groups,
47–48
during Industrial Revolution,
55–57
in Italy, 19
blacks, 235
Bohai Sea, fisheries in, 86
Boulding, Kenneth, 159
Brandt, Willy, 151
Brazil, 214, 232
deforestation in, 112, 115–16,
187
food production in, 75–78
migrations in, 62
British Columbia, deforestation in,
117–18
Brown, Edmund G. "Jerry," 98
Brown, Lester, 28, 72, 109, 122
Brundtland, Gro Harlem, 182, 192
bubonic plague, 142–43, 147
Bush, George, 22, 138, 195, 240–
241

CFCs, see chlorofluorocarbons
California Medfly disaster, 98
Californians for Population
Stabilization (CAPS), 246
Campbell, Tom, 239–40
Canada, 56, 64, 84, 119, 167, 193

cancers, 34, 124–25, 134
carbon dioxide (CO₂), 58–59, 91,
    253, 257
    from burning forests, 112, 115–
    118, 124
    from burning fossil fuels, 111,
    113–15, 132–33
    food production and, 119–20
    retarding build-up of, 221–22
carrying capacity, 38–40, 62, 64
Carter, Jimmy, 194
Catalyst Group (in India), 71–72
Catholic Church, 21
    birth control policy of, 18–20,
    241–42
    on food production, 19–20
Census Bureau, 228
Center for Conservation Biology,
    248
Centers of Disease Control, 148
Central America, 79, 117, 213–14
children, hunger among, 67
Chile, food production in, 79
China, in history, 54, 141–43
China, People's Republic of, 76
    acid rain in, 123
    CFC use and, 125–26
    deforestation in, 116–17
    desertification in, 129
    droughts in, 16–17, 122
    energy use in, 113–15
    environment impact of, 58
    fisheries of, 86
    food production of, 69–70, 86
    foreign aid to, 218
    population control in, 194, 203,
    205–10, 214, 216, 228
    resurgence of fertility in, 61
    water crisis of, 29–30
chlorofluorocarbons (CFCs), 58,
    125–26, 176, 222
cities, 43, 153–57
Clark, Colin, 159
Clean Air Act, 138
climate, 25, 34, 132, 176–77, 260–
    261
    agriculture sensitive to, 89–90,
    95, 120–23
    alteration of, 121, 171–72, 187–
    189

of Europe, 90–91, 99
    genetic variability and, 33
    global warming and, 112–13,
    119–20, 171–72
climatic belts, migration of, 119
Club of Earth, 18
coal, 25–27, 55, 57, 113, 166
cocoa, laboratory production of,
    108
coevolution, 32, 255–56
Commission on Population Growth
    and the American Future,
    156
commons, 171–73
Congress, U.S., 195
    on agricultural policy, 98
    on global warming, 120
    writing to members of, 239–40,
    245
conscious evolution, 189
consumption, 240
    environmental impact per
    quantity of, 58
    individual responsibilities in,
    228
    among rich, 18, 21, 113–15
contraception, 19, 196–97, 199–
    202
Cortez, Hernando, 140
Costa Rica, 79, 152, 190
cowpox virus, 142
craft fairs, 184
Cranston Alan, 233
crime, 23, 43, 156–57, 160, 181–
    182, 227
Crutzen, Paul, 124
cultural evolution, 48–49, 187–88,
    192–93

DNA (deoxyribonucleic acid), 125
Daily, Gretchen, 241
Daly, Herman, 160–61
dams, 167
death rates, 47, 72, 121
    coping with massive rises in,
    179
    declines in, 51–52, 55–56
    demographic momentum and,
    59–60
    historical, 48

death rates (cont.)
  during Industrial Revolution,
    55–57
deforestation, 53–54, 62, 95, 101,
    132, 177, 211, 214
  in Brazil, 112, 115–16, 187
  in Central America, 79
  CO_2 produced by, 112, 115–18,
    124
  food production threatened by,
    71, 73–75
  reversing present trends of, 221
  of tropical Andes, 79
  in U.S., 118, 232
Delhi Planning Authority, 154
demographic momentum, 59–61,
    212
demographic-transition theory, 56,
    214–16
deoxyribonucleic acid, see DNA
desalinization, cost of, 94
desertification, 17, 36, 54, 95, 101
  in Africa, 83, 127–28
  global warming and, 126–29
  halting and reversing of, 221
  migrations caused by, 62, 105
deserts, natural creation of, 90
Deukmejian, George, 243–44
developed nations, see
    industrialized nations
developing nations, 176
  access to natural resources of,
    41–44
  agricultural inputs of, 92–93
  agricultural policies of, 104–6,
    108
  CO_2 produced by, 113–15, 132
  deforestation in, 115–17
  demographic momentum in, 59
  food production in, 69–83
  foreign aid to, 108, 218
  fuelwood crisis in, 221
  global warming responsibility
    of, 132–34
  hunger in, 67, 71–72, 80–81,
    100–104
  life expectancy in, 151
  limiting family size in, 227
  migrations from, 62–65
  migration to cities in, 153–55

  overpopulation of, 238
  pollution problems of, 137–39
  population control in, 203–25,
    216–19
  population growth of, 78, 238
  poverty epidemic in, 151–52
  promise of biotechnology for,
    107–9
Dharia, Mohan, 71
dinosaurs, disappearance of, 258–
    259
diseases, ecological, 149–50
distemper viruses, 142
droughts, 10–11, 23
  in Africa, 62, 83
  deforestation and, 71
  global warming and, 16–17,
    112–13, 120–22
  migrations caused by, 62
  in U.S., 16–17, 84, 89, 99, 122

Earth:
  ancient extinctions on, 258–59
  background on history and
    functioning of, 252–61
  biotic communities of, 254–56
  ecosystems of, 256–57
  vegetation and climate of, 253–
    254, 260–61
Eastern Europe, 84, 99–100, 115
Ecological Economics, 168
economics, 37, 44–45
  and assault on biotic diversity,
    31
  of Brazil, 76
  of childbearing, 203–4
  ecological, 168
  education in, 162–63, 167–69
  failures of, 162, 164
  of growthism vs. sustainability,
    181
  infinite substitutability axiom of,
    165–67
  population growth and, 158–64,
    167–68
  transformations in, 235–36
  and unequal access to natural
    resources, 41
ecosystems, 31–32, 256–57
  agricultural vs. natural, 53

conversion from natural to
	human-dominated, 35–37
disruption of, 37, 175
health of, 110–35
ecosystem services, 31–32, 34, 74
Ecuador, food production in, 79
education:
	of economists, 162–63, 167–69
	failures of, 32
	on population issues, 189, 202,
		229–30, 233, 236
	on sexual issues, 200
	of women, 216
educational organizations, 248–49
Egypt, 53, 172
Eliot, T. S., 174
El Salvador, 79
energy conservation, 219–20
environmental groups, 98, 246–47
epidemics, 17, 23, 176–80, 238
	in Africa, 144–47
	ecological change and, 149–
		150
	in history, 140–43
	in modern environment, 143–
		146
	population density related to,
		141, 153–57
	of poverty, 151–53
Ethiopia, famines in, 80–81
ethnic groups, 182
Europe, 53, 155, 220
	acid rain in, 123
	AIDS in, 148
	birth and death rate declines in,
		56
	climate of, 90–91, 99
	completed family sizes in, 193–
		194
	economic growth in, 167
	economic transformations in,
		235
	energy use in, 115
	food production in, 84, 99–100
	overpopulation of, 39
	population density of, 38
Everglades National Park, 129–32
evolution, 22, 32
	conscious, 189
	cultural, 48–49, 187–89, 192–93

genetic, 48–49
	of Homo sapiens, 14, 186–88
exponential growth, 15–17
extinctions, 30–37, 57, 164, 177,
	188–89
	ancient, 258–59
	early Homo sapiens responsible
		for, 50
	nature's genetic library and, 32–
		37
Exxon Valdez, 45

family farms, 97
famines, 10, 17, 23, 122, 238
	in Africa, 80–81, 83, 126, 128
	in Bihar, 42
farming, see agriculture
Federal Aviation Administration,
	236
Federation for Action on
	Immigration Reform (FAIR),
	249
feminist movement, 56
fertilizer, 27–28
	as agricultural input, 92–93
	to compensate for erosion
		losses, 77
	diminishing returns from, 92–93
	European applications of, 99
	food production and, 73
	in tropics, 103–4
Fiennes, Richard, 144–45
fish, poisoning of, 74–75
fisheries, 85–88, 94, 173
floods, 17, 34
Florida, environmental disaster in,
	129–32
Florida Bay, 130–31
food, contamination of, 136
food aid, 80–82
food problem, see hunger
food production, 9–11, 66–88, 176
	in Africa, 10, 68, 80–84, 211
	in Asia, 43, 69–75, 84, 86
	Catholic Church on, 19–20
	declines in, 10, 68–69
	in Europe, 84, 99–100
	exploitation of natural resources
		in, 27–28
	global warming and, 119–23

food production (*cont.*)
    health and, 111
    importance of agricultural
        inputs to, 92–94
    in industrialized nations, 68–69,
        83–85, 99–100
    in Latin America, 10, 68, 75–80,
        84–85
    maldistribution of food and, 20–
        21, 66–67
    population growth related to,
        52–53, 68–69, 73–75
    populations supportable by, 19–
        20
    rises in, 67–68
    threats to, 70–75, 86–87, 188–
        189
food riots, 180
Food Security Act, 98
Forbes, 38–39
Ford, Gerald, 194
foreign aid, 108, 218
forest death, 23
forest farming, 104
forests, 11, 26–27, 32, 36, 78,
        101–102, 173, 261
    destruction of biodiversity in,
        33–34
    replanting of, 221
    see also deforestation
fossil fuels, 25–26
    CO_2 produced by burning of,
        111, 113–15, 132–33
    conservation of, 219–20
    consumption by wealth of, 231
    depletion of, 26–28
    see also specific fossil fuels
France, 38, 97, 115, 170
Friends of the Earth, 246
fuelwood crisis, 221

Gandhi, Indira, 182, 209
garbage disposal, 21, 32, 43, 154,
        231, 238
    in south Florida, 129–30
genetic engineering, 95
    impact of, 106–9
genetic evolution, 48–49
genetic library, nature's, 31–37,
        95

genetic variability, 33
George, Henry, 158–59
Germany, 170
Giardia lamblia, 149–50
Global Tomorrow Coalition, 248
global warming, 10–11, 43, 62,
        177, 220, 228, 231, 238–39
    acid rain and, 123–24
    air pollution and, 173
    altered rainfall patterns due to,
        172–73
    climate disrupted by, 171–72
    consequences of, 16–17, 118–
        119
    and depletion of ozone layer,
        124–26
    desertification and, 126–29
    difficulty of solving, 58–59
    droughts related to, 16–17, 112–
        113, 120–22
    food production and, 119–23
    government policy on, 120, 233,
        236–37
    health and, 111–20
    industrialized nations vs.
        developing nations and, 132–
        134
    population component of, 22
    sea-level rise resulting from,
        131
    U.S. contributions to, 232
Gorbachev, Mikhail, 175, 179, 182
Gore, Albert, 233
grain exports, 89, 99–100
grains, 68–73, 75, 81–84, 89, 100
    improvement of, 106–107
    yields of, 92–93, 95–96, 106
Grant, Lindsey, 160
grassland, 27, 36, 261
    desertification of, 128–29
grazing animals, overpopulation
        of, 128–29
Great Britain, 86, 155
Green, Marshall, 178
greenhouse effect, *see* global
        warming
greenhouse gases, *see* specific
        greenhouse gases: carbon
        dioxide, chlorofluorocarbons,
        methane

green plants, 25–26, 253–54, 260–261
  pest defenses of, 254–55
  threat of extinction to, 30–37, 57
Green Revolution, 95
  in Asia, 69–70
  biotechnology and, 106
  importance of agricultural inputs to, 92
  indigenous crops neglected by, 103
  in industrialized nations, 93
  in Mexico, 79
  in Philippines, 74
  technologies of, 69
  transfer to tropics of, 93
gridlock, 11, 23, 43, 231, 239
Grossman, Richard, 234
Guatemala, food production in, 79

Hansen, James, 22
Hardin, Garrett, 171
health, 244
  and age structure of population, 160
  ecological diseases and, 149–50
  epidemics and, 140–53
  of global ecosystem, 110–35
  global warming and, 111–20
  of poor, 151–53
  population density and, 153–57
  public, 110–11, 136–57
Health and Human Services Department, U.S., 249
Heath, Margo, 245
He Bochuan, 86, 116
Hegeman, Alanson and Marcia, 245
Heinz, John, 233
Henderson, Donald A., 144
herding, 51
Himalayas, population growth in, 34
Hollow Men, The (Eliot), 174
homeless people, 11, 43, 244
Hong Kong, 38
Humanae Vitae, 19
human beings, 16, 25, 31, 44, 66, 110, 162, 234
  averting end of, 180–84
  cultural evolution of, 48–49, 187–89, 192–93
  evolutionary history of, 14, 186–188
  first impact on flora and fauna of, 49–50
  genetic evolution of, 48–49
  land surface appropriated by, 35–37
  rise to dominance of, 46–65
  scenarios for end of, 174–80
  vulnerability to epidemics of, 142–43, 149
hunger, 9–11, 176, 178
  in Africa, 80–81
  in developing nations, 67, 71–72, 80–81, 100–104
  in world, 21
  in India, 71
  from maldistribution of food resources, 20–21
  in South Asia, 72
hurricanes, 112–13, 118, 131
hydrologic cycle, 31–32, 34

Iceland, 86
I = PAT equation, 58–59, 114, 117, 123–25, 167, 190, 193, 215, 219, 222, 228
  for developing nations vs. industrialized nations, 132–34
  reducing all factors of, 181
Imperial Valley, 94, 97
Incas, 79, 140
India, 73, 126, 172
  deforestation in, 116
  demographic momentum in, 60
  desertification in, 128–29
  early civilization of, 54
  energy use in, 114–15
  epidemics in, 143
  grain production in, 43, 69–72
  overpopulation of, 42–44, 188
  population control in, 191, 208–210, 216, 232
  population growth of, 159
  replacement reproduction in, 60, 191
  water crisis of, 29

Indonesia, 73–74
industrial agriculture, 76
industrialized nations, 176
  access to natural resources of,
    41–44
  agricultural inputs in, 93
  CO_2 produced by, 113–15
  deforestation in, 117–18
  and deforestation in tropics, 117
  economic growth in, 167
  food production in, 69, 83–85,
    99–100
  foreign aid from, 218
  global warming responsibility
    of, 132–34
  life expectancy in, 151
  limiting family size in, 227–28
  migrations to, 62–65
  overpopulation of, 39–40, 43–
    44, 194, 217, 238
  population control in, 193–96,
    214–15
  populations of cities in, 155–57
  population shrinkage in, 193–96
  threats to political and social
    stability of, 179–80
Industrial Revolution, 14
  global warming and, 111–12
  population growth and, 55–57
infant mortality rates, 67
infants, hunger among, 67
influenza, 141–42
Inner Mongolia, 129
innovation, 160–61
international conflicts, 23
International Planned Parenthood
    Federation, 194–95, 208
international regulation and
    management, 222–25
International Society of Ecological
    Economics, 168
irrigation, 52, 93–95
  epidemics caused by, 150
  global warming and, 119
  of Imperial Valley, 94, 97
  problems associated with, 36,
    93–94
  temporary nature of, 101
Israel, 170, 172, 222
Italy, 19, 196

Japan, 151, 193, 219–20
  economic growth in, 167
  economic transformations in,
    235
  energy use in, 115
  food production in, 75, 84
  foreign-aid contributions of, 218
  population density of, 38
Java, population density of, 73–74
John Paul II, Pope, 18–19, 241–42

Kampuchea, 73
Karnataka, 128–29
Kenya:
  food production in, 82
  population growth in, 14–15,
    210–12
Kesterson National Wildlife
    Refuge, 133
Korea, food production in, 75

Lake Okeechobee, pollution of,
    129–30
land, 95–96
  amount required by agriculture,
    88–89
  food production and, 70
  human appropriation of, 35–37
  population-supporting
    capacities of, 100–102
Lassa fever, 145–46
Latin America, 122
  arable land in, 96
  declines in death rates in, 56
  food production in, 10, 68, 75–
    80, 84–85
  population growth in, 78–80,
    213–14
Law of the Sea, 223–24
lead poisoning, 53
Lederberg, Joshua, 148
Leopold, Aldo, 32
letter writing, 231–33
  samples of, 239–46
life expectancies, 57, 134
  in developing nations vs.
    industrialized nations, 151
Los Angeles, Calif., 156
Lucy, 14, 48
Lyme disease, 150

MacArthur, Douglas, 104–5
McNeill, William, 140–41, 153
Madagascar, vanilla bean
    production in, 108
malaria, 144, 150
Malthus, Thomas, 168
Marburg disease, 145–46
mass-transit systems, 183
Matson, Pamela, 240
Mayan civilization, collapse of, 54
measles, 141–42
Mediterranean basin, civilizations
    of, 53–54
metals, 26, 52
methane, 91, 111, 132, 258–59
    reducing emissions of, 222
    sources of, 118
Mexico, 172, 214
    experimental agricultural
        projects in, 104
    flow of immigrants from, 63–64
    food production in, 79–80
    poverty in, 64
Mexico City, 154
Miami, Fla., 156
Miami sanitary landfill, 129
microbes, 25–26, 30–37, 57
Middle East:
    arable land in, 96
    grain production in, 72–73
    origins of agriculture in, 50–51
Midwest, U.S., weather patterns
    in, 91
migrations, 61–65
    to cities, 153–55
    of climatic belts, 119
    from desertified lands, 62, 105
military strength, population size
    related to, 170
mining, 37, 52, 71, 132–33
Missouri Botanical Garden, 112
monocultures, 103
Morrison Institute of Population
    and Resource Studies, 248
Morse, Chandler, 165–66
Moslem nations, population
    growth in, 212–13
motor vehicles, 134, 181, 183
    fuel efficiency of, 45, 220
    pollution caused by, 136, 138–39

Murphy, Dennis D., 244
mutualism, 255
myxomatosis virus, 144

National Abortion Rights Action
    League (NARAL), 246
National Academy of Sciences,
    18, 22, 112
National Aeronautics and Space
    Administration (NASA), 22
National Audubon Society, Inc.,
    229, 247
National Commission on
    Population Growth, 194
National Organization for Women
    (NOW), 249
national security, environmental
    threats to, 171–73
Native Americans, impact of
    European diseases on, 140
natural gas, 25–27, 113
natural resources, 25–45
    consumption of, 58, 240
    depletion of, 26–30
    discovering and exploiting new
        reserves of, 44–45
    early human use of, 49
    squandering of, 25–26, 37, 41, 45
    unequal access to, 41–44, 61,
        64–65
    see also specific natural
        resources
natural selection, 22, 186, 192
Netherlands, population density
    of, 38–40
Netherlands Fallacy, 39
net primary production (NPP), 35–
    37, 96
New World:
    discovery and settling of, 54–55
    origins of agriculture in, 50
New York City, 153, 155
New York Times, The, 18
Nicaragua, food production in, 79
Niger, 128
Nigeria, 82–83, 146
nitrate pollution, 149
nitrogen-fixing crops, 107
nitrogen oxides, 91, 111, 176
Nixon, Richard, 194

nonrenewable resources, 26–27,
    38–39
  depletion of, 57–58
  early human manipulation of,
    52–54
Norman, William, 244–45
North America:
  acid rain in, 123
  carrying capacity of, 64
  migration to, 64–65
  weather in, 90
nuclear power, 166, 222
nuclear terrorism, 179
nuclear war, 174–76, 238
nuclear winter, 174, 176–77
nutrients, cycling of, 32

oceans:
  changes in temperature of, 112,
    173
  pollution of, 86, 132
  see also sea levels
Office of Management and
    Budget, 22
Office of Technology Assessment,
    138
Ogallala aquifer, 95
  overdrafting of, 28–29, 133
oil, 25–28, 57, 166–67
  CO$_2$ produced by burning of, 113
  discovering and exploiting new
    reserves of, 44–45
O'nyong-nyong fever, 144–45
Orissa, 71
Ottesen-Jensen, Elise, 208
Our Common Future, 192
overconsumption, 43
overcultivation, 36, 53
overgrazing, 36, 53
overpopulation, 37–40, 190, 237–38
  carrying capacity related to, 38–
    40
  density related to, 38–40
  desertification related to, 127–28
  of developing nations, 238
  of Florida, 129–30
  of grazing animals, 128–29
  of India, 42–44, 188
  of industrialized nations, 39–40,
    43–44, 194, 217, 238

ozone, 91, 111, 257–58
ozone layer:
  depletion of, 11, 17, 58, 124–26,
    132, 173, 177, 188–89, 217,
    222, 239, 259
  formation of, 257–58
  global warming and, 124–26

Pakistan, 72, 151, 172
Paraná, erosion in, 77
Parsons, Jack, 163–64
pastures, 35–36, 78
paving, 30, 36
peat, 25–26, 55, 57
People's Daily, 116–17
Pericles, 163
Persian Gulf crisis, 45
Peru, food production in, 79, 85
pest control, 32, 119
pesticides, 27
  as agricultural inputs, 92
  environmental problems caused
    by, 74–75
  as substitutes for natural
    predators, 167
  in tropics, 77–78, 103–4
Philip, Prince (Duke of
    Edinburgh), 182
Philippines, food production in,
    74–75
Phoenician civilization, 53
photosynthesis, 35–36, 88, 115,
    119, 253, 257
plagues, 10, 142–43, 147
Planned Parenthood Federation
    of America, Inc., 208, 223, 246
plant communities, 35–36
plastics, disposal of, 166–67, 181
Poland, 105, 115
politics:
  population pressures and, 178–
    180
  and recognizing population
    problem, 21–22
  use of public pressure in, 231–
    233, 235, 239–40, 245
pollution, 27, 95
  of air, 43, 53, 136, 138, 154,
    173, 181, 220
  of aquifers, 30, 131, 178

food production threatened by,
72, 86–87
of Lake Okeechobee, 129–30
by nitrates, 149
of oceans, 86, 132
relationship between health
and, 136–39
transnational, 180
in tropics, 103
of water, 53, 72, 86–87, 136,
151, 154, 181
pond weed, exponential growth of,
15–16
population:
age composition of, 159–61,
181–82, 203
current, 9, 237
of early human forms, 47
Population Bomb, The (Ehrlich),
9–10, 22, 134–35, 177, 183,
188, 210–211, 214
population control, 190–210, 238,
240–41, 245
in China, 194, 203, 205–10, 214,
216, 228
contraception and, 19, 196–97,
199, 202
demographic-transition theory
and, 56, 214–16
in developing nations, 203–25,
216–19
government policies on, 45,
194–95, 202, 240
in India, 191, 208–10, 216, 232
in industrialized nations, 193–
196, 214–15
in Moslem nations, 213
in Philippines, 75
see also birth control
Population Council, 247
Population Crisis Committee, 247
population density, 38–40
in cities, 153–57
epidemics related to, 141, 153–57
of Indonesia, 73–74
pollution related to, 139
Population/Environment Balance, 248
population explosion:
end of, 16–17, 23, 238
fallacies about, 230

implications of, 13
individual responsibilities in,
226–51
population growth, 10, 47, 187–89,
237, 244–45
acid rain and, 123–24
in Africa, 14–15, 82–83, 210–12
annual rates of, 14–16
arguments in favor of, 159–61,
170
of cities, 153–57
climate change related to, 120–
123
deforestation related to, 115–18
demographic momentum of, 212
of developing nations, 78, 238
development of agriculture
related to, 52–53
in Eastern Europe, 84
economic growth and, 158–64,
167–68
energy consumption and, 114
environmental crisis and, 58–59
epidemics related to, 144, 149–
150, 152–53
in Europe, 99
exponential, 15–17
in Florida, 129, 132
halting of, 180
health and, 136
in Himalayas, 34
of industrialized nations vs.
developing nations, 42
Industrial Revolution and, 55–
57
labor availability related to,
160
in Latin America, 78–80, 213–
214
in Moslem nations, 212–13
news media and, 231
perpetuation of, 243–44
planning for, 37
political stability related to,
178–80
relationship between food
production and, 52–53, 68–
69, 73–75
in U.S., 156
zero, 47, 59–60, 193, 208

Population Institute, 247
population organizations, 246–49
Population Reference Bureau,
    Inc., 247–48
poverty, 42–44, 244
    absolute, 41
    in India, 42–43
    in Mexico, 64
    and population growth, 151–53
    in urban areas, 43
Powell, George, 130
press, 18, 231
Prince William Sound, 133
public housing, 155
public-interest organizations, 233,
    246–49

racism, 181–83, 204, 222, 235
radioactive wastes, 30
rainfall, 90, 261
    altered patterns of, 172–73
    in Europe, 99
    greenhouse gas build-up and, 91
    irrigation vs., 94
    in tropics, 103
Rajasthan desert, 71
Rau, Lady Dhanvanthis Rama,
    208
Raven, Peter, 112, 117
Reagan, Ronald, 43, 155, 191, 220
    population policies of, 45, 194–
    195, 240
recombinant-DNA techniques, 106
refugees, ecological, 17, 62
regional conflicts, 179
Reisner, Marc, 29
religious fundamentalism, 178,
    180
religious leaders, letters to, 241–
    242, 244–45
religious prejudice, 181–82, 222
renewable resources, 26–27, 52–54
    see also soils, aquifers,
        biodiversity
replacement reproduction, 60
resources:
    destruction of, 164–65
    substitutability of, 165–67
    see also specific kinds of
        resources

rinderpest virus, 142
Roe v. Wade, 195, 197, 245
Roman civilization, 53–54
Rowan, Hobart, 218
Roy, R. N., 71–72
RU 486, 198–99, 201

Sahel, 127–28
    droughts in, 62, 83
    famine in, 126, 128
    foreign-aid programs for, 108
San Francisco, Calif., 156, 190
Sanger, Margaret, 208
San Joaquin Valley, 29, 94
schistosomiasis, 150
Schneider, Claudine, 233
sea levels:
    food production and, 120
    global warming and, 131
    rises in, 112, 131, 178
Seattle, Wash., 156
seeds, herbicide-resistant, 107
sewage disposal, 11, 23, 137, 154
sexism, 181–83, 222
Sierra Club, Inc., 98, 247
single parenthood, 227
skin cancers, 124–25
smallpox, 140–43
social justice, 22
social systems, population
    pressures on, 178–80
soil, 9, 25–26
    depletion of, 53
    generation and maintenance of,
        32
    mining of, 71
    overexploitation of, 27–28
    plowing of, 77
    of rain forests, 78, 102
Soil Conservation Service, 98
soil erosion, 27–28, 37, 82, 95, 96,
    99
    deforestation and, 101
    food production threatened by,
        70–72, 74
    government agricultural policy
        and, 98
    in Paraná, 77
    in tropics, 77, 103–4
    limits of tolerance, 77

solar energy, 88–89, 253
  human appropriation of, 35–36
South Africa, Republic of, 83,
    167, 222
South America, 127, 213
Southeast Asia, 50, 73–74
Soviet Union, 119, 170
  agricultural policy in, 105
  arms race between U.S. and,
    175
  droughts in, 16–17, 122
  energy use in, 115
  environmental threats to
    national security of, 171–72
  food production in, 69, 71, 84,
    100
  irrigation in, 94
  overpopulation of, 39
  and World Court, 223–24
starvation, *see* hunger
"Statement on Population
    Stabilization," 191
stream siltation, 74
subsidies, 97–99, 100
Sudan, famines in, 81
Sumerian culture, 52
Supreme Court, U.S., 197, 199
Sweden, energy use in, 115
Switzerland, 97, 115
syphilis, 142

Taiwan, 38, 75
"Take-Home Messages," 229,
    231, 237–39
Tamil Nadu, 70–71
Task Force on Population and
    Earth Resources, 195
technologies:
  ecologically unsound, 18, 21, 58
  environmentally benign, 181
  of Green Revolution, 69
  individual responsibilities for,
    228–29
tectonics, 258
Temin, Howard, 143, 148
temperate zones, 90
Thailand, 73, 84
Thar Desert, 54
thaumatin protein, laboratory
    production of, 108

Thomas, John H., 242
Tokyo, 157
Tongass rain forest, 232
transnational pollution, 180
tropical agriculture, 76–79
  problems of, 77, 102–4,
    107
  successes of, 103–4
  transferring Green Revolution
    to, 93
Tunisia, 213

ultraviolet-B (UV-B) radiation,
    124–25, 173, 257–59
United Nations, 223
  on desertification, 127
United Nations Food and
    Agriculture Organization
    (FAO), 86, 96
United Nations Fund for
    Population Activities
    (UNFPA), 195, 249
United Nations International
    Children's Emergency Fund
    (UNICEF), 143
United Nations Population
    Conference, 194
urban poor, 43
urban stress tests, 155
Uttar Pradesh, 71

vanilla, laboratory production of,
    107–8
Vietnam, 170
Vietnam War, 73

Wall Street Journal, The, 234
Washington, D.C., 156, 183
Washington Post, The, 218
water, 9, 26, 55
  in agriculture, 92–95
  in Kenya, 82
  overexploitation of, 27–30
  pollution of, 53, 72, 86–87, 136,
    151, 154, 181
  salinization of, 72, 93–94, 131,
    178
  shortages of, 17, 70–74
  see also aquifers; irrigation
water vapor, 91, 111

weather:
  agriculture sensitive to, 89–91,
    95
  deforestation and, 101
  impact of global warming on,
    112–13
Weeks, John, 213
West Antarctic ice sheet, 178
whaling industry, 164
white herons, 130–31
Wirth, Timothy E., 196, 233, 245
women, 216, 235
World Bank, 223, 249
World Commission on
  Environment and
  Development, 192

World Court, 223–24
World Resources Institute, 162,
  248
World War II, 15
Worldwatch Institute, 28, 109,
  248
World Wildlife Fund, 249

yaws, 142
yellow fever virus, 143

zero population growth (ZPG), 47,
  59–60, 193, 208
Zero Population Growth
  (organization) (ZPG),
  246